HOW TO STUDY
General Editors: John Peck and Martin Coyle

PRACTICAL CRITICISM

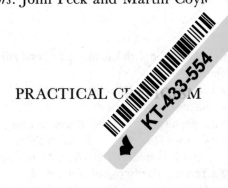

How to Study

Series editors: John Peck and Martin Coyle

IN THE SAME SERIES

PRACTICAL CRITICISM

John Peck
and
Martin Coyle

MACMILLAN

First published 1995 by
MACMILLAN PRESS LTD
Houndmills, Basingstoke, Hampshire RG21 2XS
and London
Companies and representatives
throughout the world

ISBN 0–333–63225–7

A catalogue record for this book is available
from the British Library.

10   9   8   7   6   5   4   3   2
04   03   02   01   00   99   98   97   96

Copy-edited and typeset by Povey–Edmondson
Okehampton and Rochdale, England

Printed in Malaysia

To Alison and Pam

Contents

Acknowledgements

THE authors and publishers wish to thank the following who have kindly given permission for the use of copyright material:

Faber & Faber Ltd for Paul Muldoon, 'Cuba', from *Why Brownlee Left*; HarperCollins Publishers for R. S. Thomas, 'The Welsh Hill Country', from *Selected Poems*; The Editor of *Poetry* on behalf of The Modern Poetry Association, for an extract from Lawrence Raab, 'This Day', *Poetry*, Feb. 1981 Copyright © 1981 The Modern Poetry Association; Laurence Pollinger Ltd on behalf of the Estate of Freda Ravagli for an extract from D. H. Lawrence, *The Rainbow*; Rogers, Coleridge & White Ltd on behalf of the author for Edward Lucie-Smith, 'The Lesson', from *A Tropical Childhood and Other Poems*, Oxford University Press, 1981; The Society of Authors on behalf of the Bernard Shaw Estate for an extract from *Arms and the Man*.

Every effort has been made to trace all the copyright-holders, but if any have been inadvertently overlooked the publishers will be pleased to make the necessary arrangement at the first opportunity.

General editors' preface

EVERYBODY who studies literature, either for an examination or simply for pleasure, experiences the same problem: how to understand and respond to the text. As every student of literature knows, it is perfectly possible to read a book over and over again and yet still feel baffled and at a loss as to what to say about it. One answer to this problem, of course, is to accept someone else's view of the text, but how much more rewarding it would be if you could work out your own critical response to any book you choose or are required to study.

The aim of this series is to help you develop your critical skills by offering practical advice about how to read, understand and analyse literature. Each volume provides you with a clear method of study so that you can see how to set about tackling texts on your own. While the authors of each volume approach the problem in a different way, every book in the series attempts to provide you with some broad ideas about the kind of texts you are likely to be studying and some broad ideas about how to think about literature; each volume then shows you how to apply these ideas in a way which should help you construct your own analysis and interpretation. Unlike most critical books, therefore, the books in this series do not simply convey someone else's thinking about a text, but encourage you and show you how to think about a text for yourself.

Each book is written with an awareness that you are likely to be preparing for an examination, and therefore practical advice is given not only on how to understand and analyse literature, but also on how to organise a written response. Our hope is that although these books are intended to serve a practical purpose, they may also enrich your enjoyment of literature by making you a more confident reader, alert to the interest and pleasure to be derived from literary texts.

John Peck
Martin Coyle

Preface

At the heart of the study of English Literature lies practical criticism. Every student needs to be able to do it, and to do it with confidence and skill. Far too often, however, students find themselves confronting a poem or a passage from a novel or an extract from a play and having nothing to say. Or they find themselves producing a very poor piece of writing, full of short paragraphs, with no sense of purpose behind the writing. It doesn't have to be like that. Once you realise that there are some quite straightforward rules and procedures for coming to terms with a text and building an analysis, then the whole exercise takes on a different meaning.

Central to the rules for practical criticism is the point that your essay method for practical criticism should be exactly the same as your essay method for all other papers. This is something we explain in greater detail in the following pages where we set out, in as clear a fashion as possible, the method for practical criticism – or at least the method we recommend to our students, three of whom have agreed to allow us to print one of their practical criticism analyses. The students are all in their first year at university, but the book is very much aimed at every student: it sets out the basic moves to make sense of a poem or novel or play, how to build a response and how to write an essay. In a sequence of short chapters we try to anticipate the sort of questions and problems you might have, all the time emphasising the way in which you can use a few simple controlling ideas to organise and develop your analyses. At the same time, where appropriate , we try to show you how you can take your ideas further and extend your critical skills.

Practical criticism underlies everything else you do as a student of English Literature. It is a way of reading the text closely, but with a grasp of the larger issues involved. It is a challenging way of reading that actually allows you to see things for yourself and to read the text with intelligence, with a sense of adventure and even with a certain playfulness. Certainly one of the things we wish to get across in this book is how, by following some simple steps, practical criticism becomes a way of opening up the text to different readings, with different emphases and different ideas. And this is because there is no single, correct reading of a text: there are only the readings that we construct. Which is what this book is about – how to construct your own reading and, as a result, do really well in English Literature exams.

Finally, we would like to thank our first year students at Cardiff for contributing so much to the discussions behind this book. In particular, we would like to thank: Neil Abram, Leanne Allen, Louise Bassett, Helen Cadman, Joy Cann, Louise Cooper, Clair Drayton, Karen John, Rupal Joshi, Ceri Ann Lowe, Joanna McCathie, Louise Meeson, Sarah Platts, Ben Tisdall, Kerry Thomason and Kirsten Wilcock.

University of Wales, Cardiff

John Peck
Martin Coyle

Part One
Poetry

1

Why 'practical criticism'?

1 WHAT IS 'PRACTICAL CRITICISM'?

ONE of the things you will almost certainly have to do as a student of literature is 'practical criticism'. Practical criticism is that exercise in which you are given a poem, or a passage of prose, or sometimes an extract from a play, that you have not seen before and are asked to write a critical analysis of it. Usually you are not told who wrote the poem or passage, and usually, too, you are not given any indication of what you might look for or say. We can sum it up, then, as criticism based on the close analysis of a text in isolation.

2 ARE THERE OTHER NAMES FOR PRACTICAL CRITICISM?

Practical criticism is the most widely-used name for this exercise, but it doesn't really offer a very accurate description of the activity involved. There are historical reasons why we call it practical criticism (see the answer to the next question), and people have kept on using the phrase, but it is a little misleading as it suggests there could perhaps be such an activity as 'impractical' criticism. Consequently, names such as 'analysis', 'poetry analysis', 'close analysis', 'close reading' or simply 'the criticism paper' have also become widely established, particularly in school examinations: such phrases attempt to describe rather more accurately the nature of the exercise.

3 WHO INVENTED PRACTICAL CRITICISM?

English Literature as a university subject was first taught at the University of Edinburgh in the eighteenth century. It was then introduced at the original colleges of the University of London: University College in 1828, and King's College in 1831. In America, the first Professor of Rhetoric and Oratory was appointed at Harvard in 1806. As the nineteenth century continued, English Literature became more and more widely taught. It was, however, 1894 before an honours school of English was established at Oxford University, and 1912 before the Edward VII Chair of English Literature was introduced at the University of Cambridge. As one might imagine, studying English in the nineteenth century was very different from how it is today; the dominant approaches were historical and linguistic rather than critical and interpretative. In the 1920s, however, particularly at Cambridge, there were strenuous moves towards making English a subject with a methodology of its own; a central aspect of this was much more focusing on the text. This kind of direct response is so central in literary studies today that it is hard to grasp that it was innovatory in the 1920s.

The central figure in this forging of a new methodology for literary criticism was I. A. Richards (1893–1979), who, as a lecturer at Cambridge, published *Principles of Literary Criticism* (1924) and *Practical Criticism* (1929). In the latter of these, he analysed the results of presenting unascribed poems to students and asking for their written responses to them. The disappointing, often risible, nature of the responses provided Richards with the opportunity to criticise the lack of clear principles of the then current literary criticism, and to make the case for a certain kind of detailed work on the text. His ideas about how to approach a work of literature had a profound effect upon later British critics such as F. R. Leavis and William Empson, and on a number of American critics who came to be known as the New Critics. The idea of a practical criticism, that would concentrate on the text and its verbal nuances without preconceived ideas about the author, soon found its way into the teaching of English Literature at all levels.

4   WAS I. A. RICHARDS REALLY THE FIRST CRITIC TO PAY CLOSE ATTENTION TO THE TEXT?

Practical criticism, as we are beginning to see, concerns itself with the discussion of individual works. It centres on a personal engagement with the text; theoretical principles controlling the mode of analysis and interpretation are usually left implicit. In other words, the critic starts with the text rather than with a set of ideas about texts. This became established as an approach from the late 1920s onwards, but there had, in fact, been a long tradition of applied criticism in Britain. We might mention the literary essays of Dryden, Dr Johnson's *Lives of the English Poets* (1779–81), Coleridge's lectures on Shakespeare and his notes on the poetry of Wordsworth in *Biographia Literaria* (1817), and Matthew Arnold's *Essays in Criticism* (1865 and following). But something new did begin to develop in the 1930s, something that was pushed an extreme in the work of the New Critics, who dismissed the study of literature in terms of history, morality, or any purpose outside it. They insisted upon close attention to the text itself and the virtual exclusion of anything other than the words on the page. Such thinking was most clearly defined in John Crowe Ransom's *New Criticism* (1941); from that point on, the approach of the New Critics dominated critical thinking both in Britain and America until the early 1960s.

5   WHY DO I HAVE TO DO PRACTICAL CRITICISM IN AN EXAMINATION?

As someone who is going to have to sit down and write your own response to a poem and/or a passage of prose in an examination, you might feel rather resentful that you are going to be put on the spot in this kind of way. For other papers in English you have had time to read, think and prepare, but in the practical criticism paper it is going to be a case of making it up on the spot in the frenzy of the examination. Having read the first few pages of this book, you might feel that you are being subjected to practical criticism because of a dispute I. A. Richards had with his predecessors three-quarters of a century ago. You might also feel that there is something rather unfair about a practical criticism examination: as it is just you and a poem, it might appear that it is 'you' that is being assessed. In every other subject, and in every other area of an English examination, hard work will help you get a good result, but it might appear that practical criticism sets out to test your personality rather than the effort you have made.

It is this kind of assumption that we want to dismiss in this book. There was a time when practical criticism was regarded as a way of testing the student's innate 'feel' for literature, but this is no longer the case. The main reason for this change is the more general change there has been in critical thinking since the 1960s. There has, since that time, been far more stress on the theoretical aspects of literature and criticism. The idea of an unmediated response to a text, the idea that you can simply respond to a text directly in a sort of 'pure' way, has all but disappeared. There is now a recognition that we always bring a whole range of assumptions to any text and judge it, even if we are new to the subject, by a complex set of critical principles. One effect of this is that practical criticism is no longer seen as the 'end' of literary criticism but as a starting-point for literary criticism. For the New Critics, the apparently unmediated response to the text was the sum total of criticism; as such, it became a task that was all-demanding. Today, rather more realistically, practical criticism is seen as a basic ability to comprehend a text, and, as such, stands as the foundation on which a full critical debate can be built. Practical criticism, seen in this light, is day-to-day practice on the basic manoeuvres of criticism. This is something that we will be stressing throughout this book, that practical criticism is not a complex activity, but a very basic activity, yet one which is at the heart of all good criticism.

6   WHY DOES EVERYONE DREAD PRACTICAL CRITICISM?

Dread is, perhaps, too strong a word, but most people certainly feel nervous about practical criticism examinations. This is perfectly understandable: it is fear of the unknown, that you will be confronted by something that is totally baffling, a text that you won't be able to say anything about. We want to calm these fears in this book: we want to show it is possible to take one look at a poem and immediately feel that you are going to be able to do justice to it. Analysis of a text is an academic activity, and all academic activities have established rules and procedures. The purpose of this book is to explain these rules and procedures. We will be showing you, first, how to come to terms with a poem or passage as a whole, and then, secondly, how to build upon that initial understanding as you fill out your sense of what the text is doing and saying. The rules we will be recommending are every bit as clear as the rules that you might employ in a maths exam to help you solve a question. And they are also very simple. Indeed, a point we are anxious to get across is that practical criticism is essentially a simple exercise; the end result, that is to say your answer as a whole, might be sophisticated and impressive, but everything starts from, and is built upon, some very straightforward initial moves with the passage or poem.

7 WHAT SORT OF ESSAY ARE THEY LOOKING FOR IN A PRACTICAL CRITICISM EXAMINATION?

At every stage of this book we will be stressing three points: how to understand a poem or passage as a whole, how to develop that initial understanding on the basis of closer examination of the poem, and, thirdly, how to present your response in the form of an effective essay. It is impossible to overstate the importance of a good essay method. Unfortunately, it is in the area of essay-writing that, all too often, a student's good efforts can disintegrate into nothing. At the most basic level, far too many students fail to realise they are actually required to write an essay on the practical criticism paper. There are far too many answers that aren't even divided into paragraphs, where impressions of the poem just accumulate in a manner that is not heading anywhere. An essay has to be much more structured than that. But it is also important to get the structure right. One common mistake in practical criticism is the essay that spends paragraph after paragraph explaining the content of the poem and then finishes with an extra paragraph about the formal qualities of the text. This, unfortunately, seems to be an approach that a great many students, particularly at school, are encouraged to take. It isn't a good method; it doesn't work. More often than not the person marking the paper will feel that the candidate has merely retold the story of the poem or passage at enormous length. Another approach that creates problems is that which becomes overintricate in structure: for example, a student might have a paragraph about imagery, and then a paragraph about the stanza pattern and so on. The problem with this approach is that, although it might sometimes work, it does tend to lead candidates towards tying themselves up in knots. It also gives the impression of being a sort of scientific report on the text rather than a critical reading of it.

As against these approaches, the essay method you should be aiming for is one that is clear and simple, enabling you to move steadily from paragraph to paragraph building a case. We'll say far more about this as we go along, but a point we want to establish here is that your essay method on the practical criticism paper should be exactly the same as your essay method on all the other papers in English, for practical criticism is the basis of everything else. Looking at a book as a whole or considering a poet as a whole is an extension and development of the moves that one makes in practical criticism.

8   HOW SHOULD I PREPARE FOR A PRACTICAL CRITICISM EXAMINATION?

The best preparation for anything is, of course, practice: the more poems and passages you write about, the better your work will become. But, like driving lessons, what you need is practice with guidance. We want to reiterate the point that you need to think about the activity of practical criticism in the right kind of way; it isn't just a case of 'you' and the poem, and some kind of response flowing from the inner you. On the contrary, there are procedures to go through that will enable you to get hold of, and then develop a coherent case about, the poem. Where practice will help is that it will make you a lot quicker at getting hold of a poem or passage, and a lot more nimble and assured in moving through the poem or passage.

9   THE NEED FOR CONFIDENCE

As in so many areas of life, the belief that you can achieve something is the most decisive step towards actually achieving it. Don't approach a practical criticism exam saying, 'What if I don't understand the poem?' Approach it telling yourself that you are going to be able to understand the poem, and that you are going to be able to do impressive things with it. There are good grounds for feeling confident: all of us know far more about literature than we might assume. All of us are aware of the patterns and ideas that come up in literature again and again, even if we have read very little. The thing is, however, that most of us don't realise that we know these things. This book will highlight this kind of shared knowledge about literature, particularly about poetry, that we all have, and show you how to apply it to individual works. In the case of poetry, this means 'demythologising' poetry: far too many people continue to think of poetry as saying strange things in cryptic ways. Far too many people think that there is some kind of hidden meaning in a poem, and that it is their job to get at the meaning behind the apparent meaning. It is these misconceptions that distort a sensible judgement of the difficulty, or lack of difficulty, of a practical criticism paper. Tell yourself that there is, in fact, nothing strange, cryptic or elusive about poetry, that common sense and a few sensible guidelines will soon give you a purchase on a poem, and that everything else follows logically from there.

10 WHAT SORT OF POEM IS GOING TO BE SET?

Poems come in a great many shapes and forms. A sound practical criticism method will enable you to get hold of and discuss any poem, even an enormously long one. But the fact is that, for the purposes of an examination, the kind of poem that is going to be set most often is a short lyric poem, probably no shorter than fourteen lines (a sonnet) and no longer than fifty lines. Examiners also tend to favour certain kinds of lyric poem: the sort that is set most often is one that is based on an incident or an experience in the poet's life, or something that the poet has observed. In such cases, the reader can usually get hold of the content of the poem fairly easily, but might find it hard to think of anything very much to say about the poem. Obviously, part of the purpose of this book is to tell you what to look for and what to say. At the opposite extreme from poems built around some trivial incident in the poet's life are poems where the reader can see that a great deal is going on, but then finds it hard to control the impressions the poem is making or say what they all amount to; such poems might well deal with the big themes, such as love and death, but it can be hard to pin down precisely what it is they are saying about love or death.

Other poems will strike the reader as primarily baffling. Because so few of us read poetry on a regular basis, anything from the seventeenth century or earlier is likely to strike us as puzzling. In such poems, the archaic language may act as a barrier. Somehow we have got to see through this kind of surface difficulty in order to make a start. This book will provide advice about how to overcome this difficulty. Finally, there are some poems, such as Coleridge's 'Kubla Khan', which really are deep and puzzling; we have got to find a way of coping with the genuinely unusual and difficult poem. Most poems will slot into one or more of these four categories: a seemingly trivial poem built on some observation or incident in the poet's life, a poem that is obviously dealing with big subjects such as love or death, a poem where the language is puzzling, and a poem that is really baffling. With all of them, we have got to start by establishing an initial understanding.

11 UNDERSTANDING THE POEM

Everything in practical criticism starts with reading the poem or passage carefully, and perhaps several times. In an ideal world, as you read and reread the poem, an understanding of it would gradually emerge. This, however, would take a great deal of time. We are going to suggest a more direct and practical method. Search for a central tension or opposition in the poem, a tension that will probably make itself apparent in the opening lines. We're not going to elaborate on this idea here, because Chapters 2 and 3 deal with such an approach at length, but we do want to provide one example. We turned to an anthology of poetry, opened it at random, and came across a poem that starts as follows:

> All the way to the hospital
> the lights were green as peppermints.
> Trees of black iron broke into leaf
> ahead of me, as if
> I were the lucky prince
> in an enchanted wood
> summoning summer with my whistle,
> banishing winter with a nod.

This is the opening of 'The Almond Tree' by Jon Stallworthy, but this isn't really relevant information at this point. What we are interested in is locating an opposition or tension. The easiest way of looking for a tension is to look for something positive and something negative in the opening lines, or, to put it even more simply, look for something nice and something nasty in the opening lines.

Here, for example, the word 'hospital' in the opening line suggests a negative impression, such as illness or an accident. But then everything b ɔmes very positive: the traffic lights are all green and the trees are breaking into leaf. The poet, we can see, feels special, rather like a prince, and very much in control, as if his whistle can control the seasons. But there are hints of something darker: there is the idea of something hard in the image of the trees as 'black iron' before they burst into leaf, and there is, although it is being banished, a reminder of winter in the last line. On the basis of this evidence, it seems reasonable to suggest that we already have a good idea what this poem as a whole is going to be about: feelings of joy, of being in control of life, are going to be set against more worrying ideas, images of ill-health, and of the hardness of life. We are not going to take this any further here, however, except to say that it does indeed turn out to be an intensely moving poem about a terrible burden imposed on a family at a time when everything seems wonderful in their lives. But the point we are trying to get across is that if you can spot a tension in a poem, as we have done here, it immediately provides you with a framework for shaping your subsequent impressions of the work as a whole. If you can get things off to a strong start, if you can spot a pattern in this kind of way at the outset, then everything else will follow naturally.

12 BUILDING A RESPONSE

When you have established a sense of the central tension in a poem, you have in effect defined the subject of the poem. Different readers will see it in different ways, but that doesn't matter; a poem can be read in more than one way. Building an analysis, then, amounts to looking at how the poet brings this idea to life. Essentially, most of the work will consist of seeing how the writer develops both sides of the opposition, and plays the two sides off against each other. The way in which the poet develops the subject of the poem is by the choice of words and the combination of words; poetry analysis involves looking at how the words chosen, and how the arrangement of words into patterns, bring to life the central tension. As you proceed, you will gain a sense of how the poet complicates the central tension, but this is something that should emerge as you work through the poem. In fact, it is something that should develop as your essay develops, which leads us on the next point to be considered, how to put together an essay.

13 SHAPING AN ESSAY

The major secret of essay-writing, whether it be a practical criticism essay or any other literature essay, is to get the essay itself to do a lot of the work for you. What we mean by this is that the essay's structure can help structure and direct your thoughts. This is something that we will explain fully in the course of this book, but there are some fundamental principles we need to establish here. First, use the first paragraph of the essay to get hold of the poem as a whole, in particular establishing a sense of the central tension in the work. This first paragraph should also get the 'story' of the poem out of the way, so that subsequent paragraphs can focus on how the poet brings the idea in the poem to life. Don't make the mistake of talking about content, followed by some discussion of technique; after the first paragraph of your essay, you are always talking about both, about how the formal choices the poet has made determine and develop the direction of the poem. If the poem is in four stanzas then the logical way to structure your essay is to have four main paragraphs after the introductory paragraph; if the poem has three stanzas, then your essay requires three central paragraphs. What you must also bear in mind, however, is that you are building a case, so each paragraph will have to advance your case about the poem as a whole. But the fact is that if you organise your essay as logically as we suggest here, then the structure of the essay will push you towards developing a case. The essay can then conclude with a short final paragraph where you pull the threads together, hopefully with a certain degree of satisfaction and certainty that you have done justice to the complexity and interest of the poem in question.

14 WHERE DO I GO NEXT?

There are two answers to this question. As we have already said, practical criticism isn't the end but the beginning of criticism. Every student of literature needs to become proficient at this kind of analysis of the words on the page. But this then might connect with a broader discussion of how a text functions in a certain historical period. This kind of more broad-ranging discussion does, however, have to be based upon close scrutiny of the text. We can't, for example, just suggest in a general and unsubstantiated way that Wordsworth's works were influenced by the French Revolution; we have to be able to point to specific lines in his poetry where we can detect the larger political and historical forces of the period. It is in this sense, therefore, that close work on the text – practical criticism – is the foundation on which everything else is built. There is no point in being full of big ideas about literature if you cannot see how these big ideas announce themselves in the small details of a text.

This, then, is one answer to the question 'Where do I go next?' You move beyond practical criticism, in order to confront the full range of questions and issues that come up in criticism these days, but never losing sight of the fact that you must never abandon the essential skill of an ability to do things with the words on the page. The other answer to the question 'Where do I go next?', however, is that you proceed through the chapters of this book, as we flesh out the advice given in this opening chapter. That advice adds up to the three points we will be returning to again and again: *understanding the poem*, *building your response*, and *shaping an essay*.

2

Understanding a poem

IN this chapter we concentrate on how to make sense of a poem, and then, when you feel you have got hold of a poem, how to develop your response.

Let us imagine that it is a blazing hot day in June, the kind of day when anyone with any sense would be going for a swim, but you've had to present yourself for the practical criticism exam. You've set out your pens, had a quiet laugh at those members of the class who have arranged mascots on their desks, and have now turned over the paper in order to start. You are confronted by this poem:

'The Welsh Hill Country'

Too far for you to see
The fluke and the foot-rot and the fat maggot
Gnawing the skin from the small bones,
The sheep are grazing at Bwlch-y-Fedwen,
Arranged romantically in the usual manner
On a bleak background of bald stone.

Too far for you to see
The moss and the mould on the cold chimneys,
The nettles growing through the cracked doors,
The houses stand empty at Nant-yr-Eira,
There are holes in the roofs that are thatched with sunlight,
And the fields are reverting to the bare moor.

Too far, too far to see
The set of his eyes and the slow phthisis
Wasting his frame under the ripped coat,
There's a man still farming at Ty'n-y-Fawnog
Contributing grimly to the accepted pattern,
The embryo music dead in his throat.

Step 1: Reading and thinking

The first step, obviously, is reading the poem. But, having said that, there are two different ways in which you can read a poem: an ideal way, and a less naive, slightly cynical way. In the former, you come to the poem with a blank mind, and let the poem make an impression. Your mind becomes a kind of sponge, in which ideas about and a response to the poem gradually accumulate. It's a nice idea, and it might work for some people, but it is a bit of a slow method for anyone taking an examination. It's also a method that is theoretically flawed: it assumes that the reader is innocent, that the reader has no preconceptions. But, in fact, as we'll explain, every reader, even if they are unaware of it, knows a great deal about poetry, and every reader brings this knowledge to bear in attempting to understand a poem. What we suggest, therefore, is that you read the poem in an active, almost cynical, way, with your mind buzzing with ideas as you try to sort out what is going on in the poem.

But your mind can't just buzz with ideas in an unstructured way. Your mind has to move along in a certain groove as you try to establish a pattern. This is easy to explain in relation to this poem because it is, at least to begin with, a poem that is unlikely to present the reader with too many problems. Everyone can see what the poem is about: it is about the Welsh hill country. But at that point a lot of readers might run out of things to say: they might mention that the poet describes the landscape, animal life and human life that one encounters, but, having praised the description, they could well fail to see any real point behind the description. At this stage, a lot of readers, in sheer desperation for something to say, will claim how true and accurate the poem is, as if this justifies its existence. The reality is, however, that so far we have described a reading that lacks both conviction and any real grasp of the poem.

What we are saying doesn't just apply to this poem. Time and time again, examination candidates are confronted by poems about everyday life, about the small things of life. Such poems are, in a way, trivial: the poet has noticed something or experienced something and decided to write a poem about it. There are thousands of poems that work along these lines. And, time and time again, a lot of examination candidates simply re-describe what the poet has described, and then, rather weakly, add that it is a true or moving observation on life. In all honesty, they could be analysing a proverb.

But how is it possible to break out of the trap of describing the description and then commending the insightfulness of the description? What we should be looking for, in any poem, is a larger kind of significance in the work; we should be looking for the framework of thinking that informs the poem, and which is expressed and developed in every detail of the poem. To put it another way, we are looking for 'the issue' in a poem, although we could equally well say that we are looking for the poem's 'argument'. And, as it is an argument we are looking for, the easiest way of getting at this is to look for the conflict or tension in the work.

There are simple ways of doing this: the easiest approach is to look at the opening lines and search for any positive images or impressions. Then search for any negative images or impressions. In this poem, for example, we might set the picture of the sheep 'arranged romantically' against the rather grim reference to the 'fluke' and 'foot-rot' that affects them. There is an important point that we want to make here: as you read a poem, you should be trying to detect a tension in it from the word go. You can rely upon the fact that it is always possible to detect a contrast in the opening lines of a poem. Don't worry about subsequent details, or where the poem arrives. That complicates matters in an unnecessary way; in order to start, all you need to get is an initial strong hold on the poem, almost invariably on the basis of seeing what is positive and negative in the opening lines.

But once you have got hold of a tension, what do you do with it? The idea to grasp is that the tension helps you see the larger issue that underlies and informs the poem. The poet in 'The Welsh Hill Country' is not, we assume, describing the countryside just for the sake of describing it. He must be dealing with some larger issue. On the basis of the contrast we have spotted, it seems reasonable to suggest that the poet is dealing with the difference – the tension, the conflict – between the superficial appearance of things and the grim reality of life. It is, therefore, not *just* a poem about the Welsh countryside; the poet is talking more generally about disease, waste and decay in life. At one level it is just a trivial little poem, but, as we can see, it deals with weighty themes.

That last sentence touches upon a central fact to grasp about poetry. When you are asked to read, say, a sonnet, you might wonder why people make such a fuss about something as insignificant as a fourteen-line poem. But the fact is that, in a tight and economical way, through oblique language, a short poem can deal with the weightiest matters of life and death. This is certainly true of 'The Welsh Hill Country'. But it is this 'weightiness' of poetry, the fact that a small poem may be handling enormous themes, that gives many examination candidates problems. They get the idea in their minds that there is some *hidden* subject behind the surface subject of the poem. And it is at this point that ingenuity, or, sometimes, silliness, takes over, as candidates start speculating about all sort of hidden meanings in a poem.

What we are saying is that there are *larger* meanings in a poem, but these larger issues are the *general* themes behind the *particular* examples. A poem about the death of a child, for example, will not have a hidden meaning about nuclear war, but it will have a *larger* meaning, that behind the particular example we are likely to see a consideration of issues such as death, innocence, the love of a parent, and loss. It is your job as a critic to see the larger themes that are there in the particular experience described in the poem. If this is still rather difficult to grasp, what we can add is that an effective essay format can help you spot the larger issues in a poem, because an effective essay structure helps structure and direct your thinking. And it is this, how to start establishing your response in the form of an essay that we turn to in a moment. But first, it might be helpful if we list some 'do's' and don'ts' about getting hold of a poem as a whole:

DO look for a tension, conflict or opposition in a poem.

DO look for positive images and impressions that can be set against negative images and impressions.

DO concentrate on the opening lines. You don't need to sort out the poem as a whole at this stage. You are simply concerned with getting an initial confident hold on the poem.

DO try to see the larger issue that lies behind the particular details of the poem; the tension you have spotted should help you identify a larger issue.

DON'T try to analyse the whole poem in advance. If you try to do this you are likely to tie yourself up in knots.

DON'T, at the outset, worry about details you don't understand in the poem. Such details can be dealt with later.

DON'T get side-tracked. You are analysing a poem. Concentrate on the effects that are actually taking place in the poem rather than talking about your own life and experiences.

DON'T become over-ingenious. You aren't searching for hidden meanings in the poem. Stick to the plain sense of the poem and any larger issues that the plain sense suggests.

Step 2:   Starting an essay. Summarise the poem, establish your sense of the central opposition in the poem, set up the controlling idea for your essay as a whole

Everything we are going to say about building a response to a poem is inseparable from the activity of writing down that response. Thoughts and ideas about the poem should be expressing themselves in the form of an essay, and the form of the essay should be pushing along those thoughts and ideas. But the secret of how to write a good essay is something that has to be learnt. One of the things students comment on most frequently is that they often receive poor marks for essays they have taken great pains over, whereas they sometimes receive good marks for essays they have dashed off. We are going to recommend that essays be dashed off. It is inevitable in an exam, where time is limited, but dashing off your normal essays is also a good idea (although there should always be another, and sometimes lengthy, stage with class essays of redrafting your work until it says what you want to say as elegantly and as clearly as possible).

When it comes to writing an essay, therefore, don't waste time at the outset in excessive preparation. We have seen far too many candidates making elaborate notes all over the poem on an exam paper, some even underlining and highlighting details in different colours. Why? Why go round in circles like this at the outset? You don't need to sort out every detail in advance. Another thing that is all too common is that, when they start to write, candidates often start with the closing lines of the poem. This is a fatal mistake. The poem will have arrived somewhere different at the end from where it began, but you don't need to sort this out in advance. An effective essay structure will move your argument along, enabling you to arrive at the end of the poem at an appropriate point late in your essay.

What you need to do at the outset is read the poem carefully at least twice (preferably 'out loud' to yourself). Think briefly about what is happening in the poem as a whole, but then devote your real energy to sorting out a tension in the opening lines. Once you have done this, you can start writing your essay. At the moment you haven't got a clue what you are going to say in the second or subsequent paragraphs, but that doesn't matter. Focus entirely on getting the first paragraph right. If you can get the first paragraph right, everything else in the essay will follow naturally.

You should know in advance the things you will be looking for and aiming to say in your first paragraph, and also know that it's not going to be too long: probably about ten to twelve lines. The best way to start is with a summary of the poem. This achieves two objects. First, it enables you to make sure that you have got hold of the 'story' of the poem. You aren't looking for anything elaborate at this stage. You are simply establishing your version of the plain sense of the poem. The second great advantage of starting with a summary is that it gets the 'content' of the poem out of the way. Far too many practical criticism essays spend paragraph after paragraph retelling the story of the poem. What you must realise is that this kind of retelling of the poem isn't critical analysis – it's nothing but extended summary. If, however, you get the 'content' of the poem out of the way in the first paragraph, that more or less prevents you from returning to tell the 'story' again. Instead, in subsequent paragraphs you will have to concentrate on the formal choices the poet has made to bring his or her idea to life.

A summary alone, however, won't provide you with quite enough material for your opening paragraph. You need two, or possibly more, sentences after your summary to show you can see the poem's overall argument. In order to give some direction to the story you have just retold, it is a good idea to draw attention to the tension you have observed in the poem. Then, after this, you need to step back, and make some kind of indication of the larger issue you can see in the evidence you have presented. Let's look at how, following these guidelines, we might construct an opening paragraph about 'The Welsh Hill Country':

In 'The Welsh Hill Country', the poet initially draws attention to sheep grazing. In some ways it seems an attractive picture, but reference is also made to the diseases the sheep carry. The poet then describes a house that has fallen into a state of decay, and in the third stanza a farmer, but we get an impression of a man who is wasting away. There seems to be a tension in the poem, therefore, between the superficial attractiveness of the whole picture and the underlying reality of disease and decay.

> As such, the poem amounts to far more than a mere description of a rural landscape; it seems to touch upon a large and disturbing theme of the dark reality of life.

Can you see how simple the structure of this paragraph is? Three sentences of summary, one sentence about the tension, and one sentence that steps back a little to make an initial comment on a larger theme.

It doesn't matter if you don't get things quite right at the outset. In the kind of essay structure we are describing, you can change direction, for the first paragraph contains nothing more than an initial impression; a closer look might force one to adjust that initial impression. Similarly, it doesn't matter if you can't spot a larger issue in the opening paragraph; if you have spotted a tension, you can be confident that you are starting to move in the right direction. An awareness of the larger issues inherent in that tension can develop as your essay progresses. The logic of all this might become apparent if we look at the method we are recommending from a slightly different angle. What this method amounts to is a kind of staged performance of reading the poem. In paragraph one, we look at the poem as a whole and a certain impression starts to take shape in our minds. It might at this stage be an unfocused impression, but as long as we can see a tension we are seeing a pattern, and when we have even the slightest sense of a pattern we can start to build. As we look at stanza two, in the second paragraph, we add to that initial impression; we have considered the evidence a little more, thought about it, and added to our overall impression. And so it continues: each subsequent paragraph marks another step forward in thinking about the poem. It is re-enacting, step by step, the process of reading, and slowly grasping the full implications of what we are reading.

Step 3:   Look more closely at the opening of the poem, trying to see how the poet brings the theme to life

Paragraph one has established the foundations on which we can build. Paragraph one can, and should, be fairly simple. The essay will become more complicated as it goes along, keeping pace with our developing sense of the complexity of the poem. The practical way of arranging this is that if a poem is divided into stanzas, it is best, after your general opening paragraph, to devote one paragraph to each stanza. If a poem – a sonnet, for example – isn't divided up into stanzas, create your own sections, dividing the poem into three or four parts.

In this instance, as 'The Welsh Hill Country' is divided into three stanzas, we are going to devote our second paragraph to the opening six lines, that is to say the first stanza of the poem:

> Too far for you to see
> The fluke and the foot-rot and the fat maggot
> Gnawing the skin from the small bones,
> The sheep are grazing at Bwlch-y-Fedwen,
> Arranged romantically in the usual manner
> On a bleak background of bald stone.

What do we say about these lines? The best approach is to pick out particular words and phrases for comment. You might, for example, at some point want to say something about the poet's use of Welsh place-names, such as Bwlch-y-Fedwen. It's difficult, isn't it! Not surprisingly, some examination candidates come unstuck at this point, because they can't think what to say about words or phrases from the poem, even words or phrases that have particularly caught their eye. But the fact is that if you have spotted a tension you have in your hand the key that will enable you to unlock any detail in the poem. For every detail will be adding to one side or the other of the tension you have spotted, bringing to life, and extending, the issue you have identified. The technique is to build upon what you have already established; as you do so, that will add to your understanding of the broader implications of the tension you have established.

And this is what we are going to do for the rest of this chapter. We're going to build an analysis of 'The Welsh Hill Country'. We're not going to comment all that much on what we are doing (Chapters 4 and 5 deal at length with how to develop a case), but try to see the essential simplicity of the method. We have got a sense of the tension in the poem. As we look at each stanza we should be able to fill out this idea. We don't need to comment on every word and every detail; it will prove much more productive to focus on just a few of the details, and to really do justice to them. We are, however, in order to illustrate something of the variety of things it is possible to say about a poem, going to say rather more than is necessary for an examination (we are going to write two paragraphs, rather than one, about each stanza). If our method works, and we can guarantee that it does work, by the end of the essay we should surprise ourselves with just how much we have established.

The first stanza of the poem presents, at one level, a picturesque impression of the Welsh countryside, most obviously in the reference to the sheep that are 'Arranged romantically' on the hillside. The fact of them being 'arranged', however, rather than just standing, possibly suggests there is some kind of artistic arrangement about this, as if they are on display for the benefit of a tourist, or a painter, or even a poet. All the other details of the stanza, however, undermine this romantic impression: it is as if the poet shows us both the true face of the countryside and, at the same time, in undercutting the romantic image, challenges a whole tradition in art, particularly in poetry, of looking at nature in an idealising way. This, we are led to believe, is reality: the painter, poet or tourist is 'too far' removed.

The reality is conveyed in the powerful and emotive disease words in the second line: 'fluke', 'foot-rot' and 'fat maggot'. The words and associations are unpleasant, but what is particularly disturbing is that this is a kind of rot that is eating and destroying from within. It is, as yet, difficult to see where the poet is taking us with these ideas; in a way, our experience so far is conveyed in the use of the Welsh place-name, Bwlch-y-Fedwen. It is used in a familiar way by the poet, and so, at one level, contributes to the superficial cosiness of the impression, but it is at the same time, for most readers, a strange and alien word in a foreign language. The name thus seems to underline the conflict in the poem between the real and the romantic. Here is another world, another language, a kind of mystery to which we are strangers. Possibly, however, the poem might 'translate' this world for us.

Step 4:   Look at another section of the poem, trying to build on your analysis of the poem's details

What we have said so far might seem like showing off. A reading of a poem certainly doesn't have to push things this far. But at the same time, look at how simple it all is: all we have said is that the details add to our sense of the tension in the poem. As we continue with the second stanza we should be able to take this further:

Too far for you to see
The moss and the mould on the cold chimneys,
The nettles growing through the cracked doors,

The houses stand empty at Nant-yr-Eira,
There are holes in the roofs that are thatched with sunlight,
And the fields are reverting to the bare moor.

The major impression we gain from this stanza is that nature is reclaiming the land in some way. What people have built, specifically the houses, seems like some kind of imposition on the land. The sense of nature taking over is present in a detail such as the phrase 'thatched with sunlight': the human activity of repairing and maintaining things is now in the hands of nature. And just for a moment, in this detail and at this point in the poem, nature seems warm and kind. The major impression, however, is of nature as destructive.

Nature is often associated with fertility, but in this poem (where there are sheep but no lambs), the landscape in the first stanza is 'bleak' and here it is 'the bare moor'. There is a kind of barrenness suggested in such imagery. One could interpret the whole poem in political terms, that this is an area that has been neglected, that has become depopulated, and this is the cause of the decay; that the observers, who are always too far away to see the reality, are implicitly English, and that the poem is a protest from the heartland of Wales. But, even though we cannot ignore the existence of people in the poem outside the immediate landscape, the poem seems to focus more on a slow death from within.

Step 5: Look at how the poem concludes

Too far, too far to see
The set of his eyes and the slow phthisis
Wasting his frame under the ripped coat,
There's a man still farming at Ty'n-y-Fawnog
Contributing grimly to the accepted pattern,
The embryo music dead in his throat.

It is again the case that our pretty, superficial impressions of Wales are destroyed. A familiar association of Wales is with music, but, as the last line here states, the music is 'dead in his throat'. Music in poetry suggests harmony, but here things are far from joyous; things are stuck in a rut, in 'the accepted pattern'. In so far as things move at all, they move towards death. The progression of negative images is far more pronounced and far more extreme in this stanza than in the first two: we go through illness, 'wasting', 'grimly', and then, finally, we are brought up hard against the word 'dead'. Again, however, it is a kind of wasting and slow death from within.

There is a strange and ugly word, 'phthisis'. Most readers have probably never encountered the word, but to our minds it adds to that sense of something incomprehensible in the whole experience of this landscape. It is another world, where the medical term is as unfamiliar to us as the words in Welsh. We can see so far, like the observers in the poem, but possibly we, as readers, are also included amongst the 'you' who cannot see; that we are outsiders to whom everything remains as incomprehensible as 'Nant-yr-Eira' or 'Ty'n-y-Fawnog'. We started with the idea of the gap between the superficial impression and the grim reality, but perhaps that gap is even wider and much more significant than we first realised. It is a gap that suggests how we are forever outsiders, unable to understand what we see so romantically.

Step 6: Sum up your sense of the poem as a whole

The poem moves inexorably towards death. It is a grim and startling view of this landscape. Yet, surprisingly, the poem doesn't strike us as entirely negative. The reason for this, as far as we can see, is that the speaker in the poem stands as a kind of intermediary between 'us' and 'them'. 'We' are, and will remain, total outsiders, but the poet acts as a kind of spokesperson for the community, making the case for these people. In his intermediary role, he might recognise that the rot is internal, that it is a wasting and destructive thing in nature that destroys everything, but at the same time there is perhaps a hint of accusation, a hint of recrimination against outsiders who, while they have been prepared to look at this land, have neglected any duty to protect or foster it.

We have, as you can see, come a long way in a few paragraphs, but essentially everything we have done is very simple. We started with a simple idea, a tension, and have kept to that tension. We had an idea of the gap between the superficial impression and the reality of this landscape; all we have done is explore the implications of this tension as announced in the words and ideas that constitute the poem. In other words, we have finished where we started, but in looking at the details, and relating them to our initial tension, we have arrived at a complex understanding of the poem. (It is not, of course, the only possible understanding of the poem; in Chapter 8, which focuses on essay-writing, we reproduce essays by three of our students, all of whom find their own way through the poem.) When it comes down to it the method of practical criticism is always as simple as this: practical criticism involves seeing a pattern, looking at the details, and using the details to add to one's idea of the pattern. Before we pursue this idea, however, it might prove useful to include a further chapter focusing on the first issue in practical criticism, which is how to find the tension in a poem.

3

Understanding a poem: some examples

THE first step – getting hold of a poem as a whole – is the vital one. If you can do this, then there is no limit to what you can build on such a firm foundation. This chapter is about establishing this initial understanding of a poem. We look at the openings of eleven poems (in the first two examples, just the titles), and show how easy it is to establish a sense of what is going to matter in the poems as a whole. As you read the following pages, try to see the logic of the method. Indeed, the best way to approach this chapter is as a participation exercise: see for yourself what tension and what sense of a larger issue you can establish in each case from what are very small scraps of evidence.

Example 1:   Working from a title

Sometimes – but not always – the title of a poem on its own will provide you with a great deal of information about the poem as a whole. A modern poem by Roger McGough is called **'If Life's a Lousy Picture, Why Not Leave Before the End'**. We have suggested, in the previous chapters, that you look for positive and negative impressions in order to identify the tension in a poem. It is easy to find something negative here: life is referred to as 'a lousy picture'. But what is also conveyed in the title is the idea of escape from lousiness. The title refers to watching a movie, and there is a sense in which movies offer us an escape into a fantasy world. The tension in the poem as a whole, therefore, may well be 'lousy' reality versus the possibility of escape. What larger 'issue' does this suggest? Clearly, McGough isn't just talking about going to the cinema. Implicit in the title is a broader idea of the problems people encounter in life and how they respond to these problems.

Taking this a step further, what you might pick up from the words 'why not leave before the end' is an altogether more chilling idea, the possibility of suicide. This is obviously going to be a light-hearted poem (as we can tell from the whimsical title), yet, none the less, it might touch on serious questions of life and death. In fact, the poem eventually arrives at a happy/escapist ending, but we don't know this yet, and don't need to know at the outset. What matters is that we have taken the first steps: we have detected a tension and established a provisional sense of the larger issues the poem might confront. We are, therefore, in control; we can add to, and amend, our ideas as we go along.

Example 2:   Working from a title

A lot of titles aren't going to tell you very much, but all titles are going to tell you something. When we were putting this book together, we discovered that there are a great many poems entitled 'Rain'. It is a fair bet that most poems called 'Rain' will contrast bad weather and fine weather, although sometimes a certain comfort will be found in rain. Rain in such poems, therefore, provides a focus for a consideration of the larger issue of sunshine and showers in life in general. We can anticipate a lot, then, from even a one-word title, but a longer title usually provides more help. Here is an example: **'Christmas Letter Home (To my sister in Aberdeen)'**. This says a great deal because there is such a clear tension between the idea of Christmas – a time for being at home with one's family – and the fact that the poet is away from home.

Immediately we know that the poem is going to deal with large issues such as the feeling of belonging to a family, growing up and leaving home, separation and loneliness. The words in brackets – specifically 'sister' and 'Aberdeen' – reinforce the sense of belonging to a family and belonging to a specific place. As against this, we can anticipate that the poet, in the poem as a whole, might well feel that he now lives in an alien and impersonal environment. He is likely to feel insecure, even rather frightened. Of course, as we begin to look more closely at the poem we might have to adjust this initial impression, but that is perfectly acceptable. The important point is that we have used the title to establish a foundation. If we change our ideas as we go along, it doesn't matter; all it means is that initially the poem created certain expectations, but then overturned them.

Example 3:   'Adlestrop'

Don't worry if you can't do much with the title of a poem; lots of titles aren't going to prove all that illuminating. But, almost without exception, you should be able to establish a tremendous amount from the first four to six lines of a poem. We are going to start with two twentieth-century examples, and then move back to the seventeenth century, to the kind of poems where unfamiliar language presents a problem. But first, let's consider the opening lines of 'Adlestrop', by Edward Thomas:

> Yes, I remember Adlestrop –
> The name, because one afternoon
> Of heat the express-train drew up there
> Unwontedly. It was late June.

We have suggested that you look for negative impressions and positive impressions, but an even simpler version of this is to say whether the details in a poem seem 'nice' or 'nasty'.

What about the name 'Adlestrop'? We feel it sounds rather quaint, as if it is somewhere deep in the heart of traditional England. If that is one side of things in these opening lines, what can be set against this impression? Surely the relevant detail is 'the express train', which, as against the quiet backwater of Adlestrop, reminds us of the pace of the modern world. The poem, we can anticipate, is going to be about the gap between modern life and an older, slower existence. Where the poem will eventually arrive we don't yet know, but, if it does develop in an unexpected direction, we will be well-placed to see this because we have created such a clear view at the outset.

Example 4:   'This Day'

It is easy for the reader to get started on analysing a poem if it starts with a four- or six-line stanza, but not all poems are so ordered. In the case of this poem, for example, we can't even identify a self-contained opening, as the sentences drift along in a ragged way from one stanza to the next; our quoted lines, consequently, stop rather awkwardly in the middle of a sentence:

Watching the beautiful
sticks of trees as they click and sway,
the first green unraveling,

it's easy to imagine I might
remember this day forever.
I say it to myself,

We have urged you to look for a tension in the opening lines of a poem, but you might feel that no tension is in evidence here. It seems to be just unalloyed appreciation of nature, prompting a positive mood in the poet, prompting his feeling that he will 'remember this day forever'. Spring is arriving, the seasons are in harmony, and the poet is in harmony with nature. It seems reasonable to maintain, therefore, that no tension is in evidence here.

This will sometimes be the impression at the start of a poem. What you have to do is create the tension: you have to anticipate the sourer notes that are likely to appear later in the poem. If you don't, you're not going to be able to say all that much about the poem beyond appreciating the poet's feeling of well-being. In the case of this poem by Lawrence Raab, however, it could be argued that a tension is in evidence in these opening lines, for the unusual three-line stanzas create a rather jarring effect. The overall sense of well-being in the content conflicts with this slightly discordant element in the poem's form. It is perhaps most clear in the way that the poet's sentences don't fit neatly into the stanzas; the impression that is created is that things are slightly out of control. This suggests a larger issue that we might expect to see confronted in the poem as a whole: the poem is likely to offer us some kind of reflection on the relationship between a sense of harmony in existence and a lack of harmony. Nature might be associated with fecundity and expansiveness, but, in the way the impressions expand beyond the confines of the stanzas, there is also a sense of a world that defies control.

Example 5:   'To His Coy Mistress'

In the last example, we introduced the word 'harmony'. It is a useful word to bear in mind. Most poems can be referred to as lyrics. The word 'lyric' means song; a poem can even be defined as a harmonious reflection upon experience. But we cannot have a concept of harmony without a concept of disharmony. Putting this another way, implicit in the very existence of poetry as a form is an idea of some kind of debate between harmony and lack of harmony, between a concept of order and the inevitability of disorder. The point we are really making here is that we don't just impose a tension upon a poem in order to help us understand it; on the contrary, a fundamental tension is at the very heart of poetry as an artistic form.

Such speculation, however, takes us some way beyond the limited brief of this chapter, which is simply to show how it is possible to get hold of poems from their opening lines. Let's, therefore, return to basics. Here is the opening of a very famous poem, 'To His Coy Mistress' by Andrew Marvell:

> Had we but world enough, and time,
> This coyness, lady, were no crime.
> We would sit down, and think which way
> To walk, and pass our long love's day.

The tension is perhaps, implicit rather than explicit. The poet imagines a leisurely world, where there is limitless time. Implicit, of course, is the idea that the world isn't like this, that we live in a world where time is short and where death is never far away. The poet is, then, contrasting an idealised version of life with the stark and urgent facts of life.

The additional element here, however, is the reference to his woman friend; he resents her coyness, presumably meaning her reluctance to consummate their relationship. He is likely to urge her to commit herself, for there is not enough time for coyness. It is our task as readers to look for the general issues behind this particular situation, the way in which this is likely to prove a poem that examines a world where death exists, asking how love should be regarded in such a world. If time was limitless, everything would be fine, but life is short and opportunities must be seized. But what we might also notice is that the man's desire for the woman to commit herself is also an aspect of the real world; far from being a selfless lover, he is cynical and worldly-wise, ready to exploit his argument to score a sexual advantage. The argument in the poem will go through various twists and turns, twists and turns that different readers will interpret in different ways, but we have set up the parameters of the issue with our sense of the gap between a perfect world and life as it really is.

Example 6:   'The Canonization'

Marvell is a seventeenth-century poet. It is seventeenth-century poetry that students of literature find most difficult, partly because of the language barrier and partly because a lot of it is genuinely difficult. The answer is that, at the outset, you have to try to look through the language and ignore the difficulties. You have to look behind the surface in order to establish a sense of the pattern or tension in the poem. If you can do this, you will find that a lot of the problems – both language problems and problems in understanding what the poem is saying – begin to disentangle themselves.

All of the difficulties of seventeenth-century poetry are apparent in John Donne's 'The Canonization'. It begins:

> For God's sake hold your tongue, and let me love,
> Or chide my palsy, or my gout,
> My five gray hairs, or ruined fortune, flout,
> With wealth your state, your mind with arts improve . . .

This stanza continues for another five lines, but there is quite enough here both to confuse and to help us. For a start, why is the poem called 'The Canonization', which is a reference to making someone a saint? As we begin to read the poem it seems to have very little to do with religion. That is, if we can grasp what it is about at all; it is likely to take a lot of effort before we even gather that someone has been criticising the speaker in the poem and that this is his response. It is difficult to grasp because the situation is not set up for us; on the contrary, Donne starts more or less in full flow. Rather than being eased into an argument we are confronted by a colloquial torrent. It is thus not surprising that the vast majority of English Literature students would find it very hard to say what is going on as 'The Canonization' opens.

Our advice, and this applies to every difficult poem, is, when confronted by difficulty, head in the opposite direction. This poem is a puzzling and complex structure; what you need to find, therefore, is a very simple way of gaining access to it. And the most elementary way of getting into any poem is to ask yourself 'What sounds nice?' and 'What sounds nasty?' in the opening lines. By keeping the questions as simple as this, you establish control. Asking the 'nice' and 'nasty' questions here, it seems to us that the only nice point in the opening lines is the poet's reference to love. All the other images, such as 'palsy', 'gout' and 'grey hairs' are unpleasant. Unpleasant in that they suggest illness and the onset of old age. They remind us of the 'nasty' fact of human mortality.

The tension in the poem, therefore, must be between love and the painful fact of death. In the course of the poem, Donne is likely to explore some of the ramifications of the relationship between the two. We still, of course, have no idea why the poem is called 'The Canonization', but we don't need to know at this stage. Nor do we, at the outset, have to worry about every complicated nuance in the poem. All we need is the platform on which to build, and, by asking simple questions, we have given ourselves just that. We have found love in the poem, and we have found references to illness and growing old; all the details of the poem will eventually explain themselves in the light of that basic structure.

Example 7:   'An Elegy'

As we have said, the more difficult a poem appears, the more necessary it becomes to gain access to it at a very simple level. Once you have got inside the poem you will be in control of it. Not all seventeenth-century poems are difficult, however. As in any era, there are a great many poems that are likely to strike you as simply bland or inconsequential. 'An Elegy', by Ben Jonson, might seem to be a poem of this kind. It helps if one knows that an elegy is a poem that commemorates a friend who has died. As you start to read this elegy, however, you might feel that it amounts to very little; surely a million poets have knocked off poems like this, poems full of elevating sentiments, but elevating sentiments that seem rather hackneyed or empty. This unfavourable impression might be reinforced by a feeling that the poet is using the kind of language that one only encounters in poetry, language which, on the face of it, appears to have little relationship to the real world.

The problems we have listed are probably all apparent in the opening stanza:

> Though beauty be the mark of praise,
> And yours of whom I sing be such
> As not the world can praise too much,
> Yet is't your virtue now I raise.

If your immediate response is 'boring', that's fair enough. Few people today are going to be all that strongly drawn to a poem that starts like this. If we stick with the poem, however, we might well find that it is a lot more interesting than it initially appears. In order to make such progress, though, we have got to establish our initial sense of a tension, for this will enable us to move towards a sense of the larger issue in the poem.

As an elegy, it is a poem about death, but the opening lines of the poem are given over to a very positive celebration of the qualities of the person who has died, specifically the person's beauty and goodness. An awareness of this tension leads us on to the big issue here: it is a poem that considers a world where death exists, where everything ends in decay and destruction, but it also considers the nature and value of human life in such a world. It is, then, like Donne's 'The Canonization', a poem about love and death, but the very fact that we can so easily establish a link between the two poems should underline the fact that the sense of a tension and a larger issue is simply the foundation on which we build; our pursuit of the details, in either Donne's poem or Jonson's poem, will enable us to identify the distinctive way in which they develop a familiar poetic theme.

Love and death is, in fact, such a familiar tension in poetry that we can incorporate it in the following chart of structures of organisation that you might look for in poetry.

PATTERNS OF OPPOSITION TO LOOK FOR IN A POEM

With any poem, it should help if you think about the opening lines in the light of one or more of these pairs of terms:

> Positive impressions / Negative impressions
> Nice images / Nasty images
> Harmony / Lack of harmony
> Pattern / Lack of pattern
> Order / Disorder
> Love / Death

Example 8:   'Lines Composed a Few Miles Above Tintern Abbey'

This chapter concludes with a look at the opening lines of four more poems, two from the Romantic period and two from the Victorian period. In each case, try to identify a tension and a larger issue. We supply answers, but remember that there is no one answer, that different readers will identify different tensions. Do have the confidence, therefore, to go for the pattern that you see in the opening lines of a poem; the moment you have established this sense of a pattern, you are in control both of the poem and of your reading of the poem.

These are the opening lines of a long poem by William Wordsworth:

> Five years have passed; five summers, with the length
> Of five long winters! and again I hear
> These waters, rolling from their mountain-springs
> With a soft inland murmur.

We start with five long depressing years, but, as against the impression the opening lines give of the poet's despondency, there is a sense of something that restores him in lines 3 and 4. Water in poetry can be destructive (as, say, in images of flood and storm), but here it is soft and friendly, as suggested in 'mountain-springs' and 'soft inland murmur'. Obviously more is involved than just the poet remembering this spot near Tintern Abbey; the poem is likely to deal with the sense of contentment and harmony that the poet finds in this natural setting, and how this can be set against more despondent moods. As it goes on, the poem, in fact, becomes a very complex exploration, and even questioning, of the sense of well-being that Wordsworth derives from nature, but we aren't in a position to know this at the outset. We have, though, established an initial sense of his positive frame of mind and his negative frame of mind, and this provides us with a pattern that will help us keep track of all the subsequent complications in the poem.

Example 9:   'Kubla Khan'

> In Xanadu did Kubla Khan
> A stately pleasure dome decree:
> Where Alph, the sacred river, ran
> Through caverns measureless to man
>   Down to a sunless sea.

This is very odd, so let's take it simply. The 'caverns measureless to man' and the 'sunless sea' sound rather unnerving. As against those images, the 'stately pleasure dome', although a rather exotic and esoteric image, is a *pleasure* dome. What it also represents is something built, something that is a product of human activity, and under human control. As such, it is very different from the measureless caverns.

On the basis of these images, it would seem reasonable to speculate that the larger issue the poem will deal with will be the disordered complexity and vastness of experience, and, at the same time, how people try to build something – that is to say, construct some kind or order – in such a world. The quick reader might, even this early, grasp that poetry itself can be seen as a little oasis of order in a barren world; the poet might well look at how in all areas of life, including writing, we attempt to comprehend and control unfathomable depths and immeasurable forces.

Example 10:   'The Convent Threshold'

> There's blood between us, love, my love,
> There's father's blood, there's brother's blood;
> And blood's a bar I cannot pass:
> I choose the stairs that mount above,
> Stair after golden skyward stair,
> To city and to sea of glass.

The title of this poem enables us to see that a young woman is on the verge of becoming a nun. She rejects the world, but rejects it because her love has been thwarted by enmity between two families. Blood, death and conflict deny her the possibility of love, so she has turned to the love of God – something that is presented in positive terms in the 'golden', 'skyward' and 'glass' images for life in the convent.

It would, however, seem reasonable to assume, particularly in a poem that is nearly one hundred and fifty lines long, that this rejection of the world for the love of God isn't going to be as simple as it initially appears. The poem is likely to dwell more on the disorder of daily life – including the complex emotions of sexual feelings – than on the fact of escape into life in the convent. One aspect of this is likely to be the complicated position of a woman, who, as we can see in these lines, has to operate in the shadow of her father and brother.

Given the poem's opening awareness of the complexities of the real world, the escape into the order of the convent is unlikely, when it comes down to it, to represent much of an escape at all.

Example 11:   'The Prisoner'

> Still let my tyrants know, I am not doomed to wear
> Year after year in gloom, and desolate despair;
> A messenger of Hope comes every night to me,
> And offers for short life, eternal liberty.

There is a tension here between the idea of being a prisoner – who is hounded by tyrants, who is 'doomed', 'in gloom' and in 'despair' – and, on the other hand, an idea of liberation. What we don't know is precisely what the author, Emily Brontë, means by 'messenger of Hope'. We suspect that it isn't a literal messenger, just as we suspect that the narrator in the poem isn't actually a prisoner. It is far more likely that she is talking about psychological feelings of being denied an independent existence.

Again, then, we can see the larger issue in the specific example: the poem is likely to explore feelings of being repressed and restricted. But you might feel, even at this late stage in this chapter, that you could not make this much progress this quickly. You might feel that you could not move confidently from the sense of a tension to the larger issue involved. It doesn't matter, however: if in the case of this poem you managed to establish that it sets an idea of imprisonment against an idea of liberty, then you would have established quite enough of a foundation on which to build. Your reading might be a bit limited if you kept on thinking that the prisoner is literally in jail; at some stage you would have to move on to the larger issue, to the fact that it is a psychological, social and gender-based imprisonment that the narrator is describing. But that can come in time if you can establish a tension that puts you in control; gradually, and as you work on the poem, the details will begin to make sense in relation to that basic tension, and, simultaneously, a sense of the larger issue will begin to take shape.

4

Building a response

So far we have focused on how to get hold of a poem; we now want to deal with how to develop your response. Every poem is built around a tension, but, as soon as the tension has been established, the poet has to expand it and push it in unexpected directions. In other words, where a poem arrives may be very different from where it starts. The argument in the poem will, however, have moved forward in steps. This is the main reason why we suggest that you move through a poem stanza by stanza. Don't make the mistake of immediately jumping to the end of a poem. Equally, resist the temptation to move back and forth around the text. Approach the poem logically, taking the stanzas in sequence. Don't make the mistake of discussing the content first and then, belatedly, at the end of your answer, turning to the poem's formal qualities. Throughout your answer, you should be dealing with every aspect of how the poet brings his or her subject to life.

This chapter and Chapter 5 present illustrations of how you might set about reading a poem. Try to see just how simple the method is. If you are clear about what you are doing at every stage of an analysis, and have a good idea of what you are looking for at each stage of an analysis, you might surprise yourself when you discover just how much you can find to say about any poem.

Step 1:   Reading and thinking

'The Lesson'

'Your father's gone,' my bald headmaster said.
His shining dome and brown tobacco jar
Splintered at once in tears. It wasn't grief.
I cried for knowledge which was bitterer
Than any grief. For there and then I knew

That grief has uses – that a father dead
Could bind the bully's fist a week or two;
And then I cried for shame, then for relief.

I was a month past ten when I learnt this:
I still remember how the noise was stilled
In school-assembly when my grief came in.
Some goldfish in a bowl quietly sculled
Around their shining prison on its shelf.
They were indifferent. All the other eyes
Were turned towards me. Somewhere in myself
Pride like a goldfish flashed a sudden fin.

We have decided to start with this poem, by Edward Lucie-Smith, because it is a typical example of an 'anecdotal' poem, a poem in which the poet recalls an incident in his or her life. As is often the case with such poems, you might find that you have no difficulty grasping the content, but feel that there isn't very much that can be said about the poem itself. In this instance, we have an account of the boy's complicated feelings in the period following the death of his father. It is tempting to just retell the story, and then add how true or thought-provoking the sentiments are. But this isn't analysis of a poem. We have got to niggle away at how the poet brings his subject to life, and, in doing so, we should arrive at a more complex understanding of what is involved in the poem.

Step 2:   Starting an essay. Summarise the poem, establish your sense of the central opposition in the poem, set up the controlling idea for your essay as a whole

We need to summarise the poem. If we present our summary in the first paragraph of our essay, this will help us establish a firm grasp of what the poet is writing about. In addition, presenting a brief summary at this stage will get the 'story' of the poem out of the way; having told the story once, we should be able to resist the temptation to keep on retelling it throughout our answer.

In 'The Lesson', the speaker is called into his headmaster's office to receive the news that his father has died. He bursts into tears, but it isn't so much grief at the loss of his father as relief that the school bullies are likely to ignore him for a week or two because of his loss. In the second stanza, he describes how he became the object of attention in school assembly, and then, making use of the image of a goldfish, he describes a certain pride he feels. This final point about pride – particularly as it is connected with the goldfish – is a difficult point to grasp, but we can ignore it for the moment. There is no use getting distracted at this stage by the way in which the poem concludes. What we need to concentrate on is how the poem begins. If we look for a tension, one side of the tension is obvious whereas the other side is implicit. The obvious negative point is the death of the boy's father, leaving the child on his own in the world. As against that, we can set ideas of security, of belonging to a family, of being a part of things.

The poem, it seems, isn't just about the death of this boy's father. There are broader issues involved: it is exploring the experience of childhood, the securities and insecurities of childhood, and the process of growing up. A psychiatrist could write a long paper about the issues in this poem, but, as is often the case with poetry, the poet manages to say more in a couple of stanzas than could be said in many pages of a psychological or sociological report.

Step 3:   Look more closely at the opening of the poem, trying to see how the poet brings the theme to life

We have established a tension – between a sense of security and a sense of loss, of being on one's own. We have also established a sense of the broader issue, that the poem is looking at the securities and insecurities of childhood. As we look at the poem we should be able to fill out and develop these ideas. Because this is a two-stanza poem, the obvious tactic is to divide each stanza into two, in order to provide us with the material for four central paragraphs of an essay. Let's start, therefore, with the opening lines:

> 'Your father's gone,' my bald headmaster said.
> His shining dome and brown tobacco jar
> Splintered at once in tears. It wasn't grief.
> I cried for knowledge which was bitterer
> Than any grief.

We need to focus on two or three of the details in these lines, trying to see how the details contribute to the poem and, also, how a consideration of these details advances our overall grasp of the poem.

Consider, for example, the 'bald headmaster', his 'shiny dome' and his 'brown tobacco jar'. All the time in poetry analysis we have to ask ourselves why the poet chose the particular detail and how it contributes to the poem. The fact is, of course, that ninety-nine people out of a hundred asked why the poet refers to the 'bald' headmaster wouldn't know what to say, but this is where having a method not only helps but can provide answers when things seem baffling. The clue to interpreting any detail is to look at it in the light of the tension already established. We have set security against insecurity. Does the image of the 'bald headmaster' add to our impression of security or insecurity? We feel it is a rather cold image: he is physically bald, but he is also bald in the sense of being direct or unadorned in his presentation of the harsh news to the child. The detail, therefore, begins to fill out our sense of the world the child occupies. The headmaster, as a kind of substitute father figure, could offer the child comfort, but he is unfeelingly masculine. We can add that the child's response, bursting into tears, is a response traditionally thought of as feminine. The child, presumably at boarding school, is at a remove from the warmth of a family, occupying a world which is cold and unfeeling. It is no wonder the child feels insecure, for the structure in which he finds himself offers very little sustenance (significantly, there is not a single reference to a woman in the poem).

Can you see what we have done? By focusing on just one detail we have already filled out our sense of the initial tension. We started with security and insecurity; we now have a sense of the shortcomings of the world the child occupies, how it is a world where feelings and emotions are excluded. If we turn now to the image of the 'brown tobacco jar', it should add to this picture that we have started to build. To our mind, it reinforces the sense of a male environment where feelings are contained. The image of the tobacco jar, therefore, helps pinpoint further a sense of a delicate child who is at a remove from the routine trappings of the male world.

Step 4: Look at another section of the poem, trying to build on your analysis of the poem's details

> For there and then I knew
> That grief has uses – that a father dead
> Could bind the bully's fist a week or two;
> And then I cried for shame, then for relief.

We are again going to focus on a few details. When we have selected the details, we are not going to rush along with a clever or flashy reading of them. On the contrary, we need to relate each detail back to the ideas we have already established. In this way we can steadily accumulate a solid and sensible reading of the poem.

Let's start with the words, 'For there and then I knew/That grief has uses'. Does it suggest security or insecurity? Oddly enough, a little of the child's insecurity seems to have disappeared. Saying that 'grief has uses' is almost cynical. What it suggests is that the bad news has made the child a little less of a child; abruptly he has acquired a degree of knowingness about the ways of the world. The next sentence, with its reference to the school bully, extends the impression we formed in the opening lines about the nature of the world, for bullying suggests a world dominated by male aggression. The phrase 'a week or two' is interesting: even the bully has some sensitivity, but it won't last long, traditional male bullying will soon reassert itself. As against this, the child in the poem is crying, but, as he says, it is not grief; within one paragraph he cries for knowledge, shame and relief. We are struck by the rapidity of movement of the child's feelings; it's something that needs to be set against the unchanging face of the school.

We have, so far, commented on how the words chosen bring the idea to life, but in talking about poetry we also need to consider the overall structure of the poem – the ways in which its formal qualities as a piece of patterned writing complement, indeed help define, the theme of the poem. In a poem like this (anecdotal, colloquial, unrhymed), the fact that there is some technique dictating its structure might not be all that apparent. In such instances, the thing to consider is the fact of the order and pattern of the poem. We are struck by the fact that a shape – the shape of the poem – is imposed upon the child's feelings. His thoughts and feelings stray, but, as we have already suggested, he is, at the same time, beginning to acquire some 'knowingness' about the world. There is a sense in which the poet's use of the structured order of the poem is a reflection of the way in which he has accepted the disciplines and constraints of the adult world. Equally, there is a kind of disjunction between the formal neatness of the poem and the unfathomable fact of death, but, oddly, the child is moving towards the forms and manners of the world around him.

Step 5:   Look at another section of the poem, trying to build on your analysis of the poem's details

The second stanza begins, 'I was a month past ten when I learnt this'. It is a moving line, for this is the first point at which we become aware of how young he was. The frailty of his position is, consequently, underlined. Yet, at the same time, in mentioning this the poet has detached and distanced himself. His ability to look at himself places him firmly, even confidently, in the adult world. Where does this get us? The point is that the poem is built on a tension, but, as with any poem, as it progresses the tension becomes more complicated. The complication here is that we begin to see how the speaker has come to embrace the masculine values of the adult world. He remains critical of such coldness, but has absorbed a degree of cold distance and discipline into his own personality.

It is an impression that is extended in the image of the goldfish in the bowl. Society is rather like a goldfish bowl: we are trapped inside, just as the boy is trapped and on display in assembly. A goldfish is a pretty miserable creature, but the name actually suggests something rare and precious. Here is something rare and precious stuck in a goldfish bowl. In the same way, a child is rare and precious, but the child in this poem is robbed of his childhood and freedom. He grows up quickly and becomes part of the conventional order.

Step 6:   Look at how the poem concludes

> All the other eyes
> Were turned towards me. Somewhere in myself
> Pride like a goldfish flashed a sudden fin.

You might find these closing lines impossible to relate to the poem as a whole. Why go on about the goldfish again? As always, when stuck the thing to do is to return to the pattern you have established so far in order to interpret the puzzling details. We have been talking about the difference between childhood and the way of the world at large. Which side of this tension is most in evidence here in the reference to his pride flashing like a sudden fin? It seems to us that the line suggests a kind of arrogance, a belief in himself, which is similar to the aggressive confidence he has encountered in the world at large. It is evident in the way that 'flashed a sudden fin' sounds more like the movement of a shark than a goldfish; the poem ends on a note of hardness and aggression.

Step 7: Sum up your sense of the poem as a whole

The experience of loss could have affected the child in one of two ways. He might have become desolate with the sense of loss, but what in fact happens is that he is dragged, painfully but quickly, into a world of aggressive values. A poem is always saying something larger than its plain 'story'. In this poem, the writer has moved beyond what is, presumably, a memory of childhood to offer a complex sense of childhood, of the values that operate within society, and how he has come, at least in part, to share these values. The sense of the person he has become is most obviously conveyed in the image of male aggression with which the poem ends, but the fact that there is another side to his personality is conveyed in the fact that he still looks back to this moment from his childhood.

This is probably a good point at which to formulate a list of the strategies we have employed to construct this analysis of 'The Lesson'. Exactly the same strategies can be employed with any poem.

BUILDING A RESPONSE TO A POEM: STRATEGIES TO EMPLOY

1. Build your response to the poem in paragraph steps.
2. Start by summarising the poem, and establishing a central tension.
3. Establish, if you can, your own sense of the larger issue in the poem.
4. See how the words and phrases the poet uses bring the tension in the poem to life.
5. Try to see how the structure of the poem complements and helps define the subject matter of the poem.
6. Keep moving in on details, but then, at every stage, pull back, trying to add to the case you have been building.
7. At the end of each paragraph of your essay you should be able to add to your overall sense of the 'issue' in the poem.
8. It is ATTENTION TO DETAILS in combination with BUILDING A LARGER CASE that matters. By the end of your analysis, you should feel that you have achieved a sense of how the poem works and what it is saying.

One further point we should stress again before going any further is that there is no single 'correct' reading of a poem. You might look at 'The Lesson' and form an impression of what is going on in it that bears no resemblance to our reading. That is, of course, exactly how it should be. A poem can support a wide variety of readings – but you must make sure that your reading does grow out of the actual words of the poem, that is to say that it is a reading that is consistent with the evidence rather than a merely fanciful interpretation.

'The Lesson', as we said, is an anecdotal poem. It is also an accessible poem, written in language that is easy to understand and dealing with an experience that we can all sympathise with. A lot of poems, however, are likely to prove far from accessible. 'Virtue', the poem we turn to now, is a good example of the kind of poem that might leave many readers uninterested and unmoved. Let's see what we can do with it.

Step 1:   Reading and thinking

'Virtue'

Sweet day, so cool, so calm, so bright,
The bridal of the earth and sky:
The dew shall weep thy fall tonight;
For thou must die.

Sweet rose, whose hue, angry and brave,
Bids the rash gazer wipe his eye:
Thy root is ever in its grave,
And thou must die.

Sweet spring, full of sweet days and roses,
A box where sweets compacted lie;
My music shows ye have your closes,
And all must die.

Only a sweet and virtuous soul,
Like seasoned timber, never gives;
But though the whole world turns to coal,
Then chiefly lives.

We suspect there are two very common responses to this. One is a feeling of alienation, a feeling that the language and sentiments are remote from life today. Secondly, many readers might feel that both the thought and the expression in the poem are hackneyed: the poem doesn't seem to offer much more than a platitude, that everything in life dies, but the virtuous soul lives. This will hardly serve, though, as our total analysis of the poem; if we are going to do justice to it, we need to start analysing the poem in an ordered and systematic way.

Step 2:   Starting an essay. Summarise the poem, establish your sense of the central opposition in the poem, set up the controlling idea for your essay as a whole

The poet – the seventeenth-century writer, George Herbert – talks about the 'sweet day', but then, after describing its attractive qualities, moves to an idea of the end of the day, of the day 'dying'. He then goes on to describe the beauty of a rose, but this will also die, just as spring, a season we associate with rebirth, will die. In the final stanza, however, we are told that the 'sweet' and 'virtuous' soul will live. There is, then, an obvious tension between images of attractive things and the idea of death; something reassuring, like a 'sweet day', is set against an idea that is threatening or disturbing. The broad contrast, therefore, is between a sense of the beauty of life and a sense of how things must die. As such, it is more than just a poem about a 'sweet day'; in some way, which we have not yet fully fathomed, it is exploring large questions of life and death.

Step 3:   Look more closely at the opening of the poem, trying to see how the poet brings the theme to life

The opening paragraph of our essay has summarised the poem and identified a central tension. We now need to look at a selection of the details in the poem to see how Herbert brings his theme to life. Let's look at stanza one:

> Sweet day, so cool, so calm, so bright,
> The bridal of the earth and sky:
> The dew shall weep thy fall tonight;
> For thou must die.

If we take the image of 'sweet day', we can see immediately that it is a concrete, natural image that is easy to understand. When the poet adds 'cool', 'calm' and 'bright', he underlines the simple appeal of the day, a fact which is reinforced by the repetition of the word 'so' before each of the words. It is, in fact, a very clever opening line, because it works in such a simple way to suggest the mood and feel of the day. It is all the more extraordinary when we consider how the simplicity of statement of the first line moves to the portentous statement 'The bridal of the earth and sky'. What does this convey? As it is puzzling, we need to refer back to the pattern we have already established, our sense of the opposition between the beauty of life and the fact of death. The word 'bridal' is a marriage image; it is as if the earth and sky are to be joined together in marriage. The effect is to link together nature and the social institution of marriage; both are parts of a grand pattern. In fifteen words, therefore, as this poem begins, Herbert has created an extremely positive sense of something attractive that exists in life.

If we can pause to draw attention to the method of analysis we have employed here, try to see the simplicity of the informing logic. Wishing to find an explanation for Herbert's use of the word 'bridal', we started from the assumption that it must contribute to either the positive or negative side of the poem. It is clearly a positive word, but then, when we had seen this, it enabled us to *add* to our sense of the positive statement the poem is making. We managed to move beyond the straightforward impression of attractive images and make a point about the interconnection of things. As against such a positive train of thought, we can anticipate that the poet is going to introduce negative ideas. These come in the second half of the stanza: the word 'fall', for the fall of the day, suggests an ending that might resemble defeat in battle. Just as a 'bridal' is a beginning, this is an ending.

Step 4: Look at another section of the poem, trying to build on your analysis of the poem's details

> Sweet rose, whose hue, angry and brave,
> Bids the rash gazer wipe his eye:
> Thy root is ever in its grave,
> And thou must die.

This stanza is structured in exactly the same way as the first, with two lines about the beauty of the rose and then two lines dealing with its death. But there seems to be something going on in the two lines about the rose that is rather more complex than the straightforwardly positive image of the day in the first stanza. For example, the word 'angry' in relation to the rose seems to jar. And we can see the complication in the second half of the stanza where, in talking about the root in its grave, Herbert begins to convey the sense that death is not just an enemy but entangled in the very being of the rose.

What we see happening here is a not unfamiliar effect in poetry. The poet sets up a tension, but then, as he or she explores the tension, it begins to become complex, even to break down as a tension. In the first poem in this chapter, 'The Lesson', we saw how there is no absolute split between the world of the adult and the world of the child, how the child found himself absorbing the values of the adult world. In 'Virtue' we can see that life and death are not really opposites, for death is entangled with the very existence of life as a positive concept. Over and over again in poetry criticism, the great advantage of establishing your sense of a clear opposition in the opening paragraph of an essay is that such a steady starting point enables you to appreciate how the poet complicates this initial position as the poem advances.

Step 5: Look at another section of the poem, trying to build on your analysis of the poem's details

> Sweet spring, full of sweet days and roses,
> A box where sweets compacted lie;
> My music shows ye have your closes,
> And all must die.

Herbert starts again with a 'sweet' image, but something rather odd is beginning to happen here: the word 'sweet' is repeated three times in the first two lines. There's a kind of excess about this, as if this day is a touch too rich. The other point we might notice is that 'thou' in the last line of the first two stanzas has now become 'all': it isn't just the day or the rose but 'all' that will die. A word that surprises is 'box' for spring, a box where sweets are packed together; suddenly, because a box is a confined and restricting container, there begins to seem something rather limited about mere earthly beauty. It is as if, in the stanza as a whole, Herbert is sated with the beauty of life, becoming more and more aware of the transitoriness of sensuous things, and contemplating the fact of death more seriously.

Step 6:   Look at how the poem concludes

Where a poem arrives can come as a surprise. The poet sets up a tension, begins to explore its implications, and, as a result of this exploration, might shift his or her ground by the end. We saw it in 'The Lesson' where the poet moves to some unexpected thoughts about becoming the centre of attraction. In 'Virtue' we can see that Herbert changes direction in the last stanza:

> Only a sweet and virtuous soul,
> Like seasoned timber, never gives;
> But though the whole world turns to coal,
> Then chiefly lives.

The pattern of the poem is reversed: the emphasis is no longer on how things die but upon what lives, the sweet and virtuous soul. The word 'sweet' is still being used, but, as against ephemeral things, such as a rose, it is now applied to the moral condition of a human being. When Herbert uses the phrase 'seasoned timber' it again contrasts with the images used so far, for this suggests maturity and what lasts, rather than the ephemeral things of life. When 'coal' is introduced as an image we are at an opposite remove from the brightness with which the poem started, but by this stage the delights of the world have been put in perspective. What matters are eternal things, eternal values, a value such as virtue.

Step 7:   Sum up your sense of the poem as a whole

The poem began in a simple manner: it set the delights of the world against the fact of death. But Herbert has made us reflect on the superficial nature of earthly things. He has made us see how eternal values matter more than sensory delights. But try to see how he has never directly said any of this; everything has been conveyed by implication and suggestion. There isn't an argument we can extract from the poem. If we have derived a meaning it is because the poetic images have created these impressions for us.

  This is both the difficulty and pleasure of poetry: it isn't an art of direct statement. We have to infer meanings. Because these meanings are suggested and not stated, and because the meaning shifts depending upon how the individual reader responds to the images, a poem, even within fourteen to sixteen lines, has the capacity to say, in an indirect way, a great deal. 'The Lesson' deals with the transition from childhood to a form of maturity; 'Virtue' deals with the transitoriness of earthly pleasures: in other words, substantial themes are dealt with in the brief canvas of each poem. In discussing a poem, we should feel that we eventually arrive at a sense of this full weight of the words. This is what makes practical criticism a worthwhile activity; there are students who regard it as a burden or imposition, but it is only through close analysis that we are likely to arrive at an appreciation of the complexity of the issues that can be examined in a poem.

5

Discussing a detail, building a case

We have, essentially, already said everything that need be said about a method for poetry analysis. It is a case of getting hold of the poem at the outset, and then building a response. You need to turn to details (a few details will do; there's no necessity to discuss every word and every line), and then to move out from the details in such a way that your overall sense of the poem advances. We can summarise the process as follows:

---

1. Read the poem.
2. Here's my initial response.
3. Here's how a detail relates to my initial response.
4. This is how this detail advances my overall understanding of the poem.

It is a cumulative approach: at the end of each paragraph of your essay, having looked at two or three more details, you should be able to add to your overall sense of the poem.

We can, however, see the problems you might encounter in trying to follow this approach. We have stressed that it is easy to build a response. And it is, for people like teachers, who have been teaching poetry for years. But when you haven't read much poetry – and let's be realistic, hardly anyone studying English at school or university has read all that much poetry – you might lack the confidence to plunge into interpretation of a detail. You might find yourself staring at the words on the page for ages without a thought coming into your head. And, if it takes confidence to do something with a detail, it takes a great deal more to move forward, to say how the detail advances your overall sense of the poem.

There are no quick answers here. Practice, of course, makes perfect. The more poems you analyse, the better your analyses will become. And the methods we recommend in this book should help you to make the right moves in the right direction. But inevitably there comes a point at which you will have to wrack your brains to get a result. Practical criticism is, after all, an intellectual exercise. Having said that, however, we do want to focus a little more in this chapter on how to discuss a detail and how to extrapolate a larger point from a detail. This will be the emphasis of our discussions rather than any fuller analysis, on how to move from a detail to the larger issue or idea in the poem.

Step 1:   Reading and thinking

'Tears, Idle Tears'

Tears, idle tears, I know not what they mean,
Tears from the depth of some divine despair
Rise in the heart, and gather to the eyes,
In looking on the happy autumn-fields,
And thinking of the days that are no more.

Fresh as the first beam glittering on a sail,
That brings our friends up from the underworld,
Sad as the last which reddens over one
That sinks with all we love below the verge;
So sad, so fresh, the days that are no more.

Ah, sad and strange as in dark summer dawns
The earliest pipe of half-awakened birds
To dying ears, when unto dying eyes
The casement slowly grows a glimmering square;
So sad, so strange, the days that are no more.

Dear as remembered kisses after death,
And sweet as those by hopeless fancy feigned
On lips that are for others; deep as love,
Deep as first love, and wild with all regret;
O Death in Life, the days that are no more.

Both of us can recall having to write about this poem as undergraduates; we can vaguely recall saying that the poet feels sad, but our understanding of the poem more or less stopped at that point.

Step 2:   Starting an essay. Summarise the poem, establish your sense of the central opposition in the poem, set up the controlling idea for your essay as a whole

There is no obvious 'story' to the poem. It is more a case of the poet's musings. It starts with a feeling of sadness prompted by thinking about happy times in the past. In the second stanza he talks of the sadness and yet the freshness of the past, and in the third stanza he comments on the sadness and strangeness of the past. In the final stanza he reflects on death, love and life. It is a difficult poem to summarise, partly because of the lack of an organising thread of a story, but also because it contains so much imagery, and images which yield to each other with great rapidity. It is this verbal complexity of the poem that makes it all the more essential to pin down an initial simple view as the starting point of our analysis.

The obvious broad tension to recognise is the contrast between present feelings of unhappiness and past feelings of happiness. It seems reasonable to speculate that any poem working from this basis will deal with larger issues such as time passing, happiness in life, and even the question of whether life has any meaning or purpose. What the poet will decide, we don't know yet; we could look at the end of the poem to see, but, as the end of the poem is congested with imagery, we would tie ourselves up in too many knots if we tried to work everything out in advance. It is going to prove much more productive if we make a slow start, and then gradually accumulate a larger case as we go along.

Step 3:   Look more closely at the opening of the poem, trying to see how the poet brings the theme to life

> Tears, idle tears, I know not what they mean,
> Tears from the depth of some divine despair
> Rise in the heart, and gather to the eyes,

In looking on the happy autumn-fields,
And thinking of the days that are no more.

The easiest thing to get hold of in the opening lines is how things used to be: the phrase 'happy autumn-fields' evokes a simple yet happy idea of the past. It is a totally uncomplicated image. It is, however, more difficult to pin down the poet's present feelings. He uses the word 'tears' three times, emphasising his sadness, but there is also something strange about the feelings he is experiencing. He tells us that he doesn't know what these tears mean; they seem involuntary. As against the tangible happiness of the past, there is an indeterminate and rather baffling feeling of unhappiness.

As you can see, so far we have worked from just two details – the happy autumn image, and the word 'tears'. As a general rule, when a poem proves difficult, reduce the amount of evidence you are going to consider. A baffling stanza is likely to remain a baffling stanza unless you extract from it two sharply opposed images or ideas, and use these to gain control of the stanza. It is a case of trying to get hold of the basic pattern that informs the poem at this stage. But how do we advance the case? As always, we need to review the position we had reached before looking at the stanza, and then we need to think about what we can now add. In the case of 'Tears, Idle Tears', we started with past happiness and present unhappiness. After looking at the first stanza, the point we have now reached is that this present unhappiness is rather baffling, that even the poet doesn't understand it.

At this point, it might appear that we have lost control of the poem, because of our inability to explain the poet's feelings. But, taking things slowly and steadily (and ignoring, for the moment, subsequent developments in the poem), it should become apparent that the feeling of being baffled is there in the poem itself at this stage. Our point is that you don't need to master the whole poem from the word go. If a stanza becomes confusing, your point can be that a feeling of confusion has been created. Subsequent stanzas might sort things out, but you are doing your job as a critic if you simply keep pace with the stanza-by-stanza development of the poem. In other words, you can feel quite happy if you make only a modest move forward at the end of each stanza. You don't have to make a great leap forward every step of the way. As long as you can add a little to the impression you had formed before looking at the stanza in question, then you can feel confident that you are getting somewhere.

Step 4:   Look at another section of the poem, trying to build on your analysis of the poem's details

This is the second stanza of the poem:

> Fresh as the first beam glittering on a sail,
> That brings our friends up from the underworld,
> Sad as the last which reddens over one
> That sinks with all we love below the verge;
> So sad, so fresh, the days that are no more.

Once again, we want to focus on how to build outwards from a few details. As always, look for both positive and negative images. 'Fresh as the first beam glittering on a sail' is clearly positive. It is an image that suggests the rising of the sun, and the start of a new day where everything is bright and hopeful.

Then, however, the poet's thoughts turn to death, as we can see in the reference to the 'underworld'. It is a gloomy impression that is continued in the next two lines. These lines do contain an attractive image of the sun setting, but the attractiveness of this is rather negated by the poet's reference to it sinking 'with all we love'. It seems that whatever image he considers, his thoughts always turn to death; he always sees the gloominess that is the other side of anything encouraging.

We have again kept our analysis simple. We have kept to a very small number of the details, and then worked on the implications of these details. By limiting our focus in this way, we have maintained control of the poem. But the process of analysis isn't complete until we consider where this gets us; we need to spell out how our overall case has advanced. At the end of stanza one we were struck by the poet's feeling of bewildered unhappiness. The additional point we can make now is that he sees unhappiness in everything: the images from the past retain their freshness, but any positive effect is immediately undercut as he draws attention to the depressing associations that are inherent in any positive memory. The image of the day beginning, for example, leads him on to the fact that the day ends. Where this might eventually take us we don't know yet, but we don't need to know at this stage; it is sufficient that we are tracking the poet's thoughts on a stanza-by-stanza basis, using the details of the text to try and fill out the sense of the poem's argument and ideas.

Step 5:   Look at another section of the poem, trying to build on your analysis of the poem's details

> Ah, sad and strange as in dark summer dawns
> The earliest pipe of half-awakened birds
> To dying ears, when unto dying eyes
> The casement slowly grows a glimmering square;
> So sad, so strange, the days that are no more.

Look at the image of 'dark summer dawns'. The previous stanza started with the image of first light, and dawn should be an image of first light, but here it is associated with darkness. More precisely, it is a kind of in-between world, hovering between light and dark. The gloominess is underlined by the use of the words 'dying ears' and 'dying eyes' within one line. A lot of the images in the poem are attractive, but it is as if the poet can do nothing positive with an attractive image; everything makes him think of death.

Trying to explain this, it seems reasonable to suggest that this is an expression of a state of mind. The poet cannot respond to positive stimuli in a positive way; his mind circles morbidly. There is a sense of desire for what he has lost, but that former sense of wholeness can never be restored. His mind is, consequently, dominated by thoughts of loss and what he lacks. But none of this is really explained: indeed, the poet stresses the inexplicable nature of his feelings, but this is perhaps as it should be – these are irrational feelings and, as such, defy rational explanation.

Step 6:   Look at how the poem concludes

> Dear as remembered kisses after death,
> And sweet as those by hopeless fancy feigned
> On lips that are for others; deep as love,
> Deep as first love, and wild with all regret;
> O Death in Life, the days that are no more.

If stanza three focuses on death, stanza four makes more of love. Memories of the past are associated with images of love, such as 'kisses' and 'lips'. The way to get hold of what is going on here is to remind yourself of the patterns of opposition that appear over and over again in poetry. One of these is love versus death: we live in a world where death exists; the only thing that can be set against death is love, whether that be love of God or love of a fellow human being. It is not surprising that a poem that has focused as much on death as 'Tears, Idle Tears' has should eventually consider love.

The general point here is that an awareness of, and recognition of, the patterns that repeat themselves in poetry should help you come to terms with any individual poem. But, when you have identified the familiar pattern, you then have to consider the new things that are done with an old pattern in the poem under consideration. In this poem, there is a powerful sense of love, as evoked in the images of 'remembered kisses' and 'first love', but all the love images are marred or incomplete in some way. The lips were for others, there is regret, there is a feeling that fancy has feigned love. It is as if the poet has tried to use love to resolve the poem, but even love fails him – it is insufficiently strong to dislodge his thoughts of death.

Step 7:   Sum up your sense of the poem as a whole

'Tears, Idle Tears' is a disturbing poem. It is so because of the extent to which it stresses the negative side of things. There are positive images in the poem – and these positive images are delicate and attractive – but the poet (it is, in fact, the Victorian poet Tennyson) only seems to see the failure of life and love. The poem, as such, is an intense expression of a gloomy psychological mood (although, someone looking at Tennyson in his Victorian context might wish to take things further, seeing an expression of more general Victorian anxieties in the poem. In a practical criticism exercise, however, you would not be expected to see the poem in a historical context in this kind of way. Looking at the poem in context is really the next step in criticism, the thing you do after you have done your close work on the text, a point that we touch on in Chapter 9).

Let's take stock of how we have arrived at this final view of the poem. We worked from an initial premise of happiness versus unhappiness, but at the end of each paragraph of our analysis we found more evidence of unhappiness. As we tracked this, stanza by stanza, we were struck by the poet's sense of loss and lack. There is a sense, of course, in which our analysis merely repeats our initial impression that this is a sad poem, but, in fact, through building a case in a careful and steady way, we have managed to say some quite precise things about the poet's feelings of sadness, and to gain an impression of how he uses the four stanzas of the poem to frame and develop this feeling. (Obviously you could add more to the analysis, but in the chapter we have been concerned with showing you how to make the most of just a few details, especially when dealing with complex texts.) It is a depressing poem because, in the last stanza, it undercuts love, the one thing that the poet might have hung on to, but it is also a powerful poem in the way in which, through oblique imagery, it suggests the state of mind of the poet. And it is also a very skilful poem in that, in four stanzas, it manages to say a great deal about life, love and, above all, death.

Let's try an equally simple step-by-step approach with another poem, 'London' by William Blake. This time, however, rather than offering you our analysis, we will point out some of the questions you can ask which will allow you to build a more complex case out of the details of the text.

Step 1: Reading and thinking

'London'

I wander thro' each charter'd street,
Near where the charter'd Thames does flow,
And mark in every face I meet
Marks of weakness, marks of woe.

In every cry of every man,
In every Infant's cry of fear,
In every voice, in every ban,
The mind-forg'd manacles I hear.

How the Chimney-sweeper's cry,
Every blackning Church appalls;
And the hapless Soldier's sigh
Runs in blood down Palace walls.

But most thro' midnight streets I hear
How the youthful Harlot's curse
Blasts the new-born Infant's tear,
And blights with plague the Marriage hearse.

All of us can probably see that there is a sort of cry of rage here, a protest against a state of affairs which is wrong or corrupt in some way. But we need to be more precise about what the poem says, and, as always, the only way to achieve that is by looking closely.

Step 2:   Starting an essay. Summarise the poem, establish your sense of the central opposition in the poem, set up the controlling idea for your essay as a whole

The speaker in the poem describes his progress through the streets of London, where he encounters widespread misery. He hears the cry of men, and the cry of babies. He draws attention to the chimney-sweep, and to the soldier. Then, in the final stanza, he mentions a young prostitute before concluding with an image of plague. There is clearly something amiss in the London of Blake's day. With a poem like this, examination candidates are sometimes distracted into focusing on the poet's anger and sense of social injustice (using this as the justification for offering their own social views), but what we need to focus on is the details of what the poet is actually saying.

The poem starts with the line, 'I wander thro' each charter'd street': 'charter'd' here means 'legally defined' or 'constricted'. That, surely, provides us with our central tension for the poem: as against the image of the poet wandering, there is an image of constriction. The tension, therefore, is between an idea of freedom and the constraints that are placed upon people. The controlling issue in the poem is, therefore, the ways in which freedom is stifled, denied or repressed.

Step 3:   Look more closely at the opening of the poem, trying to see how the poet brings the theme to life

So far we have established the broad issue in the poem. What we are most interested in, however, is how Blake brings his ideas to life, for this will, eventually, enable us to arrive at a fuller understanding of the poem.

> I wander thro' each charter'd street,
> Near where the charter'd Thames does flow,
> And mark in every face I meet
> Marks of weakness, marks of woe.

In the case of this first stanza, you might wish to focus on the two words 'wander', as Blake wanders through the city, and 'flow', which he uses in relation to the Thames. What do these two words suggest? In what ways can we link these two words together? What is the bigger idea that is conveyed by the two words?

We have already mentioned how 'charter'd' suggests an idea of confinement or restriction. What other negative images can you find in the opening stanza? What is suggested by the word 'marks' in the line 'Marks of weakness, marks of woe'? What is the effect of repeating the word? Can you explain how the words flow and mark suggest opposing ideas? When you have asked yourself these and similar questions about the details in the stanza, you will need to take stock of your case so far. We started with an idea of freedom and restriction. Have we added to that idea, or do we now simply have a more vivid sense of how Blake sets up the issue in his poem?

Step 4:   Look at another section of the poem, trying to build on your analysis of the poem's details

> In every cry of every man,
> In every Infant's cry of fear,
> In every voice, in every ban,
> The mind-forg'd manacles I hear.

Are there any positive images in this stanza? An image of a child in a poem can be an image of hope for the future; is that the case here? What connects the man and the infant, in lines 1 and 2 of the stanza? What is the effect of repeating the word 'cry'? The first stanza offered us an idea of constriction; in what ways does this stanza continue and extend an idea of repression (both at a physical and mental level)? Does the form of the stanza (that is, its neat, regular pattern) suggest an idea of freedom or confinement? When you have thought about the details of the stanza, what do you feel you can add to your overall sense of the poem? Our feeling is that in the first stanza the idea of freedom versus constriction was set up very forcefully as a general idea, but what is added in this stanza is an impression of how people are affected. It is as if they do not even have the freedom to speak, for all we hear is a cry. But this is not just physical repression, for, as 'mind-forg'd manacles' suggests, it is also a form of ideological repression.

Step 5:   Look at another section of the poem, trying to build on your analysis of the poem's details

> How the Chimney-sweeper's cry,
> Every blackning Church appalls;
> And the hapless Soldier's sigh
> Runs in blood down Palace walls.

If there is freedom and if there is repression, that means there must be victims and oppressors. Who in this stanza would you say are the victims and who are the oppressors? In what ways might the chimney-sweep and the soldier both have to pay a high price for their livelihoods? We might be able to see why Blake links the 'Palace' with the suffering of the soldier, but why do you think he also singles out the 'Church' for criticism? We have had the word 'cry' repeated several times already in the poem, and now Blake adds the word 'sigh': what do such words tell us about the manner in which he is presenting the hardships that people endure? Pulling everything together, how has our case advanced? One approach that it would be possible to take would be to suggest that, whereas stanza two concentrated on the victims, Blake now identifies the oppressors. At the same time, the suffering people have to endure is even more gruesomely described as a physical attack on their bodies.

Step 6:   Look at how the poem concludes

What you should be endeavouring to keep track of is how Blake, having set up an opposition, develops it. You should be trying to show how the words and ideas chosen expand the proposition offered in the first stanza. As always with poetry, it is the economy of the method that is interesting. A social critic could write many pages in prose showing how the Church is complicit with authoritarian rule and the denial of freedom in society, but in Blake's poem a single reference to the Church conveys this idea. And, as we can see, it does it powerfully; one aspect of this is that the reader is having to play an active part, the reader is having to make the connection, linking the image to the overall theme of the poem.

What we also know about a poem is that the tension is going to become more complex as the work continues, and that the end of the poem is often going to offer a very complex impression. This certainly seems to be the case in the last stanza of 'London':

But most thro' midnight streets I hear
How the youthful Harlot's curse
Blasts the new-born Infant's tear,
And blights with plague the Marriage hearse.

Why should the predicament of the harlot be the one that strikes
Blake with most force? This is the first person in the poem who is
identified as female, and it is the woman who suffers most of all: what
might we infer from this about the nature of the authoritarian powers
that govern society? The poem has already presented images of
physical suffering: what kind of physical suffering might be
experienced by the prostitute? How does it add to the impression
the poem makes that Blake doesn't just call her a harlot but also
'youthful'? Those who run society usually claim to uphold moral
standards: what does the existence of the prostitute tell you about the
actual sexual morality of society?

When Blake refers to the prostitute's 'curse', he might mean that
she swears, but what else could he mean? How could her curse affect a
new-born infant or blight a marriage? If, as seems likely, Blake is
referring to venereal disease, what does this tell us about the
hypocrisy of respectable society? In what ways is a reference to
venereal disease a particularly vivid image for suggesting something
rotten in the London of Blake's day. The poem ends with a reference
to the 'Marriage hearse'. Marriage often appears at the end of a
literary text as an answer, that people in love join together within the
framework of society. Does Blake's closing image, however, refer more
to love or death?

Step 7:   Sum up your sense of the poem as a whole

The poem starts with a very simple opposition between freedom and
the denial of freedom as Blake sees it expressed and exemplified on the
streets of London. By the end, most readers are likely to feel that they
have read a very strong, very forceful poem. But if you analyse the
poem, taking up the kind of points we have suggested here, you
should find that you can offer a much more precise sense of why the
poem strikes you as forceful. What impresses is the cumulative force of
Blake's critique, the way in which it builds stanza by stanza, and, in
addition, the way in which the individual images suggest complex
points about the nature of suffering and oppression in society. By the
end of 'London', we have arrived at a sense of something rotten and

rotting at the very heart of society. Everywhere we turn there is ideological oppression which expresses itself as physical oppression. Things are, indeed, so rotten that the very existence and continuation of society, as reflected in new birth and marriage, is threatened.

6

Twenty questions

THIS chapter, which is, admittedly, a bit of a rag-bag, sets out to answer a miscellaneous range of questions about the practice of practical criticism. It includes basic guidance, summarising some of what we have said already, and also some tips which might prove useful but which don't really have a place in any of the other chapters. This isn't a technical chapter, however; there are technical terms that have a place in poetry criticism, and which, if used judiciously, can help your response, but we deal with such matters in Chapter 7. This is a looser, less specific chapter; a chapter that is made up of advice, hints and tips that should enable you to produce a better analysis of a poem.

1   WHAT IS THE WORST MISTAKE ANYONE CAN MAKE IN POETRY CRITICISM?

Practical criticism is an exercise in which you analyse the poem and build a response to the poem. You need to keep close to the words on the page and build your case on the basis of the evidence of the words on the page. There are some people who can never grasp these basic points. They might read a poem about, say, a country cottage, and then embark upon pointless stories about country holidays they have enjoyed, and how much they like the poem because it reminds them of things they have seen and experienced. Don't fall into this trap! The examiner doesn't want to read your life story. The examiner wants to see you attempting to come to terms with the poem you have been asked to analyse.

2   WHAT IS THE SECOND WORSE MISTAKE ANYONE CAN MAKE IN PRACTICAL CRITICISM?

Story-telling! When they are about eleven, school-children are often asked to write a review of a book. Most children tell the story and then add, 'It was very good. I would recommend it for other children my age.' There's nothing wrong with that – if you are eleven. But something a bit more demanding is being asked for in practical criticism. There is no point in devoting most of your answer to merely retelling the story of the poem in your own words. A summary is not an analysis.

3   WHAT IS THE THIRD WORST MISTAKE ANYONE CAN MAKE IN PRACTICAL CRITICISM?

Far too many examination candidates spend the greater part of an answer dealing with the content of a poem before adding an additional paragraph in which they talk about the formal properties of the poem. This is a poor approach because it makes such a rigid distinction between the theme of the poem and how the theme is brought to life. By far the best approach is to deal with the story of the poem in your opening paragraph, before devoting the rest of your answer to analysing the choices the poet has made, that is to say how the words chosen bring the theme of the poem to life. As you discuss how the poem works you will be adding to your overall sense of its content. A mistake some students make is to devote a paragraph to imagery, then a paragraph to structure, and so on. This doesn't work very well because it is a cumbersome approach; it fails to capture how a poem creates an impression as the reader moves from one stanza to the next.

4   WHAT SHOULD I BE DOING IN A PRACTICAL CRITICISM ANALYSIS?

The ideal analysis recreates the reading process. You read the poem as a whole and certain ideas take shape in your mind. As you read more closely these ideas develop and even change direction. As you move through the poem you reflect on details and these add to your sense of what is going on. By the end, your attention to the details of the poem, accompanied by your piecing together of your impressions, will enable you to arrive at a coherent understanding of the poem as a whole.

5   IS THERE ANY DIFFERENCE BETWEEN A POETRY ANALYSIS AND WRITING AN ESSAY?

No, none at all! This is where examination candidates often go wrong. They fail to see that in the practical criticism paper, just as much as in any other paper, they are being asked to write an essay. An essay can be defined as a clear argument that you build from the evidence of the text. A lot more is said about this in Chapter 8, but the most important point to grasp is that you must build a case and this case must advance in coherent paragraphs. Far too many practical criticism candidates just list the things they have spotted in a poem. There is a lot more involved in essay-writing than just listing impressions. Fortunately, the fact that poems are often written in three or four stanzas provides you with a ready-made format for constructing an essay; in addition to an introduction and conclusion, simply devote a paragraph to each stanza. If a poem isn't divided into stanzas, you will need to split it into three, four or five sections. If it is a very long poem, you won't be able to deal with every part of the poem; the best tactic is to divide the poem into four, and pick out a few details from each section. Discussing a few details as thoroughly as you can creates the impression that you have discussed the whole poem, whereas if you try to discuss every line it will look as if you have merely dashed across the surface.

6   WHERE DO I DISCUSS THE RHYME SCHEME OF A POEM?

We pose this question because over the years we have read so many answers that begin, 'This poem employs the following rhyme scheme: *ababcdcdefefghgh*'. Apart from being a dull way of starting an answer, why would anyone bother to list the rhyme scheme in this kind of way? The thing to realise about the rhyme scheme of a poem is that it helps the poet bring to life the subject of the poem, but you have got to *start* with the subject. At a subsequent stage in your answer you might deal with how the poet's use of rhyme helps create the meaning of the poem, but we can't think of any situation in which it would ever prove necessary to list the entire rhyme scheme of a poem.

7   WHAT IF I KNOW THAT THE POEM IS WRITTEN IN IAMBIC PENTAMETERS?

Some students acquire an understanding of the metrical patterns of verse. This is tremendously useful knowledge to possess, but it is knowledge that you need to deploy with some care in an answer. Technical information should be used to support and explain an insight. There is no point is simply stating that a poem is written in iambic pentameters; what you should be aiming to do is to show how the poet's use of a certain metrical form helps create the meaning of the poem.

8   WHAT ASSUMPTIONS CAN I BRING TO A POEM?

A poem is a curious thing. It obviously deals with some aspect of life, but the odd thing is that the poet has decided to write about life in the patterned format of a poem. Implicit in the very existence of poetry, therefore, is a tension between the openness of life and the ordered structure of verse. This fact makes it possible to start our examination of any poem by looking for an inherent tension. The sense of a tension will invariably provide you with both the foundation and framework for your analysis.

9   DOES THE END OF A POEM PROVIDE A RESOLUTION?

Shakespeare's comedies always end with marriage. Marriage provides a resolution. There have been disputes and differences along the way, but now the characters come together within the social institution of marriage. Some poets conclude their poems as neatly as this. In a number of George Herbert's poems, for example, he finds himself in dispute with God, but at the end of the poem his

Maker speaks to him and he makes his peace with God. Most poems, however, don't end as neatly as this. Most commonly, a poet, having set up a tension, will explore it and develop it, and often shift it into a new area by the end, but the poet isn't 'tidying' things up at the end. If we consider, for example, a poem that deals with the death of a child, it would seem inappropriate if the poem found an 'answer'. But what the poem can do is make us aware of the complexity of the feelings of loss and the puzzling nature of death. At the end of a poem, therefore, we might often feel more unsettled than consoled.

10   HOW CAN SOMETHING AS SLIGHT AS A SONNET BE REGARDED AS A MAJOR WORK OF ART?

There are three sorts of poetry: lyric poetry, narrative poetry and dramatic poetry. Dramatic poetry is the term used for the verse we encounter in, say, a Shakespeare play. (Browning wrote dramatic monologues: poems in which an imaginary speaker addresses an imaginary audience.) Narrative poetry is, quite simply, poetry that tells a story. (Milton's *Paradise Lost* is an example of a narrative poem.) Just about all the rest of poetry, with some curious exceptions such as Pope's *Moral Essays*, is described as lyric poetry. What we usually mean by the term 'lyric' is a fairly short poem expressing the thoughts or feelings of a single speaker. One of the most popular lyric forms is the sonnet, a poem of fourteen lines that conforms to a a number of set patterns. Many sonnets, particularly from the Renaissance period, are about love. How, you might ask, can a short poem in a conventional form on a well-worn subject amount to anything substantial? The point is that, although the poet deals with a specific incident or experience, implicit is a much larger consideration of important issues in life. Poetry is a peculiarly compressed form of expression; within the compass of one short poem, dealing with one concrete experience, large questions about love, life and death can be raised.

11   WHY ARE THERE SO MANY POEMS ABOUT LOVE?

Up to and including the seventeenth century, religion was often the central subject in poetry. If a poet dealt with problems, including the problem of death, the love of God would always be the answer. When literature moves in the seventeenth century from spiritual to secular experience, love remains as a positive force. Part of the appeal is that one of life's obvious tensions is between men and women; in the experience of love, however, the difference and distance between a man and a woman is eliminated, even if only temporarily. Most love poems, however, are by men; the woman is the object of attention and praise, but there is, more often than not, a sense in which the woman is being used. It is not an equal relationship; the man often treats the woman as a possession, or focuses entirely on her beauty. Inherent in a love poem, therefore, is the idea of harmony between the sexes, but there is also a niggling sense that the relationship between the man and the woman is far from equal.

12   WHY ARE THERE SO MANY POEMS ABOUT DEATH?

Whatever other problems a poet may consider, the problem that ultimately has to be considered is that we live in a world where death exists. This fact raises questions about the value of all that we try to construct in a world where everything ends in nothingness. In an elegy, for example, that is to say a poem that deals with the death of a friend, the poet is likely to ask what point there is in writing, indeed in trying to achieve anything at all in life, when we live in a world where death can intervene so unexpectedly and so destructively. Religion is one solution to the problem of death, but, alongside religious love, human love is also often seen as a positive force in poetry.

13   WHY ARE THERE SO MANY POEMS ABOUT NATURE?

It would require a whole book to provide a satisfactory answer to this question, but one thing we might point out is that nature is cyclical. Things in nature die, but in the spring they renew themselves. As such, there is a beauty in nature that is not tragic, for even as it wastes away that is not the end of things. Human beings, however, simply die; there is no renewal. Religion, of course, offers a sense of renewal and continuity, but for the most part in poetry dealing with nature there is a sense of the gap between nature's order and the lack of any such order in human life.

14   WHY IS THE WORD 'O' USED SO OFTEN IN POETRY?

This might seem a flippant question, but it is prompted by our answer to the previous question about nature poetry. In Keats's 'Ode to a Nightingale', he is aware of a world of pain and suffering, where men die young. Keats, however, escapes into another world, a world of nature that he has created in his imagination. This escape into another world begins with the words 'O, for a draught of vintage'. If you see the word 'O' in a poem it is a helpful signal to you that the poet is escaping into a world of the feelings or the imagination. In any poem employing the word 'O', there is always going to be a clear tension between lines dealing with the disordered reality of the world and the line starting with the word 'O', which will be dealing with a ordered, rarefied existence.

15   WHAT ARE THE MOST COMMON IMAGES IN POETRY?

Just about every poem ever written uses light and dark imagery. 'Light' imagery will always represent a positive state of affairs, 'dark' imagery will always suggest the disturbing side of things in the poem. One of the most common forms this takes is setting images associated with the day against images associated with the night. Looking for light and dark images will help you spot the tension in a work, but, if you can already see the tension, a consideration of the poet's use of light and dark imagery will help you see how the poet brings his or her subject-matter to life.

16   WHAT IS THE SIGNIFICANCE OF WATER IMAGERY IN POETRY?

Water imagery – covering everything from storms at sea to something as mundane as a drink of water – is extremely common in poetry. Its appeal is that it can suggest a great many different ideas. Storms, rain, waves and floods can suggest destruction. But water can also be the water of baptism, or a life-saving drink. In the Bible, the story of Christ walking on the waves is a poetic image of chaos and disorder being transcended. In Milton's *Lycidas*, an elegy, his friend has drowned but by the end of the poem Milton's fresh hope is expressed through his use of gentle and attractive water images. The attraction of water imagery to a poet, therefore, is the fact that it can be manipulated to support and illustrate both sides of the tension in a poem. Water imagery is the kind of detail you should be looking for when you are attempting to explain how the poet brings his or her ideas to life.

17   ARE THERE OTHER IMAGES THAT I CAN EXPECT TO ENCOUNTER AGAIN AND AGAIN IN POETRY?

Yes, there are. If the poet wants to convey a reassuring impression he or she will use names of specific places and people; if the poet wants to disturb, things will remain anonymous. Naming and labelling orders and controls the world. What you can rely upon in poetry is that if the poet uses names there will also be points in the poem where names are deliberately not used; in other words, if one kind of image is used in a poem, the contrasting image will also be used. For example, a poem that refers to a healthy body is also likely to use images of illness or disablement. Such use of paired images is inevitable, for imagery is the device a poet employs to bring to life the tension in a poem, and if one side of the tension is developed the other side has to be developed as well. You might, therefore, find it rewarding to look for some of the following paired image patterns in poetry: images of peace and war, silence and noise, social order and social disruption, domestic order and domestic disorder, good weather and bad weather, male and female, soft and hard, east and west, as well as those listed above: light and dark, wet and dry, nature and society.

18   HOW DOES RHYME FUNCTION IN POETRY?

The range of devices available to a poet is limited. The poet selects words, combines words, and organises the structure of the poem. In the last few answers we have concentrated on the poet's use of words, specifically the use of imagery, but the structure of the poem also has a crucial role to play in determining what the poem says and its effect. One aspect of structure is rhyme. The most obvious thing to say about rhyme is that, for the most part, it endorses a sense of pattern. As against a sense of disorder, rhyme can surreptitiously suggest an idea of order.

19 WHY IS SOME POETRY UNRHYMED?

It is, of course, only the makers of greetings cards who believe that all poems must rhyme. Lots of poems don't rhyme. But what you might want to look out for are those poems that do rhyme, but where the rhyme suddenly goes askew. Look at this example from Alexander Pope's poem 'Epistle to Dr Arbuthnot':

> Half froth, half venom, spits himself abroad,
>   In puns or politics, or tales, or lies,
>   Or spite, or smut, or rhymes, or blasphemies.

Pope is condemning a man he detests. Usually in his poetry he uses rhyming couplets, and he usually controls this very tightly, but on this occasion the rhyme goes slightly wrong when 'lies' is matched with 'blasphemies'. Pope's use of rhyming couplets suggests his liking for order and balance; he always writes satirical attacks on rogues and villains, and there is an effective discrepancy between their disorderly behaviour and the sense of order that is implicit in his verse form. At this point, however, the rhyme scheme falters. Why? The answer, surely, is that blasphemy, an offence against God, is so extreme an offence that it disrupts Pope's pattern; this is the extreme example of disorder, pernicious enough to undermine any hope of, or attempt at, order. It is this kind of small but effective way of expressing and extending the central idea of a poem that you should constantly try to be aware of in practical criticism.

20 WHAT IS THE PRACTICAL CRITICISM EXAMINER LOOKING FOR?

The person marking the practical criticism paper expects to see a number of things:

1. That you have grasped the meaning and significance of the poem.
2. That you can discuss the poem in some detail showing how it brings its theme to life.

3. That you can build a response in such a way that, by the end of your essay, there is a sense that you have really come to terms with the poem.
4. That you can express and develop your analysis of the poem in a coherent, literate essay.

If you do all these things you will, of course, receive a very good mark. But there is one more quality that the examiner is looking for. Practical criticism is a serious exercise, but practical criticism is also a test of your cleverness, of your creative ability to read a poem imaginatively. This is tricky advice to offer because it might seem to imply that you are meant to attempt ingenious readings of poems. This is not the case. But you will impress the examiner if you can do more with a detail than other people taking the exam. Don't, therefore, rush along too quickly. Once you have set your essay up, linger over some of the details, trying to see if you can do more with them, trying to see if you can establish additional ways in which the details reflect and extend your sense of the issues in the poem. It is that kind of creative reading within the format of a solid and well-organised essay that really impresses the examiner.

7

Technical terms

THERE are a great many technical terms, such as alliteration and assonance, which are the correct descriptive names for the various effects we encounter in poetry. It is quite possible to be a very good critic of poetry without knowing any of these terms; sometimes, indeed, knowledge of the correct name for an effect can actually weaken an analysis. What we mean by this is that when you are writing about poetry it is important that you describe what you can see happening in the poem. It could be the case that your analysis might work better if you present a vivid description of the effect you have noticed, rather than just saying, as some students do, 'this line contains a lot of alliteration'. The rule is, therefore, that it is never enough just to name the device or feature that you have spotted in the poem, you must also make sure that you describe how the device or feature functions in and contributes to the poem. A fuller sense of what we mean should become apparent in the following glossary, where we not only define terms but also try to show these concepts at work in poetry.

Alliteration. Repetition of the same letter (or, more precisely, sound) at the beginning of two or more words in a line of poetry. For example, describing a river in 'Kubla Khan', Coleridge writes 'Five miles *m*eandering with a *m*azy *m*otion'.

Alliteration is easy to spot in a poem, but you will receive no credit at all for merely noting that the poet has made use of the device. It is the same with any feature that you notice in a text: far too often students point out a detail, but fail to justify its presence. The rule is, when you spot something of interest, go on to discuss how it functions in the poem. In the line from Coleridge, for example, the use of alliteration serves to reinforce the meaning of the words which are intended to create a vivid impression of a meandering river. In discussing alliteration, resist the temptation to invest letters with some special sound quality; it is not the repetition of the 'm' sound that suggests the meandering, dream-like movement of the river but the meaning of the words themselves. The alliteration simply serves to link the words together at the level of sound. The 'm' sound in itself suggests nothing: it is the meaning of the words that is important.

A poet who makes extensive use of alliteration is Spenser: a Cave of Despair is described as 'Darke, doleful, drearie, like a greedie grave'. Depressing and frightening words are clustered together; the impression that the words convey is made more forceful because the use of alliteration establishes a link between them. It is the same when he writes 'So faire and fresh, a freshest flower in May': the 'f' sound in itself suggests nothing; it is the clustering of attractive words that is important. Spenser was writing in the late sixteenth century and alliteration is a central feature of his poetry; his epic poem *The Faerie Queene* tells the stories of knights on quests encountering temptations, and his bold use of alliteration helps make clear the nature of the people and the things encountered on the journeys.

Subsequent poets, perhaps because their intentions are not so straightforward, are far more sparing in their use of the device, using it only occasionally to create a special effect. An exception is Hopkins, a late-nineteenth-century poet. The main theme of his poetry is the wonder he finds in God's world. In order to stress this wonder, Hopkins employs both unusual language and an unusual degree of alliteration. In 'Pied Beauty' he writes,

> Whatever is fickle, freckled (who knows how?)
> With swift, slow; sweet, sour; adazzle, dim;
> He fathers-forth. . .

The words and ideas, all of which are in praise of God, acquire additional force because they are linked together through the alliteration. This is the main purpose of alliteration, to lend ideas and images additional emphasis and force.

Assonance. Repetition of the same vowel sound in two or more words in a line of poetry. When Wordsworth writes of 'A host of golden daffodils' there is a repeated 'o' sound. This reinforces the meaning of the words and gives them emphasis.

A common mistake is to exaggerate the importance of sound effects in poetry, spotting assonance (and alliteration) everywhere, and arguing that certain repeated sounds are crucial in creating the effect of a poem. It is, however, the meaning of the words that is important, and sound has only a minor role in underlining that meaning. Most poets use assonance sparingly and always in a straightforward way. For example, Keats's 'Ode on a Grecian Urn' begins,

> Thou still unravished bride of quietness,
> Thou foster-child of silence and slow time.

What attracts Keats to the urn is its ideal innocence and stillness: it is words such as 'bride', 'quietness', 'child' and, 'silence' that principally suggest this, but the assonance on 'i' helps reinforce the impression because it links and emphasises these words. There is a slight jarring note with the one important word in the first line that does not fit into this pattern: 'unravished' carries within it a hint of its opposite, the idea of aggressive assault. Something less harmonious and peaceful is thus hinted at in the word itself, and this idea is underlined by the slight discordance of this word amidst a sequence of words employing the same 'i' sound. In itself, however, the repetition of the 'i' sound does not convey anything: it only becomes significant in the context of these specific words. The thing to avoid is the idea that certain sounds have inherent significance: they do not. If you comment on assonance, try to see how it is used to support the meaning of the words.

A related device is **consonance**: the repetition of the same consonant sound before and after different vowels in two words: for example, '*live*' and '*love*'. Wilfred Owen, a First World War poet, often uses consonance instead of rhyme, as in this extract from 'Strange Meeting':

> It seemed that out of battle I escaped
> Down some profound dull tunnel, long since scooped
> Through granite which titanic wars had groined.
> Yet also there encumbered sleepers groaned.

The subject matter is the nightmare of war. It is principally the imagery that creates a terrifying impression, but the half-rhymes (when consonance replaces rhyme it is called **half-rhyme**) are important as well. Whereas rhyme in such a poem would seem far too neat and orderly, the half-rhymes add to the shock of the language which is deliberately clumsy and unlyrical or unharmonious. They also stress the brutal ugliness of the meaning of the words. Half-rhyme is a central device in Owen's poetry, which always concentrates on the pain and suffering of war, and is also used by other poets, particularly twentieth-century poets, when they want to suggest a world in fragments, a world where things will not hold together in an ordered way.

Free verse. Poetry written in irregular lines and without any regular metre. To grasp the significance of this we need to know that other forms of verse are based upon a regular metrical pattern. Most commonly in English poetry poets write in ten-syllable lines, with five stresses in each line, called iambic pentameters (*see* **Metre** below). Free verse, however, abandons any such regular pattern, and usually also abandons rhyme. Widespread use of free verse is a recent innovation, beginning with the nineteenth-century American poet Walt Whitman's *Leaves of Grass*. In the twentieth century free verse has become very common. T. S. Eliot, Ezra Pound, William Carlos Williams, Wallace Stevens, and D. H. Lawrence are just some of the modern writers who have used the form. It is possibly the case that modern poets, confronting a very disorganised world, distrust any notion of a regular pattern and so prefer free verse, which seems to acknowledge the untidiness of life and of the mind.

Eliot's 'Ash Wednesday' is in free verse:

> Because these wings are no longer wings to fly
> But merely vans to beat the air
> The air which is now thoroughly small and dry
> Smaller and dryer than the will
> Teach us to care and not to care
> Teach us to sit still.

This is difficult to understand out of context, but what Eliot is writing about are his feelings of uselessness coupled with his desire to accept God's guidance. As in all poetry, the poet is seeking order in an often bewildering world. Rather than using a traditional poetic frame to organise his thoughts, though, Eliot opts for the much looser form of free verse which allows him to trace the pattern of his thinking in all its disorder and confusion. Free verse is well suited to this sort of excursion of the mind. Repetition of word and phrase is important in introducing some element of organisation: Eliot alights on a word and it becomes a touchstone as he advances to his next proposition. The technique suggests both the untidiness of a bewildered response and the desire to try and establish some degree of coherence and continuity of thinking. A free-verse poem is irregular, but the poet seeks the occasional moment of symmetry: Eliot, in fact, employs rhyme in the lines above to suggest that search for order. The effect is that we gain a sense of how bewildering the overall picture is, but equally sense the poet searching for even a fragment of order.

In most free-verse poems we are stuck by the impression of a poet struggling to make even a little sense out of a very confusing world. Whitman however, is a system-maker. His poetry celebrates the diversity of America, but he also offers us his personal credo. His beliefs, though, are very individual, even quirky, as they are not developed in a context of traditional poetic frames. Yet, as with all successful free verse, Whitman's poetry presents a vivid impression of a complex mind grappling with the world.

Heroic couplet. A pair of ten-syllable lines (i.e., iambic penta-meters, *see* **Metre** below) that rhyme: a poem as a whole can be written in a sequence of heroic couplets. First used by Chaucer, and later by Spenser, Shakespeare, Donne, Byron, and Browning amongst others, the form is, however, always most associated with the poetry of Dryden and Pope. It was the most popular form of poetry in the eighteenth century.

When couplets are used in narrative poetry (for example in *The Canterbury Tales*, or Keats's 'Lamia') we are not all that conscious of the rhymes, as the writers keep the couplets open, allowing the thought to run on rather than the pattern of the verse being allowed to dominate. In such poetry, heroic couplets are almost as flexible as blank verse, letting the story progress with only a gentle reminder of the presence of the poet. Dryden and Pope, however, usually write in closed couplets (with a semi-colon or full stop at the end of the second line), and this serves to draw attention to the rhyme. This suits their intention as writers: both are satirists, mocking folly, and the balance of the couplet serves as a repeated reminder of the sort of simple balance and order that should prevail in society. An idea of balance is implicit in the couplet form, but they accentuate this – so successfully, indeed, that we now always think of heroic couplets as the appropriate verse form for satire.

When the couplets are closed the thought in each couplet often inclines towards a kind of epigrammatic neatness, as if an issue is wrapped up in the neat form of the two lines. One way of approaching Pope's couplets in particular is to regard them as something like miniature stanzas in which he confronts a problem but exerts his poetic control over the material presented. For example:

> Some have at first for wits, then poets pass'd,
> Turn'd critics next, and prov'd plain fools at last.

Pope writes of things getting out of hand: there is instability, people chopping and changing, but the anarchy that almost takes over in the illustrations is always dominated by Pope exerting his own authority in a couplet as a whole. It is often the case that the themes of the whole poem (here *Essay on Criticism*) are crystallised in every couplet. Pope also uses couplets effectively to state his own principles directly: on these occasions the whole progress and organisation of the lines suggest order and good sense. From the same poem:

> True wit is nature to advantage dress'd,
> What oft was thought, but r.e'er so well express'd.

The lines themselves, in their structure and expression, are a perfect illustration of the sentiment they contain.

Metre. Metre means the pattern of stressed and unstressed syllables in a line of poetry. The most widely-used line in English poetry is the iambic pentameter: this is a ten-syllable line with five stresses or emphases.

For example, the following line from Gray's *Elegy* has ten syllables:

> 1   2   3   4   5   6   7   8 9   10
> The plowman homeward plods his weary way.

When we read the line our voice goes up and down because of the different stresses we naturally give the ten syllables. In poetry we mark these differences by using signs: ˘ for an unstressed syllable, ´ for a stressed one, and this reveals the metrical pattern:

> Thĕ plówmăn hómewărd plóds hĭs wéarў wáy.

As you can see, an unstressed syllable is followed by a stressed one. Each little unit or group of syllables is called a foot: in this case each foot is an iambic foot because it has the pattern unstressed–stressed syllable. The conventional way of marking off the feet from each other is the sign ' : thus, Gray's line has five iambic feet:

Thĕ plów-'măn hóme-'wărd plóds ' hĭs weá-'rў wáy.'

Do not worry if you cannot hear this pattern: nobody actually reads poetry in this broken, halting way. What we are doing is scanning the line, looking to see what its metrical pattern is. Instead of saying that the metrical pattern is five iambic feet, we use the technical term iambic pentameter ('penta' means five).

Metre seems a frighteningly technical topic, but it becomes less frightening as soon as we realise that the bulk of English poetry, both rhymed and unrhymed (unrhymed lines in iambic pentameter are called blank verse; Milton's epic *Paradise Lost* is written in blank verse, as are most of Shakespeare's plays), is written in iambic pentameter, with the same pattern as that illustrated above. A pattern is created in the verse, but it is a fairly natural pattern as the speaking voice does rise and fall in this way. Indeed, the easiest way of thinking about metre is as a regular rise and fall pattern.

Often, however, poets will disrupt this regular pattern or rhythm to produce certain effects in the verse. The reason for this is that a poem written in a totally predictable and regular pattern would become very mechanical. The regular metre of Gray's line suits its sense: it describes the laboured, tired journey of the ploughman. Not every line, however, will have five clear stresses in this way. Often, indeed, we may only hear four, as in this first line from Milton's *Paradise Lost*:

Ŏf mán's fĭrst dísŏbédiĕnce ănd thĕ frúit

Milton is writing about troublesome concepts: the fall of Adam and Eve and the relationship of humankind to God. A totally regular metrical pattern would suggest this was an easy thing to do, that some simple order can be found, whereas this is not so.

The pattern of the verse, then, can vary to suit the subject. The metre, however, still remains iambic pentameter because metre describes the most frequently occurring pattern in the poem. This is the case even when a poet introduces variations into the poem by using a different sort of foot. Variation stresses different words and emphasises them unexpectedly. The most common way of varying the iambic pattern is to start the line with a strong stress instead of a weak one. When Pope writes,

Óft shĕ rĕjécts, bŭt névĕr ónce ŏffénds

the word 'Oft' is unexpectedly emphasised and so its meaning is stressed. This sort of reversed foot, with the stressed syllable appearing first, is known as a **trochaic foot**, or **trochee**. The only other significant variation is the **spondee**: this is a two-syllable foot where both are stressed, as in this line from Keats:

Thŏu fóstĕr-chíld ŏf Sílĕnce ănd slów Tíme

Once again the effect is to emphasise the meaning of the words. This is true of metre as a whole. Metre is one way in which the poet orders language to make it more meaningful than ordinary language, compressing it into a pattern.

We have called this pattern both metre and rhythm. The difference between these, strictly speaking, is that metre is something the poet imposes on the words, arranging them into a pattern. Rhythm, however, is something that comes with the language itself because of the way we speak. In reading a poem it is the rhythm of the language we hear, its movements and flow. Indeed, the only way to spot the stresses in a line of poetry is to read it as you would normal prose, noticing which syllables you emphasise. Most of the time the pattern of syllables will be straightforward. When it is not, then the poet will be varying the metre to suit his or her theme.

Not all poetry is written in five-feet lines. There are names for every length of line (length means how many syllables and feet in a line): the most significant are the tetrameter, which has eight syllables divided into four feet, and the hexameter, which has twelve syllables divided into six feet. If the feet in an hexameter line are iambic it is called an alexandrine. Such conventions do not apply to Old English poetry and medieval alliterative poetry, where syllables do not matter, only stress. The name for this is pure-stress or strong-stress metre, and there are always four stresses to every line, regardless of the length.

A form of pure-stress metre is found in the work of the late-nineteenth-century poet Gerard Manley Hopkins. He experimented with his verse a great deal but essentially he works in free verse with strong stresses in each line. Hopkins called this 'sprung' rhythm because he felt we had to spring from one strong syllable to the next without any pause between. This is a line from 'The Wreck of the *Deutschland*':

> The sóur scýthe crínge, and the bléar sháre cóme.

It has six strong stresses according to Hopkins, though the reader has no way of knowing this. What Hopkins is getting away from is the discipline of the traditional iambic pentameter. He is writing in free verse; there is no regular metre or line length, but the verse is still patterned, most often by the repetition of words or by parallel sentences. In other words, such verse is rhetorical rather then metrical – its effect is that of speech, not of organised rhythms.

There are three other technical terms related to prosody (prosody is the study of versification, especially metre, rhyme, stanzas) which it can prove useful to know: (a) **caesura**: a pause in a line of poetry, often marked by punctuation; (b) **end-stopped lines**: a pause at the end of a line of poetry, marked by punctuation; (c) **run-on lines**: there is no pause at the end of a line. This running-over of the sense of one line into the next is also called **enjambement**, meaning a striding-over.

Rhyme. Identity of sound between two words extending from the last fully stressed vowel to the end of the word: for example, 'hill' and 'still', 'follow' and 'hollow'. Rhyme is usually employed at the end of lines, but poets can make use of internal rhyme. Rhyme suggests harmony and order: the poet finds connections between words, if only at the level of sound, but the connection made suggests a broader idea of finding an order in things. This search for order will be most apparent in what the words of the poem say, but the verse form, including rhyme, helps realise the idea.

In these lines from Yeats's 'Sailing to Byzantium' he makes a plea to priest-like figures:

> O sages standing in God's holy fire,
> As in the gold mosaic of a wall,
> Come from the holy fire, perne in a gyre,
> And be the singing-masters of my soul.
> Consume my heart away; sick with desire
> And fastened to a dying animal
> It knows not what it is; and gather me
> Into the artifice of eternity.

In this instance the actual sense of the words might be difficult to grasp, but the use of rhyme (including the internal rhyme of 'fire' / 'gyre' in line 3) helps create a pattern in the verse which actually helps us grasp what is being said: that he wants to escape to a rarefied, ritual-like life outside time.

Rhyme can link problematic words. Marvell's 'To His Coy Mistress' begins:

> Had we but world enough, and time,
> This coyness, Lady, were no crime.

'Time' and 'crime' are troublesome ideas, but they are absorbed in a couplet: we feel that the poet has got control of the concepts. So rhyme has an ability to unify and connect disparate entities, finding similarity in dissimilarity. It is never enough to point out that a poem rhymes; you have to construct a case about how the use of rhymes contributes to the overall meaning and effect of the poem. The answer, however, will always be that rhyme contributes to a sense of order.

What is also worth looking out for are the occasions on which the rhyme pattern falters. In Yeats's poem we might expect line 6 to rhyme with line 2 or line 4, but they do not quite rhyme. The idea in the line is a painful one, that of the 'heart fastened to a dying animal', and serves to remind us of the impossibility of escape for the poet, but the poem's failure to rhyme perfectly also contributes to the sense that the disorder of the real world is breaking up the pattern of the poem. There is a similar effect in Marvell's poem. Suddenly the rhyming pattern falters:

> And yonder all before us lie
> Deserts of vast eternity.

It only just fails to rhyme, but the break in the poem's orderly pattern is sufficient to underline the idea of the vastness of eternity, an idea too big to absorb into Marvell's ordered response to life.

There are technical terms for the different kinds of rhyme, which it can prove useful to know:

(a)   **end rhyme** occurs at the end of lines
(b)   **internal rhyme** occurs within lines

(c) **masculine** or **strong rhymes**: a single stressed syllable – 'hill'
     and 'still'
(d) **feminine** or **weak rhymes**: two rhyming syllables, a stressed
     one followed by an unstressed one – 'hollow' and 'follow'
(e) **eye rhyme** or **courtesy rhymes**: words spelt alike but not
     actually rhyming – 'love' and 'prove'
(f) **imperfect rhymes** (also called **partial**, **near**, **slant** or **off-
     rhymes**): words which do not quite rhyme and so produce a
     sense of discordance – 'soul' and 'wall'
(g) **half-rhymes** (also called '**consonance**') repetition of the same
     consonant sounds before and after different vowels – 'groaned'
     and 'groined'

The conventional method of referring to the rhyme scheme in a poem
is to work through the alphabet, assigning the same letter to the lines
that rhyme: a poem in rhyming couplets could be said to rhyme *aa bb
cc dd ee*, etc.; a four-line stanza might often rhyme *abab*. This, however,
does not tell us anything important about the poem; we always have
to go further and talk about the rhyme words themselves. For
example, in Yeats's lines above, the rhyme between 'me' and
'eternity' reinforces the idea of the poet's yearning for an ideal world
by connecting the two words through sound.

Rhythm. Rhythm means the flow or movement of a line, whether it
goes fast or slow, is calm or troubled. But how do we know whether a
line is fast or slow? The answer is that the meaning of the words tell
us: rhythm and meaning cannot be separated.
     For example, in the closing stanza from Hardy's 'The Voice' he
is haunted by a woman's voice, a woman he still loves even though
she has gone:

>   Thus I: faltering forward,
>   Leaves around me falling,
>   Wind oozing thin through the thorn from norward,
>   And the woman calling.

Cold images of falling leaves and the north wind suggest his mood of
despair. Turning to the rhythm, the first line is about the poet's
faltering: the idea is suggested by the break after 'Thus I'. The
rhythm falters, but the meaning of the words has told us what to

expect in the rhythm. Similarly, the second line mentions the falling leaves, and the rhythm itself is falling – as we read the last word our voice trails away. The rhythm thus matches and reinforces the sense of the words. It is the same in the third line: it is tempting here to say that the line imitates the noise of the wind, but it does not. The description of the wind is an image that expresses the poet's feelings of pain. So the depressing, lifeless rhythm of the line matches the speaker's feelings. As always the rhythm supports the real meaning of the line.

The way in which rhythm supports meaning can be seen again in Donne's 'The Sun Rising':

> Busy old fool, unruly Sun,
> Why dost thou thus,
> Through windows and through curtains call on us?

The language is colloquial, the rhythm almost chatty but also angry. We can set the lively, questioning manner of this against the lines from Tennyson's 'The Lotus-Eaters':

> There is sweet music here that softer falls
> Than petals from blown roses on the grass.

The scene is attractive – the words make that clear – so Tennyson opts for a contented, rather dreamy rhythm. Rhythmic effects are always as simple as this. If the speaker is troubled, then the rhythm will be troubled. If the speaker is happy and excited, so too will the rhythm be. If he or she is calm and contented the rhythm will be relaxed. It is always best to work from the meaning back to the devices of the poem, such as rhythm, rather than trying to guess the meaning from the rhythm.

Stanza. A sixteen-line poem might be divided into four equal units of four lines: these units of verse, separated by a space in the printed text, are called stanzas. Four-line units (quatrains) are the most common, but the term refers to any such group of lines. Each unit normally contains the same number of lines, and usually the same rhyme scheme is employed. In long poems, where there are divisions at irregular intervals, each unit of verse is referred to as a verse paragraph.

Below we list some of the great number of English stanza forms, but such technical description is less important than understanding the role of stanzas in poetry. There must be some reason, connected to the overall meaning of the poem, why a writer might chose to organise a poem in this way. A stanza from George Herbert's 'Jordan I' provides a clue:

> Who says that fiction's only and false hair
> Becomes a verse? Is there in truth no beauty?
> Is all good structure in a winding stair?
> May no lines pass, except they do their duty
>   Not to a true, but painted chair?

Herbert is criticising the elaborate images and ideas that poets are so fond of. One thing he criticises is a structure like a winding stair – that is, a poem that ties itself up in knots in pursuit of its idea. The verse states this, but Herbert's point is supported by his use of a regular five-line stanza (rhyming *ababa*), which stands as a counterweight to the convolutions of writing he is so much against.

Stanza patterns usually operate in this way. By employing a regular pattern the poet offers an idea of order within the work. Within the stanza all kinds of complications can occur, but this is held in tension with the overall desire for a pattern. We can see this in Browning's 'Two in the Campagna': he is trying to define the essence of love, but it is difficult, as the chopped syntax of the poem indicates:

> No. I yearn upward, touch you close,
> Then stand away. I kiss your cheek,
> Catch your soul's warmth – I pluck the rose
> And love it more than tongue can speak –
> Then the good minute goes.

The rapid move from idea to idea suggests the intangibility of what Browning is trying to define, but the overall stanza pattern stands as a testimony to his desire to understand and order experience.

The logic informing the use of stanzas is simple, but always worth commenting on, particularly if you feel that the stanza pattern falters at any stage in a poem, as this is an effective way of enacting the difficulty the poet is having in ordering his or her view. Many stanzas have no special name, and often a poet will invent a stanza form for a particular poem. But there are some patterns that are widely used:

(a) **couplet**: a pair of rhymed lines
(b) **heroic couplet**: rhymed lines in iambic pentameter
(c) **tercet** or **triplet**: three lines with a single rhyme
(d) **quatrain**: a four-line stanza
(e) **rhyme royal**: a seven-line stanza in iambic pentamenter rhyming *ababbcc*
(f) **octava rima**: an eight-line stanza rhyming *abababcc*
(g) **spenserian stanza**: a nine-line stanza rhyming *ababbcbcc*; the first eight lines are iambic pentameter, the ninth an alexandrine
(h) **sonnet**: a fourteen-line poem in iambic pentameter. There are variations on the sonnet, such as a shortened form invented by Hopkins called the curtal sonnet. This has two separated stanzas, one of six lines, the other of four – with a half-line tail-piece
(i) **canto**: a subdivision of a narrative poem

Symbol. An object which stands for something else (for example, a dove symbolises peace). In a poem it is a word which, while signifying something specific, also signifies something beyond itself.

People are often unclear about the difference between an image and a symbol. The difference is that what an image is associated with is stated in the poem, but with a symbol we have to infer the meaning and association. An example might make this clearer. A poet who compares his or her lover to a rose is using a figurative image, associating the lover with something from a different realm of experience. In this poem by Blake, however, a rose is used as a symbol: we suspect that he is not only talking about a rose, but what the rose stands for or is associated with is not stated:

> O Rose, thou art sick!
> The invisible worm
> That flies in the night,
> In the howling storm,
>
> Has found out thy bed
> Of crimson joy,
> And his dark secret love
> Does thy life destroy.

Reading the poem we might work out that Blake is talking about something evil destroying something beautiful, possibly corrupt passion destroying a young woman's innocence and beauty. The poem does not, however, state this, yet it is effective because it is so indirect.

It is easy to make the mistake of thinking that symbols are rampant in poetry, and so read poems in a naive way in which everything is assumed to have a hidden meaning. The truth is that most poems are far more direct, stating an idea and usually using imagery to add associations and complexity to the idea. Symbols are only used when a writer wants to express an apprehension of something which is not directly observable in the everyday world. The writer has to use a symbol because he or she can only convey this non-rational apprehension of something by using objects and words from the familiar world. Symbols are first used a lot in romantic poetry, where the poets often want to express their sense of an unseen world in the imagination. Coleridge's 'Kubla Khan', with its creation of a mythical world which does not have an obvious meaning but seems somehow to reflect the fantasies of the unconscious, is a good example of a symbolic poem. A poet can, however, start with an object in the real world and make it symbolic by loading it with meaning which is not explicitly stated: for example, the solitary figures Wordsworth encounters become symbolic, and Keats's nightingale, in 'Ode to a Nightingale', is something he sees but then invests with a tantalising significance.

The danger with symbolism is that the poet can lose all touch with the ordinary world. This happens in some of Blake's longer poems where he explores the inner mind, using symbols, but the symbolism has become so private that we can see no meaning in it. Successful symbolism – as in 'Kubla Khan', or in 'Ode to a Nightingale', or when Yeats creates the world of Byzantium in his poems – is rather more of a compromise, in that we can fairly confidently infer a meaning, and see how the imaginings of the mind relate to ordinary experience.

8

Writing a poetry practical criticism essay

WE have offered a great deal of advice so far, some of which you may have found useful and a lot of which you might choose to ignore. As we all know, however, what really matters is that day when you have to sit down in an examination and respond on the spot to a poem you haven't seen before. The obvious, if rather smug, thing to say at this point is that if you have had a lot of practice writing analyses of poems, then you are going to find it relatively easy on the big day. But practice also involves knowing exactly what you are doing in an essay, and why you are doing it. The earlier chapters of this book have already covered many of the issues involved, but this chapter deals directly and exclusively with the technique of writing a practical criticism examination answer. You might choose to reject our advice. It could be that you feel you have been taught a better method, and we are obviously happy to accept that there is more than one way to write a good essay. The advantage of the method we suggest, however, is that it makes active use of the essay format itself to help you write a good essay. Or, to put that another way, the essay structure does a lot of the work of writing the essay for you. This is something that should soon become apparent as you look at the following examples.

EXAMPLE ONE: WRITING ABOUT A SINGLE POEM

Step 1:   Reading and thinking

'Dover Beach'

The sea is calm tonight.
The tide is full, the moon lies fair
Upon the straits; on the French coast the light
Gleams and is gone; the cliffs of England stand,
Glimmering and vast, out in the tranquil bay.

Come to the window, sweet is the night-air!
Only, from the long line of spray
Where the sea meets the moon-blanched land,
Listen! you hear the grating roar
Of pebbles which the waves draw back, and fling,
At their return, up the high strand,
Begin, and cease, and then again begin,
With tremulous cadence slow, and bring
The eternal note of sadness in.

Sophocles long ago
Heard it on the Aegean, and it brought
Into his mind the turbid ebb and flow
Of human misery; we
Find also in the sound a thought,
Hearing it by this distant northern sea.

The Sea of Faith
Was once, too, at the full, and round earth's shore
Lay like the folds of a bright girdle furled.
But now I only hear
Its melancholy, long, withdrawing roar,
Retreating, to the breath
Of the night-wind, down the vast edges drear
And naked shingles of the world.

Ah, love, let us be true
To one another! for the world, which seems
To lie before us like a land of dreams,
So various, so beautiful, so new,
Hath really neither joy, nor love, nor light,
Nor certitude, nor peace, nor help for pain;
And we are here as on a darkling plain
Swept with confused alarms of struggle and flight,
Where ignorant armies clash by night.

Read the poem several times, making sure that you read it in an
active way – looking for a pattern, looking for a tension, looking for
some sense of how the poem is organised. Remember that, as the

poem progresses, it is likely to go through a number of twists and turns; for the moment, ignore the complications in the latter stages of the poem. Concentrate on the opening. If you can establish a tension in the first few lines, then you will have established the pattern on which the rest of your answer can build.

This poem is arranged in four irregular stanzas; it might be a good idea to number them, to remind yourself that each stanza is going to require a separate paragraph as you build your essay. If a poem isn't divided into stanzas, it will help your answer if you divide it into four (or, sometimes, three or five) sections. Remember that your way into a poem should be simple and straightforward. This poem, for example, starts with a number of calm and reassuring images; it is easy to anticipate that some form of disturbance will soon arrive in the poem. This is as much as you need to establish in order to get started. You don't need to work everything out in advance; nor do you need to make masses of notes all over the poem as it appears on the examination paper. You don't need to do these things because the format of your essay will steer you towards the things that need to be spotted as your answer develops. So, the starting point is:

---

1. Read the poem several times.
2. Focus on the opening lines, trying to see a tension that is central in the poem.
3. Don't become immersed in detailed analysis in advance of writing your essay. You can feel confident that the essay itself will do the work of steering you along.
4. Establish the foundation on which you are going to build your case.

Perhaps the most important point is not to over-burden yourself at the start of your analysis. One book about practical criticism that we looked at suggested that candidates should begin by 'looking for recurring words, contrasts, a relation between the beginning and the end of the poem, and the nature of the imagery'. In other words, look at everything at once and tie yourself up in impossible knots. We think it is a much better idea to establish a simple tension at the outset, introducing the complications later.

Step 2:   Starting an essay. Summarise the poem, establish your sense of the central opposition in the poem, set up the controlling idea for your essay as a whole

Start your first paragraph with a brief summary of the poem. Make sure that you summarise what the poem actually says. In the case of 'Dover Beach', for example, some readers might start speculating about the identity of the speaker or why he is in Dover. You don't need to make up a story behind the poem in this kind of way. Don't speculate; stick to the task of describing what you actually encounter. Then try to establish a sense of a tension in the poem; you don't need to look for anything at all complicated at this stage. You are simply making a reasonable assumption about the possible overall direction of the poem. If you can see a larger issue that is implicit in what you have written so far, draw attention to this in the last sentence of your opening paragraph.

Applying this approach to 'Dover Beach', a summary would have to start with the poem's initial peaceful view of the straits of Dover. The speaker goes on, however, to describe the grating roar of withdrawing pebbles, and this brings melancholy thoughts into his mind. In the second stanza, he mentions how Sophocles heard the same sound, which made him think of human misery. In the third stanza, the poet compares a kind of high tide of the 'Sea of Faith' with this melancholy withdrawal. This sad mood in the poem leads directly into the fourth stanza, where he implores his love that they be true to each other in such a frightening world. The obvious tension is between a sense of security and well-being, and an idea of disturbance. The poem clearly amounts to more than just a description of the view from the poet's window as Dover; we might say that it is dealing with larger issues of security and insecurity in life in general.

Step 3:   Look more closely at the opening of the poem, trying to see how the poet brings the theme to life

We now have a steady opening paragraph, a paragraph that should help frame and direct all our subsequent impressions. We have a sense of security and insecurity, and an impression that the poet, Matthew Arnold, is dealing with more general questions of what we cling on to and what might unsettle us in life. Make sure that you write one clear paragraph to set up your essay. One of the most common mistakes made by examination candidates is writing an essay with two opening paragraphs; what we mean by this is that they get started, and then write a second paragraph where they go over the same ground again. This weakens an essay. You must ensure that you get off to a purposeful start, which means one clear paragraph to launch the argument. Remember, too, that English is a subject where your writing matters. Make every effort you can to write in grammatical sentences; pay attention to your spelling, and, when you quote from the poem, make sure that you quote accurately. This kind of attention to detail might sound pedantic, but it is in fact essential to the smooth running and progress of your essay.

With your first paragraph written, you now need to concentrate on the second paragraph. At the heart of this paragraph will be a close consideration of a number of details from the poem's opening stanza. As the earlier chapters of this book have explained, the sense of a tension that you have established will enable you to justify and explain the poet's choice of details, while, at the same time, close discussion of these details will advance your overall understanding of the poem. In the case of 'Dover Beach', you might want to explain how the opening images create a sense of security. It is not just the images chosen, but also the simplicity and regularity of these opening lines (in particular, the sense of balance in the monosyllabic, equally-divided line 'The tide is full, the moon lies fair'). There is an overwhelming impression of peacefulness and order. The sea in literature can suggest chaos and destruction, but here it is 'calm' and 'tranquil', and the cliffs of Dover reinforce this comforting impression, as they seem to represent a defence against any potential threat.

A threat does arrive, however, in the second half of the stanza where the initial quiet of the poem yields to the harsh 'grating' noise of the withdrawing pebbles, and where a sense of violence appears as Arnold uses the word 'fling' to describe the movement of these pebbles. The term 'moon-blanched' is interesting: this is no longer the reassuring moonlight of the opening lines. There is something cold and drained of colour about this image, and, as such, it helps change the initially reassuring land and seascape into an impression that is anonymous and unsettling. Arnold's play with light is also evident, we can now see, in the reference to the light on the French coast that 'gleams and is gone'. At first this seemed just a part of the generally attractive picture, but we can now see that it might be more complicated than that, for it is an impermanent light; we are soon plunged back into darkness.

As you can see, we haven't looked at all the words in the stanza. There's no need to, and, indeed, an answer would be weakened if you attempted to look at too much. Look at enough to see how the poet develops the two sides of the tension in the poem. At the end of the paragraph, however, you must take stock of where you have arrived. It is our impression that, at a thematic level, 'Dover Beach' is still keeping things fairly simple: Arnold's initial effort has gone into establishing a sense of security and insinuating a shifting, uncertain, rather harsh sense of insecurity.

Step 4:   Look at another section of the poem, trying to build on your analysis of the poem's details

The first paragraph, and the last paragraph, of an essay should be relatively short: just enough to set up the poem, and then, finally, to pull the strands of your argument together. All the central paragraphs of your essay, however, need to be rather longer, and, ideally, all more or less the same length, as these are the solid steps in the building of your argument. At the end of each paragraph you must say to yourself, 'What, on the basis of looking at these details, can I now say about this poem that I couldn't have said before?' You must ensure that each paragraph does arrive somewhere and does advance your case in this kind of way. A good tip to bear in mind is that if you find yourself quoting any of the words of the poem in the last sentence of a paragraph then you are still rather too close to the evidence. You will need to add another sentence, a sentence in which you can stand back and take stock of what you have proved so far. You might, of course, object that this seems a rather schematic approach to essay-writing, but essay-writing needs to be schematic; you must have a plan that ensures that you keep paying attention to the words of the poem, and you must make sure that you are advancing an argument. By far the best method of organising this is to stand back as a paragraph concludes and take stock of your progress.

In the case of 'Dover Beach', by the end of our second paragraph we had arrived at a point where, rather than just talking about security and insecurity, we could say something about the unstable, shifting and unnerving nature of the feelings that disturb Arnold. Stanza two should start to fill out and develop this idea. It isn't quite as straightforward as this, however. This is the second stanza:

> Sophocles long ago
> Heard it on the Aegean, and it brought
> Into his mind the turbid ebb and flow
> Of human misery; we
> Find also in the sound a thought,
> Hearing it by this distant northern sea.

In our experience, a lot of students are 'thrown' by this stanza. They can't see why Sophocles suddenly appears, or what he has got to do with anything established so far. If you get stuck in poetry analysis, however, it is always easy to find an answer to your dilemma. The more puzzling a detail, the more essential it becomes to return to first principles. Encountering this reference to Sophocles, you have to ask yourself whether he has more to do with 'security' or 'insecurity'. Possibly the name suggests both ideas. Sophocles is, after all, part of our cultural inheritance. But, after the familiarity of the view at Dover, it is an abrupt shift to Sophocles, and, as the stanza continues, there is a sense of a huge time-span and disconcerting distances. As against this large sense of the past, the static security of a moonlit night in Dover seems very small, almost trivial. There is even something rather touching about the poet holding on to his educated knowledge, his familiarity with the thoughts of Sophocles, in such a frightening world. It is as if he needs touchstones, things or names or impressions that provide him with some kind of security.

How has this advanced our overall grasp of the poem? What can we say now that we couldn't have said at the end of the previous paragraph of our essay? We have, in fact, made a fairly substantial move forward. Previously we had an idea of the shifting and unnerving nature of the world, but now we have moved on to a sense of the frightening immensity of the world and, given our own smallness in this world, how we need to cling on to things (a seascape, a sense of England, a cultural inheritance). We have, therefore, made a big step forward in our understanding of the poem, but we have managed to do this as a result of our simple method of analysis: we started the paragraph with some ideas, looked at some details, and this enabled us to add to and develop our ideas. The running conclusion we have arrived at is, of course, not the only view that could be arrived at here; there is no single correct reading of a poem and every reader will interpret the evidence in his or her own way. But the important point is that you do try to advance your case in this kind of way.

Step 5:   Look at another section of the poem, trying to build on your analysis of the poem's details

> The Sea of Faith
> Was once, too, at the full, and round earth's shore
> Lay like the folds of a bright girdle furled.
> But now I only hear
> Its melancholy, long, withdrawing roar,
> Retreating, to the breath
> Of the night-wind, down the vast edges drear
> And naked shingles of the world.

If you have established control of the first two stanzas, essentially using the structure and format of the essay to help you achieve control, then you will be well-placed to tackle this stanza. If, however, your essay has failed to advance in paragraph steps, you might flounder with this stanza – for the obvious reason that you will have no sense of a developing picture in which to place the details you encounter here. As an illustration of what we mean by this, let's consider the phrase 'Sea of Faith'. We have seen essays where the candidates have no idea what Arnold means by this, but these essays also lacked any sense of a developing argument: consequently, the candidates lacked a key that would have enabled them to decode the detail.

The way to make sense of 'Sea of Faith' is to work from the ideas established at the end of the previous paragraph. The point we arrived at was the frightening nature of the world, and how people need to hang on to things that provide some sense of security. The 'Sea of Faith' is clearly one of these things that we cling on to; more precisely, it is religion, and the first few lines of this stanza provide a sense of how religion provided comfort and protection. A neat illustration of this is that it is referred to as like 'a bright girdle'; this clothing image can be set against 'naked shingles' in the last line of the stanza. On the one hand there is the protection of clothes, on the other the exposure of nakedness. What can we now say, however, that we couldn't have said before? The obvious point is that the idea of security has now been directly associated with religious faith, but Arnold writes as if the security of religion is a thing of the past, that we live exposed lives in a harsh world where we are on our own.

Step 6:   Look at how the poem concludes

The poet sets up a tension and then develops that tension. What we can anticipate is that, rather than resolving the tension, the poet will push it further or in a new direction at the end of the poem. We need to look at the last stanza of 'Dover Beach', therefore, to see what Arnold adds to the picture we have established so far. As we have said all along, it is best to concentrate on just a few words from the stanza. In this instance, however, we are going to say far more than is necessary in an essay, to show how it is possible to 'play' with a text. There is an important point involved here. An examiner will want to see you looking closely at the details of a poem, and will want to see you building a sensible case – and if you do both these things you will receive a good mark. But an examiner is going to be even more impressed if you can push things a little bit further, if you can spot things that other people aren't spotting. We are not talking about a silly or over-ingenious reading of a poem. What we are talking about is a demonstration of your ability to read creatively, to 'play' with details and ideas. What we have in mind should become apparent in the following comments on the last stanza of 'Dover Beach'.

> Ah, love, let us be true
> To one another! for the world, which seems
> To lie before us like a land of dreams,
> So various, so beautiful, so new,
> Hath really neither joy, nor love, nor light,
> Nor certitude, nor peace, nor help for pain;
> And we are here as on a darkling plain
> Swept with confused alarms of struggle and flight,
> Where ignorant armies clash by night.

The stanza starts with the words 'Ah, love'. In the course of three stanzas, Arnold has developed a sense of a frightening world and what people cling on to in such a world. What he turns to in this last stanza is a personal relationship: the bond between two individuals provides some sense of connection in a universe where we are all too aware of the separateness of every pebble. This is something that works on a timeless basis – that love is one thing that we can hold on to in a world where death exists – but it also works within a more specific historical context. With the loss of religious faith, as referred to in stanza three, there is a loss of the sense of a greater power outside the individual; consequently, there is a turning-in on the personal. The human subject is placed at the centre of experience. This connects with an impression in the last stanza of a retreat from the world into domesticity; it is a way of keeping the world at a distance.

But the hint of imploring in 'Ah, love, let us be true/To one another' perhaps indicates that he can see the essential falseness of the connection he is proposing. It seems small recompense for the loss of religious faith, particularly when we note, a few lines later, that Arnold denies the existence of love in the world: 'the world . . . Hath neither joy, nor love, nor light'. The denial of love is, of course, incompatible with his plea to his 'love', except in so far as he is prepared to cling on to an illusion in the absence of anything else. Indeed, the whole stanza is characterised by a kind of cold reality that denies illusions. One way in which this comes across is that the three positive words – 'various', 'beautiful' and 'new' – are followed by the list of six negatives. It is not too fanciful to suggest that a trinity is challenged by something that is twice as powerful.

The poem throughout its four stanzas makes effective use of the contrast between named places and anonymous tracts of land and time. The sense of a bleak landscape is at its most powerful at the end. The poem is irregular in structure, the uneven length of the stanzas and the rather arbitrary use of rhyme managing to suggest a world where order is now only a dim memory. And a sense of disorder is the note on which the poem ends. Unpredictably, Arnold moves to an image of battle, an image that has no connection with anything that has preceded it in the poem. We are, indeed, on a 'darkling plain', where all the images of light with which the poem opened have been lost. Most telling of all, however, is the image of conflict with which the poem ends: two anonymous armies clash, seemingly with no sense of the cause or purpose of their battle. All sense of order and design – including God's design for the world – has gone.

You would not, of course, be expected to say even a fraction of the things we have said here about the last stanza of 'Dover Beach' in one paragraph of a practical criticism essay, but, if you can find interesting or unusual ways in which the subject of the poem is conveyed and expanded in the details of the poem, it is well worth pursuing your hunch.

Step 7: Sum up your sense of the poem as a whole

Our essay has moved through five paragraphs so far: one to set the poem up, and then four of steady analysis. We need one final paragraph to pull everything together. Sometimes this will be a fairly routine paragraph, in which you merely sum up what you have established about the poem, but sometimes, if your analysis has worked well, this might be a paragraph where you are brimming over with things to say – brimming over because your analysis has led you to discover dimensions to the poem that you had no idea were there when you started your essay, and which you want to report on in an excited way. One thing to avoid in this concluding paragraph is a dismissive judgement on the poem: you aren't going to gain any marks for saying 'I don't like this poem' or 'I don't think this poem works very well'. It's much better to end on an upbeat note, drawing attention to just how much is going on in the poem you have been discussing; indeed, your analysis, if it has worked as planned, should have provided ample evidence of just this, the interest and complexity of the poem under consideration.

EXAMPLE TWO: WRITING ABOUT A SINGLE POEM

It is quite possible that the length of our discussion of 'Dover Beach' might have obscured the simplicity of the step-by-step method we are describing. With this second example, therefore, we want to convey the same advice in a much more condensed form.

Step 1: Reading and thinking

'A Church Romance'

She turned in the high pew, until her sight
Swept the west gallery, and caught its row
Of music-men with viol, book, and bow
Against the sinking sad tower-window light.

She turned again; and in her pride's despite
One strenuous viol's inspirer seemed to throw
A message from his string to her below,
Which said: 'I claim thee as my own forthright!'

Thus their hearts' bond began, in due time signed.
And long years thence, when Age had scared Romance,
At some old attitude of his or glance
That gallery-scene would break upon her mind,
With him as minstrel, ardent, young, and trim,
Bowing 'New Sabbath' or 'Mount Ephraim'.

Read the poem several times, making sure that you are reading it in an active way – looking for a pattern, looking for a tension, looking for some sense of how the poem is organised. Concentrate on the opening. If you can establish a tension in the first few lines, then you will have established the pattern on which the rest of your answer can build.

Step 2:   Starting an essay. Summarise the poem, establish your sense of the central opposition in the poem, set up the controlling idea for your essay as a whole

Start your first paragraph with a summary of the poem. Then try to establish a sense of a tension in the poem; you don't need to look for anything at all complicated at this stage. You are simply making an assumption about the probable overall direction of the poem. If you can see a larger issue that is implicit in what you have written so far, draw attention to this in the last sentence of your opening paragraph.

It is easy to summarise this poem, but perhaps a little more difficult to establish a tension. A woman in church looks at the church band (a minor obstacle for many readers would be not knowing that in rural areas in the Victorian period many churches had a band rather than an organ); one member of the band seems to send her a message in his playing. Years later, as a married couple, romance has yielded to routine, but some mannerism of the man will suddenly make her see the scene when they were both young, and he was her minstrel. It is easy to see what is positive in the poem: it is love. What we set against this, however, is less clear; perhaps we should take note of the last line of the opening stanza with its reference to 'the sinking sad tower-window light'. It is an image that suggests decline and the end of the day. Implicit in such a tension is something bigger than the mere 'story' of this poem: in this small poem Hardy has found a way of exploring love, youth and growing old.

Step 3:   Look more closely at the opening of the poem, trying to see how the poet brings the theme to life

There are three stanzas in this poem; you need to think, therefore, in terms of a five-paragraph essay: one paragraph to set things up, three of analysis, and one to pull everything together at the end. At the heart of the second paragraph you will need to present a close consideration of a number of details from the poem's opening stanza. As the earlier chapters of this book have explained, the sense of a tension that you have established will enable you to justify and explain the poet's choice of details, and, at the same time, close discussion of the details will advance your overall understanding of the poem. At the end of this paragraph (and at the end of the following paragraphs), you will need to see how your case has advanced, asking yourself 'What can I say now that I couldn't have said before?' You must make sure that each of the central paragraphs of your essay does advance your understanding of the poem.

In the case of 'A Church Romance', the sort of thing you might decide to focus on is a kind of grand demeanour in the young woman, who seems to rise above her pew as she sweeps her eyes over the gallery. And how, in the word 'caught', there is a kind of chase or pursuit which is not entirely at one with the context of the church; indeed, there is a kind of restlessness about the young woman, who seems to strain against the formal context – and formal language – in which she finds herself. We receive a strong sense of an individual and, moreover, a woman who is seizing the initiative as she plays her youthful, flirtatious game. The only note that strikes a different chord is the reference to the 'sinking sad tower-window light', an image that suggests decline and darkness, in fact everything that is the opposite of youthful energy. We started with a sense of love versus the passing of time. We now have a much more confident sense of the energy and exuberance of youth.

Step 4:   Look at another section of the poem, trying to build on your analysis of the poem's details

> She turned again; and in her pride's despite
> One strenuous viol's inspirer seemed to throw
> A message from his string to her below,
> Which said: 'I claim thee as my own forthright!'

It is again a case of looking at details, and then seeing how your case has advanced. You might decide to pick up the musical references, for music always suggests an idea of harmony. Or you might be interested in the respective position of the man and the woman, how the poet repeats the point that it is him above and her below. Yet it is more complex than that, for she is in charge of the situation, she is the one who interprets his playing in a certain way. And this can be connected with the way in which she is larger than the church which would attempt to contain her. Where does this get us? We could continue talking about the poet's presentation of youthfulness and romance, but there seems to be another dimension as well, perhaps turning on issues of power in male–female relationships. Love, in the hands of this young woman, becomes a kind of rebellious energy.

Step 5:   Look at how the poem concludes

With the passing of time, romance has given way to routine. But occasionally she thinks of the young man, and she is back in her former years. Within the person who is growing old is the young person, still with memories of the freshness of romance, still capable of thinking of her husband as a 'minstrel' who is wooing her. The last line contains the names 'New Sabbath' and 'Mount Ephraim': these names mean nothing to the modern reader, but can you see how they are rather cold and formal names, in keeping, in fact, with the formal language of much of the poem. But amidst such formality, including the formality of religion, there is a restless energy in evidence.

Step 6:   Sum up your sense of the poem as a whole

In your final paragraph you need to pull everything together. It is only at this point that you can do this as it has taken this long for the overall picture to take shape. What might strike you here is that, in a form that rather conceals the fact, the poem is a sonnet. There seems something appropriate about this, as if it is a form well-suited to a theme of love and time passing. The sonnet is a tight, formal structure, but with an energy inside it that challenges the form; in the same way, the poem has dealt with youthful energy within an established order. It is the proximity of the two ideas in the poem that makes Hardy's presentation of the attractiveness and defiance of youth all the more forceful. It is this kind of sense of something complex having been achieved within the small frame of a poem that, perhaps more than anything else, you should be attempting to convey in an essay.

EXAMPLE THREE: REAL ESSAYS

If we were reading, rather than writing, this book, we would by now have a number of points that we would want to raise. Points like these: everything that has been said so far might be perfectly true, but does it apply in the real world? For example, tips about how to write an essay might sound plausible, but do they actually work? The advice to focus on just a few details sounds plausible, but precisely how few or how many details is one meant to focus on, and how much is one meant to say about each detail in the course of assembling a paragraph?

It is to meet questions like this that we want to turn now to some real essays by real examination candidates. Here are three essays about R. S. Thomas's poem 'The Welsh Hill Country', the poem we discussed in Chapter 2. They are 'real' essays in various senses: one is that they have weaknesses as well as strengths. In assembling a book like this, it is tempting to include the best essays from students that one has ever read as examples of how practical criticism can be done. But such essays are more likely to intimidate than encourage. These are representative essays written in forty-five minutes by first-year university students; all three students are good at English, but at the same time they would admit to finding this kind of exercise far from easy. As you will see, all three more or less follow the approach we describe in this book, but not slavishly. After each essay we have added a brief comment, but as you read the analyses try to judge for yourself the quality of the answers you are reading. It might be a good idea if we include R. S. Thomas's poem again here.

'The Welsh Hill Country'

Too far for you to see
The fluke and the foot-rot and the fat maggot
Gnawing the skin from the small bones,
The sheep are grazing at Bwlch-y-Fedwen,
Arranged romantically in the usual manner
On a bleak background of bald stone.

Too far for you to see
The moss and the mould on the cold chimneys,
The nettles growing through the cracked doors,
The houses stand empty at Nant-yr-Eira,
There are holes in the roofs that are thatched with sunlight,
And the fields are reverting to the bare moor.

Too far, too far to see
The set of his eyes and the slow phthisis
Wasting his frame under the ripped coat,
There's a man still farming at Ty'n-y-Fawnog
Contributing grimly to the accepted pattern,
The embryo music dead in his throat.

'The Welsh Hill Country'
by Louise Meeson

The poem describes a Welsh scene: the sheep grazing on a farm, the decaying buildings, and the kind of man who lives here. The poem suggests that there is far more in the world than our superficial gaze can see. Thomas reveals this by his use of contrasting images, showing the darker and bleaker side which underlies the 'romantically' depicted outer image. In this way a more serious and painful world, where everything is in decay, is shown.

In the first stanza, Thomas evokes the feeling that nature itself is decaying. He begins with the line 'Too far for you to see'. Obviously the Welsh countryside is impossible for everyone to see, but this line also refers to the fact that finer details are missed by humans as they survey the world around them. The poet draws attention to small details which are unpleasant in themselves but which also evoke an idea of natural decay: 'foot-rot', and the 'fat maggot' who is 'gnawing the skin from the small bones'. This unpleasant imagery is the reality behind the 'country' life, rather than the image that most people hold of sheep 'arranged romantically'. The last line of the stanza also emphasises the contrast between the true reality shown and the romantic notion held by many of what country life is like: Thomas conjures up an image of 'a bleak background of bald stone', which contrasts with our usual idea of fields. Thomas has shown nature in decay and reveals that the vision the reader holds is a façade.

In the second stanza, the first line repeats the statement made at the beginning of the poem. As it is repeated emphasis is added, and we are made aware that we really are 'too far' away to receive the full picture. Once again, unpleasant imagery is revealed: 'moss', 'mould', 'cold chimneys'. In this stanza decay of a material kind is portrayed as he describes the state of the house: 'nettles growing through the cracked doors'. And a feeling of emptiness is evoked by referring to the empty houses and the bare moor. The bleak images are contrasted with the hope offered by the 'sunlight', but the overwhelming fact is that everything material is decaying. It appears, indeed, that the whole world is 'reverting to the bare moor', implying that one day the whole world will be barren.

In the third stanza, Thomas almost repeats the line used at the beginning of the other stanzas, but this time the sentence has become more of an accusation as it is emphasised so much. Throughout the stanza, human suffering and decay are portrayed, which develops the theme established earlier. Gradually, however, the form of decay has changed from natural to material until finally it becomes human decay. The poet shows us human decay through referring to a single farmer. He describes his decaying appearance: 'Wasting his frame under the ripped coat'. Thomas then goes on to reveal the monotony of this life, the man merely contributing to the 'accepted pattern'. The decay of the human spirit is also suggested as the farmer's sadness is shown and his lack of vitality: 'The embryo music dead in his throat'. Such monotonous decay is, in fact, just as destructive as the 'fat maggot' or as the 'mould' on the chimneys, as it too has consumed its surroundings. It seems a slow, perpetual decay.

The poem is, therefore, divided into three stanzas depicting natural, material and human decay. All of the stanzas are linked; as one process takes place, so do the other two. They are bound together. In addition, these forms of decay are a cycle that repeats itself again and again, something that is echoed in the repetition of the opening line. The empty houses are almost like a metaphor for the emptiness of human life. All that can be set against such decay is an image of 'sunlight'. In a way, however, people have provoked this decay by farming until nothing is left but the bare moor. We are left with a sense that there is a darker side to everything; that nothing should be taken at its romantic face value.

Louise's essay is obviously good: it starts with a good opening paragraph, and is well-organised throughout. At every stage she pays close attention to the words on the page, and always takes great care to really do something with each detail. There is a real sense of building a case. In each paragraph there is a sense that she has added a fresh dimension to her overall case. If there is a weakness, it perhaps begins to become apparent in the last paragraph, which flags a little. Possibly the case could have been pushed further; it might have been a good idea to have paused a little longer at the end of each paragraph to state more fully how the case has advanced. By doing this, Louise might have discovered some more dimensions to the poem, some levels of meaning and significance that she has missed. But this is harsh criticism of a good piece of work, the kind of essay that would always receive a good mark.

'The Welsh Hill Country'
by Kerry Thomason

The poem draws our attention to a Welsh scene, looking at the countryside, the buildings on the landscape and a farmer. From the title, 'The Welsh Hill Country', one's expectation is that this is going to be a poem describing the beauty of the Welsh countryside. As early as the second line, however, it is clear that this is not going to be a conventional poem of praise but a poem that looks at things in a more realistic light.

From the opening line the reader is put at a great distance from this vision of the Welsh countryside. 'Too far for you to see' suggests that we do not have a clear vision, especially for detail, for when we look at this typical scene of sheep grazing we see only a romanticised version of fluffy white animals. The poet's next line brings us in a lot closer, destroying the illusion and pointing out the realities: the 'fluke' and the 'fat maggot/ Gnawing the skin from the small bones'. There is no softness or compassion here; all we see now are the less than attractive features of the sheep. These are dirty animals, living wild, and diseased. This is underlined by the use of alliteration, the words 'fluke', 'foot-rot' and 'fat maggot' being linked together through the association of sound and, as such, creating a nasty, unpleasant feel to this line. There is a reference to our conventional glossy tourist's image in 'Arranged romantically in the usual manner', but the setting is then described as much barer and less green than we might have imagined: 'On a bleak background of bald stone'. The setting of the poem has, therefore, been established: the images are not pleasing but close to the truth of how sheep actually look on a desolate Welsh landscape. For the reader who has not seen such a landscape, however, romantic illusions have been shattered.

The second stanza moves from the hillside to the houses. Welsh country cottages are usually thought of as pretty, homely and picturesque. But here we are shown the reality. The first line again stresses that this is 'Too far for you to see', and then in the second line the poet's attention zooms in closer. There is again use of alliteration – 'moss and mould' – to reinforce the impact of the unpleasant images. The 'cold' in 'cold chimneys' suggests the bleakness of these houses; there is no warmth, no domestic fire in these chimneys. The nettles that are growing everywhere suggest neglect and decay. When, in describing the houses, the poet says 'There are holes in the roofs that are thatched with sunlight', it could be a way of suggesting that the sunlight is deceptive, it covers over the holes, and so covers over the truth. The word 'thatched' indeed seems out of place here, as we associate it with a pretty cottage not with a slate roof; there seems to be a mixing of the superficial appearance (as things might appear in sunshine) and the uninhabitable reality. More illusions are shattered in this stanza: the fields are even 'reverting to the bare moor'. Not only the sheep, therefore, but also the houses are undesirable in what we might, at first sight, have regarded as a beauty spot.

The final stanza turns to a farmer. It starts in the same way as the other two stanzas: we are at a distance and then we move in. The farmer is not our usual stout, jolly image of a farmer but a man who is as much in decay as the sheep and the houses. Even his coat is neglected and shabby, like everything else around him, and he too is affected by disease. The final three lines of the poem are a comment on the whole setting. In 'There's a man still farming', the word 'still' suggests that time has moved on but not on this Welsh hillside. The man is described as 'Contributing grimly to the usual pattern' as if everything is in a rut, a cycle that gets nowhere. There is no happiness: he even works 'grimly'. In the same way as the poem, the whole setting is an 'accepted pattern' that has been reversed by the bluntness of the language and images in the poem. Life has stopped. 'The embryo music dead in his throat' shows a slide towards staleness, old age and death. The music has not progressed further than his throat – it has not come into the open air. Again an 'accepted pattern' has been reversed: we associate Wales with male voice choirs, but here the music is 'dead'.

The 'accepted pattern' of this poem is important. On the one hand we have the actual regular pattern: three regular stanzas opening in the same manner and with the same sort of stark description throughout – no praise, no optimism, no glamour. And there is also a pattern of alliteration to underline the ugliness of it all. On the other hand, the poem mocks a conventional view of the countryside. It is as if we get closer to an unpalatable truth as we see the unconventional things the poem suggests as it undermines its own accepted pattern. Life in the country might seem ideal from a distance (and this poem looks conventional at first sight), but the reality is far less comfortable and attractive.

This essay is another very good piece of work. It has many of the same qualities as Louise's essay. Kerry has organised herself well: she starts with a simple paragraph to set the poem up, and then builds a case in a very sensible and steady way. In the same way as Louise, she picks out details and then really tries to do something with the details; she consistently manages to show how they work and how they add to our overall sense of the poem. But the essay also has another quality. Kerry pushes things as far as she can take them. Look at the things she says about the thatched appearance of the roof in the third paragraph of her essay. She has already established her ideas, but the 'thatched' image enables her to provide, in a creative and inventive way, another impression of how the poem conveys its subject. Kerry does this in the right place; it is at the end of paragraphs that one should try to extend the case, one should try to spot things that other people aren't going to spot. This doesn't mean that a reading has to become over-ingenious, simply that the poem probably announces and develops its theme in ways that are not immediately apparent.

Kerry also pushes things at the end of her fourth paragraph, where she plays with the idea of the 'accepted pattern'. It is again the case that another dimension to the poem is opened up; Kerry has found another way in which the poet conveys his theme. And, in the case of this essay, it is just the touch of inspiration that Kerry needed to inspire her last paragraph, where she sees how the idea of the 'accepted pattern' will enable her to pull everything together. The great merit of this essay, then, is that it is solid and sensible, but it also takes a chance when it can in order to push the argument along. It's not easy to do this (students are often aware that their sentences strain in trying to express the point when they try to take things further), but it is worth taking the risk because such inventive reading gives an essay an extra dimension of sharpness and interest.

'The Welsh Hill Country'
by Helen Cadman

'The Welsh Hill Country' presents a rural picture: its three stanzas offer an impression of three faces of country life. It is ostensibly a poem indicating what a visitor or onlooker does not see when visiting the area. The poet writes, 'Too far for you to see': this shows that the current situation is a deeper one than the superficial, purely visual image might suggest. There is more to it than sheep grazing 'Arranged romantically'.

This idea of the sheep 'Arranged romantically' perhaps shows the trivial nature of sight-seeing, for are sheep really an appropriate symbol of romance? This in itself suggests that the viewpoint of the sight-seer or tourist is ridiculous, a kind of cliché. The reality behind the image is highlighted in the second and third lines:

> The fluke and the foot-rot and the fat maggot
> Gnawing the skin from the small bones.

These images of death and disease contrast sharply with the picturesque, calm scene described in the second half of the stanza. The foot-rot and fat maggot indicate the chaotic state of reality, for maggots, disease and death are the reality for both the sheep and those who farm them. It has little to do with the orderly image of domesticated beasts arranged romantically. As the poem opens, therefore, we see a striking contrast between an orderly surface appearance and grubby reality.

But it goes further than this. There is a suggestion in the poem of a crumbling civilisation:

> The moss and the mould on the cold chimneys,
> The nettles growing through the cracked doors . . .

Although the 'cold chimneys' and 'cracked doors' suggest total desolation, this is not the case for the vegetation is thriving and 'growing'. This seems to suggest that although human civilisation is in decline, nature is taking over and reclaiming land lost to humans. For example, the line 'And the fields are reverting to the bare moor' indicates a return to nature. The moor might be 'bare' and 'bleak' but this is its natural state. The chaotic state of reality is again clear in the way that the vegetation rambles in an undisciplined way all over the houses. The poem, as such, seems to have moved beyond the idea of the reality behind the superficial appearance and to be suggesting something about the fragility of a whole social order.

The idea of a breakdown of regimented order is also evident in the last stanza. Thomas writes about the farmer's illness 'Wasting his frame under the ripped coat'. The use of the word 'frame' suggests a structure – the structure of a man – but this structure is crumbling. The man's ripped coat also implies decay. The atmosphere of futility is something that dominates the final two lines:

> Contributing grimly to the accepted pattern,
> The embryo music dead in his throat.

The fact that the man is 'grimly' working suggests that he is aware of the futility of his actions, but he will not deviate from the 'accepted pattern'. A refusal to deviate is perhaps why the 'embryo music' – a chance of harmony – dies in his throat. All in all, it is as if Thomas is not just showing us the reality the tourist does not see but also trying to see what has gone wrong, why this community is dying.

Hope is present as suggested in the fertility of nature, the way that nature rambles over the empty house. And there is the reference to the holes in the roofs being 'thatched with sunlight': the sun mends and restores. This could suggest an answer to decay: allowing nature to take its course, not subjecting it to arrangement or a framework. The use of Welsh place-names in the poem is also interesting. A name such as 'Bwlch-y-Fedwen' implies the exclusion of the visitor who has come merely to look at the countryside. Certainly, as an English reader of this poem, I feel it creates an atmosphere of separation and exclusion; these names have meaning, but if one does not speak Welsh the meaning remains a secret. In fact, the poem as a whole seems to present a secret, mysterious, dying civilisation, caught between nature and outsiders; it is a poem that examines the decay and slow death of this civilisation.

Helen's essay is rather different from the other two. It is again a very well-organised piece of work, in which she works from the evidence all the time, and keeps on making sure that she is building a bigger case. The difference, however, is that Helen focuses more on the 'larger issue' that she can detect in the poem. The first two essays talk about the reality of the Welsh countryside; Helen talks about the death of a whole civilisation. As you can see, her analysis of details is a little less thorough than in the essays by Louise and Kerry, but this is perhaps inevitable, as she puts so much of her energy into seeing what implications, what larger issues, she can extract from the details. Helen would probably get a higher mark than Louise or Kerry, because her reading is more adventurous and creative, but students don't get good marks merely on the basis of having clever ideas. As in Helen's essay, the case has to be well-written, coherent and well-organised, and must emerge from close consideration of the evidence of the text. The ideal essay – not just in practical criticism but in any area of literary studies – is simultaneously solid and adventurous, sensible and inventive.

EXAMPLE FOUR: COMPARING TWO POEMS

This has been a long chapter, but it needs to be as essay-writing is the most important skill that has to be learnt when you are studying literature. We are, however, almost at the end of what we want to say about essay-writing. There is just one more question to deal with, the problem of how to discuss two poems in one answer. This is a difficult task if you insist on turning it into a difficult task, but a straightforward task if you set about it logically.

Sometimes you will be confronted by an examination paper which, rather than asking you to discuss one poem, asks you to compare two poems. What you can take for granted is that there will be some kind of connection between the two poems, or else the examiner would not have linked them together in one question. It is reasonable to assume, therefore, that there will be plenty of scope for comparing and contrasting the two poems you are confronted with. The major decision you will have to make is whether to discuss one poem first and then the other, or whether to discuss the two poems together. Some people might offer you different advice, but our feeling is that it is very unwise to attempt to discuss both poems at once. If you try to do so, you are likely to tie yourself up in the most elaborate and awkward knots. It is a far better idea to consider one of the poems first, and then consider how the other poem compares, or contrasts, with it.

You will, however, have to refer to both poems in the opening paragraph of your essay. Summarise one of them and try to identify a tension, then summarise the other and try to see a tension. It is at this point that the area of overlap between the two poems should become apparent; you should be able to conclude your first paragraph with a confident statement of the common ground you can see between the two poems: both, for example, might be poems about loss or love or war, or a vast array of other subjects. When you have established a very simple idea of the area of connection between the two poems, you can feel confident that you have set your essay up in a useful and constructive manner. What the rest of your answer will have to do is explain the different ways in which the two poems handle a similar theme.

Even when you are writing about two poems, it is best to think in terms of a six-paragraph essay: a paragraph to set things up, two paragraphs for each poem, and a final paragraph to pull everything together. It is a good idea to start with the poem that you find less impressive or less interesting of the two that you have been asked to consider; it might seem a cynical approach, but this enables you to say in the first half of your answer that poem A deals with certain matters in a certain way, and then, in the second half of your answer, that poem B also deals with these matters, but does so in a much more interesting way.

Obviously, when discussing two poems you won't have time or room to go into as much detail as you would with just one poem. In the second paragraph of your essay, therefore, look at a handful of details from the first half of poem A; at the end of the paragraph, as always, make sure that you spell out what you can say so far. Then, in paragraph three, look at some more details from the second half of poem A, at the end of the paragraph moving towards your summing-up of your sense of what is going on in this poem. Paragraph four can then start by suggesting that there are links between poem A and poem B, but also substantial differences. Again, focus on a handful of details, trying to explain what you can see in the first half of poem B. There's no need to refer to poem A as you are making this analysis; at the end of the paragraph, as you offer your running conclusion on poem B you must make sure that you stress how it both resembles and differs from poem A. Repeat the same steps with paragraph five. Then, use paragraph six to draw the strands of the argument together.

As you can see, this is very straightforward advice. Where students' essays about two poems go wrong is that all too often they strangle themselves with the mechanics of their essays; they are so busy darting back and forth from one poem to the other that they don't really have much of a clue about where they are meant to be heading. The kind of simple structure we have described, by contrast, will help you remain in control of the poems and in control of your essay.

One final point, a point that doesn't just apply to writing about two poems. It is, in fact, something that applies to essay-writing across the whole field of literary studies. Nobody expects perfection! Nobody is capable of perfection! Essays will have weaknesses, but the more essays you write the better your essays will become. You might make mistakes in your analysis of a text, but the examiner isn't going to penalise you for the things you got wrong; the examiner is going to reward you for the bits in your essay that worked well. And what you can always be confident of is that if you produce a well-written, coherent essay, that works from the evidence and builds a case in a series of substantial paragraphs, then that kind of essay is sure to get a very good mark; if you can add a little bit more, if you can read creatively and inventively, then the sky's the limit.

9

Taking things further

WE have already touched on the point that practical criticism is the beginning rather than the end of criticism. There was a time – the period up to and including the 1960s – when the critic's intense response to the isolated text was seen as the most important thing in literary studies. Everything was felt to emerge from the critic's emotional and intellectual encounter with the words on the page. Nothing outside this one-to-one relationship (for example, the historical context of the text) was felt to be of all that much consequence. It is the legacy of this kind of approach that, perhaps, still makes practical criticism seem a frightening examination paper. There is the feeling that one's intelligence is on trial in a particularly exposed way.

What we have been arguing, however, is that there is nothing particularly difficult or demanding about practical criticism. It is simply an academic exercise and, as with all academic activities, has established rules and procedures that enable you to perform the task in a professional way. This book has presented one view of these rules and procedures. Our down-grading of the difficulty of practical criticism is an important point to grasp. Practical criticism represents the kind of basic manoeuvres on a text that you need to be able to perform as the basis for anything else you might want to say. It is important, because all criticism should pay close attention to the words on the page, but what is also important is where you go next.

In the past twenty years or so, a lot of new ideas and approaches have emerged in literary studies. Anyone going to university to study English, for example, will soon become aware of terms such as structuralism, poststructuralism, deconstruction, Marxist criticism, feminist criticism, psychoanalytic criticism and New Historicist criticism. What links all these new approaches is that they involve radical questioning of the ways in which people have assessed and interpreted literature. It is easiest to explain this in relation to feminist criticism. There is now a widespread recognition that texts were, in the past, almost invariably read from a male point of view. Nobody ever questioned the fact that the majority of love poems were written by men, nor the fact that most love poems presented the woman in a very standard way. Feminist criticism started by drawing attention to such assumptions, but has subsequently developed into a much broader consideration of how the whole of society is organised on the basis of gender. The effect of a movement such as feminism, therefore, has been the introduction of new thinking into the general sphere of intellectual and political debate; specifically in the area of literary studies, it has opened up new ways of thinking about and talking about what is going on in a text.

Initially such new thinking might not seem to impinge all that much on the activity of practical criticism, until you stop to think that, for the most part, practical criticism interprets texts in the light of common sense and received social attitudes. The moment you adjust your theoretical stance, however, as university students of English soon discover, you begin to see additional dimensions to literary texts. What also soon becomes apparent is that discussion of the text cannot stop short as a self-contained exercise; you need to look beyond the text, relating it both to our current social and political climate, and to the historical and social context in which the text was produced. In other words, new approaches will affect your view of the words on the page, and then, as you look at the words on the page, you will find yourself wanting to move out into broader considerations. The skills involved in practical criticism remain vitally important, however, as, when it comes to the crunch, you have to be able to demonstrate large ideas from the evidence of specific details in a text.

All of this might sound rather daunting. It is, however, less complex than it seems. What we are really talking about is how close work on the text can both combine with and provide the basis for a much broader consideration of the text, for example the social and political implications of the text and its function in the period of its production. In order to illustrate this we are going to look at a modern poem, 'Cuba' by Paul Muldoon. The main point that might strike you in the analysis of this poem is that, whereas the previous analyses always stopped short at a certain point, here we follow through the implication of our reading. The same approach could be applied to all the poems we have already looked at. In the case of Matthew Arnold's 'Dover Beach', for example, we mentioned how the poem conveyed a sense of being on his own in a frightening world. We stopped at that point, however; if we were discussing the poem in this chapter we would want to relate this to the impact of Darwin's ideas on the nineteenth century, and we would also consider Victorian ideas about the self, the ways in which the Victorians constructed an idea of the individual subject. In the case of Thomas Hardy's poem 'A Church Romance', we might want to use our work on the words on the page as a route into talking about Hardy as a poet poised between the nineteenth and twentieth centuries; in addition, although we did touch on the sense of woman conveyed in the poem, we might want to press further with a consideration of the gender politics of the poem.

What we are talking about, therefore, is the next step; how to take things further when you have gained control of the poem. Although we are taking things further, do try to see that our usual structure of step-by-step analysis and step-by-step building of a case is at the heart of the following discussion. We do not number the steps as we have done in the previous chapters, but the steps are present; the difference is that, at each stage, we speculate more widely on the implications of what we discover in the poem.

'Cuba'

My eldest sister arrived home that morning
In her white muslin evening dress.
'Who the hell do you think you are,
Running out to dances in next to nothing?
As though we hadn't enough bother
With the world at war, if not at an end.'
My father was pounding the breakfast-table.

'Those Yankees were touch and go as it was –
If you'd heard Patton at Armagh -
But this Kennedy's nearly an Irishman
So he's not much better than ourselves.
And him with only to say the word.
If you've got anything on your mind
Maybe you should make your peace with God.'

I could hear May from beyond the curtain.
'Bless me, Father, for I have sinned.
I told a lie once, I was disobedient once.
And, Father, a boy touched me once.'
'Tell me, child. Was this touch immodest?
Did he touch your breast, for example?'
'He brushed against me, Father. Very gently.'

The title of the poem, 'Cuba', is a reference to the Cuban Missile
Crisis. President Kennedy, the United States president at the time,
issued an ultimatum to the Russians demanding that they remove
their nuclear weapons from Cuba. It was an extremely tense period, a
few days when the world seemed to teeter on the edge of nuclear war.
The poem itself, however, only deals with the crisis in an indirect way.

It describes the speaker's sister arriving home in the morning
having been out all night. Her father shouts at her. He seems to feel
that her behaviour is all the more open to criticism because of the
political crisis. He tells her to go to confession. In the last stanza, we
hear her in the confessional telling the priest about a slight encounter
she had with a boy. The obvious contrast in the poem is between the
softness of the girl and the aggressive hardness of the father. It would
seem reasonable to suggest that the poem is, amongst other things,
exploring issues of gender, the different roles played by, or imposed
upon, men and women.

Looking at the first stanza, we can see how economically
Muldoon creates a sense of the girl, specifically through the reference
to her 'white muslin evening dress'. As against this delicacy, there is
the boorishness of the father who is 'pounding the breakfast-table'. In
addition, the father physically dominates this first stanza with his
tirade against his daughter. She is allowed a mere two lines before the
father embarks upon his speech. She doesn't seem to reply, and
indeed she says nothing until the last stanza when she speaks quietly
in the confessional. Traditionally we might have just regarded this as
an example of how some fathers treat their daughters, but feminist
criticism has encouraged us to look at the ways in which men silence
women. It is the father who speaks in this stanza, and, in a wider
sense, it is men (the poet, Patton, Kennedy, the priest) who are
speaking throughout the poem. The girl, as is the case with so many
women in literature, is denied a voice; she is dominated by the
discourse of men. She does, of course, speak in the last stanza, but this
is speaking on the male's terms, providing the responses that are

required of her in the confessional. Furthermore, female experience is marginalised: the father turns on her with 'Who the hell do you think you are'. It is the male who places himself at the centre of experience. What is of consequence in the girl's life is dismissed as trivial in comparison with the concern with 'important' things assumed by the male. The man, then, dominates the physical space of this stanza, and this echoes a broader pattern of domination in society. Where this gets us in terms of a critical approach is that, rather than just talking impressionistically about tensions in a family, we might, in the light of feminist thinking, see that the poem reflects a much larger idea of how the whole of society is constructed around gender roles. This domestic poem at that point becomes a political poem, examining the politics of gender and the politics of family life.

The thing about politics at a personal level is that it is a direct echo of politics at a more public level. The father, dominating the available space, is asserting his power. His behaviour is paralleled on the world stage: the Americans feel that someone else is occupying their space in Cuba and, consequently, make a display of their power. The power game at an international level, therefore, is an echo and extension of what happens in a family. Yet power is also connected with fear; the father is clearly scared by the missile crisis, and displays his fear by lashing out against someone weaker than himself. The second stanza, where the father continues to occupy all the available space, is a stanza that seems to focus on the question of men and power. The father refers to an American general, Patton, and to President Kennedy. If we move on to the next stanza, we can connect the priest with these other men in the poem, for they are all male leaders, but male leaders who in some way abuse their position of power. An interest in power, as with an interest in questions of gender, is something that is at the centre of a lot of current critical writing; such criticism concerns itself with the larger social dimension of a text, how a text reflects, and participates in, power strategies and power politics. A student wanting to look more thoroughly at a range of Paul Muldoon's work might well decide to focus on such social and political implications.

One of the political levels of 'Cuba' becomes apparent when, in the second stanza, the poem touches briefly on the issue of colonialism. The father, as Irishman, criticises Kennedy as 'nearly an Irishman / So he's not much better than ourselves'. What do we make of such self-deprecation? A few years ago critics might have dismissed this as a negligible detail, or commented upon the ability of the Irish to laugh at themselves. There does, however, seem to be more involved than this. The essential point is that Ireland has been a colonised country. It is part of the structure of colonialism that the occupying country thinks of itself as superior and belittles the colonised population, 'civilised' people needing a sense of 'uncivilised' people in order to think of themselves as civilised. It is an oppressor/ victim relationship that reproduces itself over and over again in every colonial context. The odd thing is that the oppressed people in such a relationship often start playing the role that is expected of them; in 'Cuba' the father has internalised the derogatory terms in which the English speak of the Irish, and, consequently, expresses a view of the Irish as hot-headed and spoiling for a fight. An interest in colonialism is another of the areas of concern that have become prominent in current criticism. The student who wanted to take this further might want to start investigating the distinctive position of Irish literature (part of 'English' literature, but outside it at the same time). Also relevant here is the fact that Paul Muldoon is a poet from Northern Ireland; it is likely that a full study of any poet from Northern Ireland would have to give consideration to the continuing political problems of that country, and how these problems might be reflected in poetry.

So far we have seen how a discussion of 'Cuba' might well embrace questions of gender, power and colonialism. Such issues do, of course, overlap. In colonialism, the colonial power puts down the colonised people; in gender relationships, the powerful male puts down the woman. The colonial power and the male assume they are rational; they dismiss the colonised people and women as irrational. In its three stanzas, therefore, 'Cuba' has touched on a complicated web of issues that are central to our social and political lives. What needs to be pointed out, however, is that it isn't individual perceptiveness that has enabled us to see these themes in the poem. The reason why we are aware of these issues in 'Cuba' is that current critical and theoretical thinking encourages one to look for such topics. To put it another way, it is unlikely that 'the general reader' would spot these aspects of 'Cuba', but someone who had been studying English at university, and had, as a result, absorbed the current preoccupations of criticism, would in all probability immediately start noticing these aspects of the text.

What we are talking about, then, is how practical criticism is affected by current ideas in critical thinking, both in terms of what the reader is likely to see as significant in a text and in terms of providing a direction for moving out of the text into a broader discussion. One issue that features frequently in current debates is whether a text is primarily a reflection of conservative impulses within society, or whether a literary text can play a radical and subversive role. In the case of 'Cuba', we might feel that Paul Muldoon is very sharp in his critique of patriarchal power. He even seems to criticise his own role in the poem, for, in much the same way as the father or the other men, the speaker in the poem is an oppressor. He reports on his sister's conduct, and even listens to her as she speaks in the confessional; he is a kind of spy, helping to control his sister. There is, however, more to the issue of 'control' than this. One aspect of male control of women is control of female sexuality; the father wants to control his daughter's private life, and the priest has a prurient interest in the girl's sexual experiences. The issue seems to be that men cannot understand female sexuality and, seeing it as a threat, attempt to control it. The poem seems self-consciously to present the brother as one of the controllers.

As such, Muldoon seems to separate himself from the worst traits of male aggression. His sympathies seem entirely with the whimsical, romantic girl who speaks at the end of the poem. But the way in which Muldoon imagines the girl at the end – and here we see how complicated any argument becomes that touches on the social and political implications of a text – , the way in which he conceives and presents her could be said to demonstrate the extent to which he has internalised a reductive male image of women. He might appear to be a critic of standard patriarchal ways of thinking, but his representation of the men as hard and the woman as soft is simply an echo of the conventional patriarchal view. Critics today often talk about the ideological values that are engrained in a text; Muldoon might seem to detach himself from the ideological values of the culture he is part of, but he is also, it could be argued, complicit with these ideological values, something that is apparent in his ultimately patronising attitude towards the girl.

But perhaps it's not as straightforward as this. Perhaps it is we, as readers, who are guilty of traditional patriarchal thinking when we insist on seeing the girl as romantic, delicate, whimsical and dreamy. She has after all been out all night. Perhaps she is not as innocent as she appears or sounds. And perhaps she doesn't even sound innocent. It is possible to read the last line in a whimsical way, as if the girl is drifting off dreamily with the memory of her brief romantic encounter, but it is quite possible that, throughout the last stanza, she is speaking to the priest in a defiant and amused way, teasing and mocking his interest in sex. Perhaps this is a sexually experienced person laughing at a celibate person.

How does this affect our sense of the poem? The first point is that if we think any less well of the girl when we decide to see her in this different light, then we are falling into the trap of traditional male thought. Why should it be wrong for the girl to be out enjoying herself? We suspect, in fact, that she isn't all that young, that this is a woman rather than a girl. The poem doesn't actually specify her age. Perhaps the way in which we have kept on referring to her as a girl, rather than as a woman, indicates that our response in this chapter has been permeated by conventional male thinking, that we have been seeing a girl (someone who can be controlled) and shying away from acknowledging a woman (someone who is old enough to be independent). Another point is that, if she is speaking defiantly in this last stanza, then there is a sense in which she is simply ignoring the oppression of men; she has found a way of empowering herself. If this is the case, then the poem can be seen as acknowledging a rebellious, subversive, disruptive and challenging force within the power structure of society.

You might feel that this discussion has started to go round in circles, but this is because, in the end, it is impossible to pin the poem down. That might seem frustrating, but it also provides you, as a student of literature, with a great opportunity. Final decisions about texts have never been made; texts are always open for re-examination. Readings of texts change all the time in relation to the society in which they are being read. Again, this might seem to make English an insubstantial subject, but this instability of critical judgements is what makes English an important subject, for we are not involved in arriving at safe answers but in participating in a broader social and political debate about how texts function in the past and in the present. It is this sense of the broader picture, of the implications, that is the next step after practical criticism. But you must never get too far away from the detailed evidence of the text. If you want to discuss power, gender, colonialism, race, sexuality, the role the text plays within the society of its day, the ways in which it can both challenge and be complicit with the ideological values of its day, the ways in which the poet, without realising it, can internalise conservative values which at an explicit level he or she rejects, and what is said and what is left unsaid in a text, it is no use talking about these things in general terms; you have got to be able to show how big ideas are reflected in even the smallest details of a text.

Part Two
Prose

10

Understanding a passage of prose

1 WHAT IS PROSE PRACTICAL CRITICISM?

PROSE practical criticism might be considered to be a very curious
activity. You are confronted with an extract from, more often than
not, a novel, and asked to discuss it in detail. Nobody has ever read a
novel in this way. We might read poetry slowly and carefully, but
with a novel we just dash across the surface. It is because prose
practical criticism is such a contrived academic exercise that
examination papers often provide rather more directions than with
a poem; there might be a list of questions – like comprehension
questions – asking you to look at specific aspects of a passage.
Essentially, however, as with a poem, you are being asked for your
impression of what the passage is about and how it brings its subject
to life, and at the end of the exercise you are expected to arrive at an
enhanced understanding of the passage.

2 IS THERE ALL THAT MUCH THAT CAN BE SAID ABOUT A PASSAGE OF PROSE?

Most people would imagine that there is far less to discuss in a passage
of prose than in a poem; common sense tells us that language is used
in a less intense way in a novel than in poetry. Most students,
therefore, approach prose practical criticism with an assumption that
they aren't going to find much to discuss in the passage. This is
matched by a feeling that, as the passage of prose is merely an extract,
it would be wrong to expect a design or any sense of overall coherence
in it. Indeed, how can one judge a part without seeing the whole? It is
for these two reasons – a belief that prose practical criticism doesn't
offer the reader much to write about, and a feeling that there is

something odd about looking at a random extract – that many examination candidates are even less enthusiastic about prose practical criticism than they are about analysing poetry. A poem might *look* frightening, but at least one can see that it can be discussed in a productive way. What, however, can we do with a passage of prose?

3   HOW DO I SET ABOUT DISCUSSING A PASSAGE OF PROSE?

In nearly every respect, we look at a passage of prose in exactly the same way that we look at a poem. As with poetry, we are pulling things apart with the intention of putting them back together again, but putting them back together with an enhanced understanding of what we have read. Prose might appear to use language in a less intense way than poetry, but the fact is that the operations of prose are just as complicated as the operations of poetic language. Consequently, the method we illustrate in this book for prose matches closely the method we have recommended for poetry: we begin with how to gain an initial purchase on a passage, we then focus on how to build a case, and finally we stress the importance of a good essay method. As with poetry, an essay structure that helps you organise your impressions will do a lot of the work for you.

4   HOW DO I DEAL WITH THE FACT THAT IT IS A PASSAGE TAKEN OUT OF CONTEXT, WITHOUT A BEGINNING, MIDDLE OR END?

The obvious objection to what we have said so far is that a poem, unlike a passage of prose, is a coherent whole. We can see how a poem sets up its theme, develops it, and gives it a fresh twist towards the end. A passage of prose, by contrast, is shapeless. But the assumption you have to make in a practical criticism examination is that the passage for discussion does have some internal coherence: often, for example, examiners set the openings of novels or the openings of chapters within a novel. There is, therefore, a substantial element of design in any passage that is offered. In many cases the passage will be setting up themes that are prominent in the work as a whole. You are not, however, being asked to make guesses about how a novel might develop; what you are being asked to do is spot the larger themes within the specific passage. The passage set might, for example, be about a mother and daughter: you are being asked to see how the passage is not *just* dealing with these two people, but more generally with human themes of parent and child relationships. You are, we might say, being asked to see the general in the particular.

5   DOES PROSE PRACTICAL CRITICISM HAVE ANY PRACTICAL USE?

With poetry practical criticism we were keen to stress that close analysis is the basis of the whole subject: that it is the ability to analyse an individual poem that provides a way of putting together larger ideas and impressions. It might at first appear that this does not hold true for novels, but in fact it does. You have to read a novel as a whole as the first step in studying it, but, if you are going to do justice to the novel, it is necessary to get as close as you can to the words on the page. Prose practical criticism is, therefore, essentially practice in the skill of close reading, and practice in the skill of extrapolating a larger case from close reading.

6   WHAT SORT OF PASSAGE IS GOING TO BE SET IN A PROSE PRACTICAL CRITICISM EXERCISE?

This is a difficult question to answer as you could be set anything. Extracts from non-fiction writers used to be popular; George Orwell, in particular, has been set a great deal over the years. For the purposes of this book, however, we are going to focus on extracts from novels. You are likely to be set about one-and-a-half pages of a novel. Openings of novels are popular, but the passage could come from anywhere in the work. By and large, there is a fair degree of logic informing the selection of a passage. It will often feature one or more of the principal characters in the novel, or perhaps a description of the community in which the characters live. Students tend to find passages like these easier to deal with than passages of pure description, such as, for example, nature description. One of the things we will be showing you is that you don't have to look at a passage for ages hoping that it will eventually make sense. On the contrary, you can start analysing a passage almost immediately, for there are recurrent patterns in fiction and expectations that we can bring to fiction. This and the following chapters show you what to look for.

7   HOW DO I SET ABOUT UNDERSTANDING A PASSAGE?

You must read the entire passage to begin with, preferably twice, but it is the opening lines that you will need to focus on as you will be able to spot issues here that permeate the passage as a whole. In order to illustrate this, let's look at the opening of *Schindler's List*, by Thomas Keneally. The novel, first published in 1982, was originally called *Schindler's Ark*; it was retitled after the release of Steven Spielberg's film. As you will be aware, the novel tells the true story of how Oskar Schindler saved over a thousand Jews from Hitler's death-camps. After a Prologue, the first chapter of the novel begins:

> General Sigmund List's armoured divisions, driving north from Sudetenland, had taken the sweet south Polish jewel of Cracow from both flanks on September 6th, 1939. And it was in their wake that Oskar Schindler entered the city which, for the next five years, would be his oyster. Though within the month he would show he was disaffected with National Socialism, he could still see that Cracow, with its railway junction and its as yet modest industries, would be a boom town of the new dispensation. He wasn't going to be a salesman any more. Now he was going to be his own tycoon.

In discussing poetry, we suggested a number of moves one could make in looking for a tension. In particular, we stressed the idea of accumulating negative and positive impressions. The same approach can be applied to a passage of prose, but it doesn't produce a satisfactory result with the same regularity. We do, however, need to look for a tension. Every novel tells a story. For a story or narrative to exist there has to be a problem, something that creates a disturbance within life. You couldn't really have a story which just consisted of someone being born, going to school, getting a job, getting married, having children and living happily ever after. It wouldn't be very interesting or exciting. Some conflict or tension would have to be introduced.

We can, therefore, assume that every novel is built around some kind of tension. What is also the case is that this tension is going to be set up at the opening of the novel, and it is going to reveal itself in some shape or form in every single paragraph of the novel. The most common tension in novels is between individuals and the social order they are part of: they find themselves in contention with the world they occupy. The assumption with which one can approach novels, therefore, is that there is going to be a tension, and the tension is likely to be a conflict between the individual and society. But not every passage is going to feature characters; we might be confronted by a chunk of pure description, for example a lengthy description of waves breaking on rocks. If there are no characters involved our method would appear to have come unstuck. But a passage such as that which we have described will in all probability be commenting on, or providing a contrast with, the sense of the social order in a novel. Our point is that there is a sense of social order in novels, and either people in contention with this order or other challenges to this order. The challenge might be located in nature, as if nature will not conform to society's rules and expectations. In dealing with prose passages, therefore, we will be looking for a sense of the social order, and someone in conflict with or some kind of challenge to social order.

8   WHAT CAN I SAY ABOUT THE OPENING OF *SCHINDLER'S LIST*?

If we think in terms of society and the individual, the two elements in the opening of *Schindler's List* are the German army invading Cracow and Oskar Schindler (who is part of this new order, but perhaps at the same time not part of it). We need to look at how Keneally suggests a split between the Germans as a whole and Schindler, for in doing so we will understand the implications of the passage, how, at a surreptitious level, we are already being told a lot about the large themes of the novel. Let's concentrate first on the Germans: the first sentence is full of facts as it names the general, the armoured divisions, their route, the town being invaded, the mode of attack and the date. You might argue that this is merely information that we need to know, but we are being told a great deal more than this, for the inclusion of so many facts establishes a sense of a bureaucratic, cataloguing mentality. As against this, Oskar Schindler is an unconventional maverick. This is something we might know from the film, but, even if we had never heard of the film, we can see here that Schindler regards the invasion as an opportunity to make his fortune.

The impression on one side, therefore, is of military discipline and order, whereas, on the other side, Schindler is established as an unconventional figure who isn't going to abide by the rules. It is an impression that is reinforced by Keneally telling us how quickly Schindler became 'disaffected' with National Socialism. If the German forces operate in the light of certain ideological convictions, Schindler doesn't. The tension is really as simple as the fact that first we have a sentence about the Germans and their invasion of Cracow, and then, in the second sentence, we have Oskar Schindler.

Cracow is going to be Schindler's 'oyster'. The Germans are associated with factual language, but metaphor is required for a description of Schindler's activities. The idea that he is an individual, as against the impersonal German force, is conveyed in the extent of the use of the word 'he': 'he would show that he' and 'he was going to be his own tycoon'. We don't yet know, of course, that Schindler is going to be a force for good: it would seem reasonable to assume at this stage that he is simply going to be the kind of spiv or black-marketeer who always appears in wartime. But this doesn't matter, for Keneally has established the real issue in our minds, that Schindler is in conflict with the military order of Nazi Germany.

9   WHERE DO I GO FROM HERE?

As with poetry analysis, when you have established a pattern in the text you can start to build a response, seeing how the details of the passage bear out yet also modify and deepen the pattern with which you started. All of this won't make much of an impact, however, unless you are organising your impressions in a coherent essay. As we will explain, the best approach, as with poetry, is to think in terms of a six-paragraph essay: an opening paragraph that tries to get hold of things as a whole, four substantial paragraphs of analysis, and a conclusion.

10 UNDERSTANDING A PASSAGE

For the rest of this chapter we are going to focus on how to understand a passage, but we will also flesh out our initial response, and make a few suggestions about how to handle an essay. The passage we have selected for discussion is from D. H. Lawrence's novel *The Rainbow*. The passage is about a girl called Anna; she is the daughter of a Polish woman, Lydia Lensky, who, after the death of her husband, settles in the north of England and marries Tom Brangwen:

> In Cossethay and Ilkeston [Anna] was always an alien. She had plenty of acquaintances, but no friends. Very few people whom she met were significant to her. They seemed part of a herd, undistinguished. She did not take people very seriously.
>
> She had two brothers, Tom, dark-haired, small, volatile, whom she was intimately related to but whom she never mingled with, and Fred, fair and responsive, whom she adored but did not consider as a real separate being. She was too much the centre of her own universe, too little aware of anything outside.
>
> The first *person* she met, who affected her as a real, living person, whom she regarded as having a definite existence, was Baron Skrebensky, her mother's friend. He also was a Polish exile, who had taken orders, and had received from Mr Gladstone a small country living in Yorkshire.
>
> When Anna was about ten years old, she went with her mother to spend a few days with the Baron Skrebensky. He was very unhappy in his red-brick vicarage. He was vicar of a country church, a living worth a little over two hundred pounds a year, but he had a large parish containing several collieries, with a new, raw, heathen population. He went to the north of England expecting homage from the common people, for he was an aristocrat. He was roughly, even cruelly received. But he never understood it. He remained a fiery aristocrat. Only he had to learn to avoid his parishioners.
>
> Anna was very much impressed by him. He was a smallish man with a rugged, rather crumpled face and deep eyes set very deep and glowing. His wife was a tall thin woman, of noble Polish family, mad with pride. He still spoke broken English, for he had kept very close to his wife, both of them forlorn in this strange, inhospitable country, and they always spoke in Polish together. He was disappointed with Mrs Brangwen's soft, natural English, very disappointed that her child spoke no Polish.
>
> Anna loved to watch him. She liked the big, new, rambling vicarage, desolate and stark on its hill. It was so exposed, so bleak and bold after the Marsh. The Baron talked endlessly in Polish to Mrs Brangwen; he made furious gestures with his hands, his blue eyes were full of fire. And to Anna, there was a significance about his sharp, flinging movements. Something in her responded to his extravagance and his exuberant manner. She thought him a very wonderful person. She was shy of him, she liked him to talk to her. She felt a sense of freedom near him.

A tension is set up in the very first sentence: 'In Cossethay and Ilkeston she was always an alien'. The precision of Cossethay and

Ilkeston maps out the locality: it is very English, very familiar-sounding. But the use of the word 'alien' forces us to see Anna's foreignness, that she feels she does not belong to and is not part of this world. We already, then, have the pattern of an individual at odds with society. The larger issue, as it so often is in a novel, is how individuals adjust, if at all, to the demands of society.

11 BUILDING A RESPONSE

There must be hundreds of novels in which the main character feels that he or she is a stranger in the world he or she occupies. Lawrence has, we might say, relied upon a standard pattern of fiction. But what interests us is what he does with this standard pattern. If we can see how Lawrence brings this familiar tension to life, then we will be making some real progress towards a full appreciation of what is going on in the extract.

Having set up a tension for our discussion – Anna and the rest of the world – it seems most logical to focus on the details at the beginning of the passage, the details about Tom and Fred. You don't need to discuss every detail in a passage, indeed your analysis is going to prove most effective if you concentrate on a limited number of details. What we are told is that she didn't mingle much with Tom, and didn't consider Fred as a real, separate being. We could, of course, start to make sense of this at a personal level: we could say, for example, that this is just how young children are, but such a chatty approach doesn't really hit upon the larger issues that are being raised in the passage. In order to get further, it helps if we get back to basic principles, the fundamental sense of a division between the individual and society. The impression the passage makes is that, at this young age, Anna doesn't really see herself as an individual, as a distinct subject. She sees other people as a herd, but there is a sense in which, at this stage, she is operating at an animal-like level in which she has not begun to conceptualise an idea of herself. When she meets Baron Skrebensky, though, she starts to gain a sense of people as individuals; at a more profound level, she starts to understand how the world is organised and how people relate to the world. Such ideas are in part conveyed in the curious fact that Baron Skrebensky, a Polish aristocrat, has become a Church of England minister. The oddness of this points to two things: the structures, including the class structure and the structure of organised religion, in which people live, and an individual who doesn't really fit in the structure in which he now finds himself.

What we might also notice even this early in the passage is the manner of Lawrence's writing, in particular his use of short, impressionistic sentences. How can we relate this impression to our developing sense of what is going on in the passage? One possible answer is that Lawrence is not writing in the polite style of society. On the contrary, his quick, nervous style seems to keep pace with and annotate feelings. It is, in fact, a style that seems in sympathy with the alienated individuals of his novel.

12 ORGANISING AN ESSAY

It is always best to organise your reading into a six paragraph structure. Paragraph one summarises the passage, establishes a tension, and a sense of a large theme. Paragraphs two, three and four can then start to flesh out that initial impression. Paragraph six then pulls everything together. As you move through the passage you will need to keep on stopping to take stock. You must keep on asking yourself how you are adding to your overall sense of the passage. In our consideration of *The Rainbow*, for example, we have already moved from a basic sense of Anna at odds with the world to a more complicated sense of how she begins to distinguish a concept of the self. In addition, we have begun to suspect that Lawrence's sympathies are very much with the alienated individual.

In order to add to this, let's look at another section from the passage:

> When Anna was about ten years old, she went with her mother to spend a few days with the Baron Skrebensky. He was very unhappy in his red-brick vicarage. He was vicar of a country church, a living worth a little over two hundred pounds a year, but he had a large parish containing several collieries, with a new, raw, heathen population. He went to the north of England expecting homage from the common people, for he was an aristocrat. He was roughly, even cruelly received. But he never understood it. He remained a fiery aristocrat. Only he had to learn to avoid his parishioners.

This passage begins to complicate our ideas about the relationship between individuals and society. The thing about Skrebensky is that he is at odds with the modern world: he continues to behave as an aristocrat and can't adapt to a new democratic order. It is as if he expected the Church of England to provide him with a position and status such as he might have experienced in his native Poland. It is this man, however, whom Anna sees as an inspiring figure. It seems reasonable to speculate that the novel will show Anna at odds with the world, and that part of this will be a rather arrogant assumption that she is better than the rest of the world. Lawrence provides a number of details, such as the reference to the collieries, that draw attention to the industrial context in which these events are taking place. Animating the novel, it would seem, is a rebellion against the fact of industrial Britain, but perhaps something else as well, a fear of the working class. Rebellion in the novel is not, therefore, a timeless affair, but a rejection of the modern age. Anna might well prove to be a romantic individual who desires something grander than the age can offer her. But there is the additional factor, hinted at in these early references to social class, that Anna is a middle-class character who, confronted by the working class, wants to move in the opposite direction.

Let's take stock of what we have just said. We didn't know what we were going to prove from the section of text under consideration, but, by focusing on a few details and by sticking with the terms we had already established, we have added quite a lot to our sense of what is going on in the passage. It doesn't matter whether our conclusions are right or wrong, indeed right or wrong doesn't come into it. What matters is that we have tried to keep close to the details of the text whilst at the same time trying to draw larger conclusions from these details. What we have been doing is not conjecture, as we have not been making up wild ideas about the characters. It is something far more solid than conjecture – it is a view that we have constructed from the evidence. If we were now to look at more details in the passage we would be able to add to that view.

But it is impossible to add to a view unless you can establish an initial view to add to. It is this that we turn to in the next chapter of this book: how to get hold of a passage, how to make sure that you have seized the passage and, as such, seized the initiative in constructing an effective reading. Before we do this, however, it might be useful if we list some 'do's' and 'don'ts' about the method for tackling a passage of prose:

DO look for a tension in the passage. This will allow you to get hold of the passage as a whole. The basic pattern of most novels is the conflict between individuals and the social order they are part of.

DO interpret the details you spot in the light of the overall tension you have established.

DO use a six-paragraph essay structure to control your analysis, building your response step by step. Work from the evidence of the text towards the larger issues.

DON'T guess about the characters: remember they are there to embody the issues.

DON'T get side-tracked into issues not in the text.

DON'T think of the passage as shapeless: all passages show a development of the issue in them as they progress from beginning to end.

11

Understanding a passage of prose: some examples

THE first step – getting hold of a passage as a whole – is the vital one. If you can do this, then there is no limit to what you can build on this firm foundation. This chapter is about establishing this initial overall understanding of a passage of prose. The chapter consists of the openings of typical passages that might be set in an examination, followed by our observations on how to look for a significant tension in these extracts. The best way to approach this chapter is as a participation exercise: try to see for yourself what tension and what sense of a larger issue you can establish in each case from what are very small scraps of evidence. The passages, ranging from Jane Austen to the present day, are presented in more or less chronological order. Some are novel openings, some focus on characters, and some are passages of description. All of them, you should soon begin to realise, present tremendous opportunities for analysis and discussion.

Example 1:   Jane Austen's *Emma* (1815)

This is in some ways the most straightforward example: it is the opening of the novel, and focuses immediately on the central character and the community in which she lives:

> Emma Woodhouse, handsome, clever, and rich, with a comfortable home and happy disposition, seemed to unite some of the best blessings of existence; and had lived for nearly twenty-one years in the world with very little to distress or vex her.
> She was the youngest of the two daughters of a most affectionate, indulgent father, and had, in consequence of her sister's marriage, been mistress of his house from a very early period. Her mother had died too long ago for her to have more than an indistinct remembrance of her

caresses, and her place had been supplied by an excellent woman as governess, who had fallen little short of a mother in affection.

We have suggested that you look for a tension, particularly a tension between the individual and society, but there doesn't seem to be much evidence of a tension here; Emma Woodhouse seems content with her lot and at peace with the world. She is financially secure and has a 'happy disposition'.

When the picture is as settled as this, however, we can assume that the novelist is going to disturb things, that she is going to put the heroine in situations where her sense of well-being and self-sufficiency will be challenged. But this isn't going to be just a later development in the novel; if we look more closely at the opening sentences we should find signs of disturbance being signalled from the outset. Look, for example, at how Emma 'seemed to unite some of the best blessings of existence': the choice of the word 'seemed' introduces a reservation. It is an impression that is underlined in the continuation of the sentence as Austen tells us how, in her twenty-one years, Emma has had very little to disturb her. This perhaps hints that Emma has been living in a slightly unreal world.

This might have something to do with the fact that her father is not just affectionate but indulgent. It is quite possible that Emma isn't going to find it all that easy to cope with the world after years of having her own way. There is also something more than a little strange about the family set-up in these paragraphs. The comment that Emma's mother's 'place had been supplied by an excellent woman as governess' is extraordinary. It seems to skate over a problem far too lightly. Emma might not be seen as a child in a single-parent family, but this is what she is, even though Austen's commentary seems designed to obscure the fact.

What we have at the opening of *Emma*, then, is an implicit sense of a tension between an individual and society, with just a few hints already that there is something less than perfect about society and about the individual at the centre of things here. We have our tension, therefore; the other thing we need to establish, if possible, is an idea of the larger issue implicit in the passage. The best way to get at this is to think about the narrator's stance. It is our impression that Austen speaks in the voice of polite society. One facet of this is that she likes to control the world, something that is suggested in her careful pin-pointing of Emma's character. It is also interesting that she refers to Emma as 'handsome'. Why not pretty? The problem would seem to be that the word pretty might suggest someone who is wayward and fickle. 'Handsome', by contrast, suggests soundness of character. Such details imply that Austen speaks from within society, sharing the values of society. But at the same time she has hinted at certain shortcomings in the social order. What this suggests is that the novel is going to take the form of a social critique from one who is, none the less, a member of society. The larger issue would seem to be a consideration of the well-being of the society of Austen's day, in particular focusing on what an individual makes of her life in that society.

Example 2:   Mary Shelley's *Frankenstein* (1818)

Frankenstein, the speaker in the passage, creates a living being:

> It was on a dreary night of November, that I beheld the accomplish-ment of my toils. With an anxiety that almost amounted to agony, I collected the instruments of life around me, that I might infuse a spark of being into the lifeless thing that lay at my feet. It was already one in the morning; the rain pattered dismally against the panes, and my candle was nearly burnt out, when, by the glimmer of the half-extinguished light, I saw the dull yellow eye of the creature open; it breathed hard, and a convulsive motion agitated its limbs.

It would be a very imperceptive reader who was unable to see that there are considerable differences between this passage from *Frankenstein* and the previous passage from *Emma*. The most obvious difference is that we have left the comfortable world of Emma for a very strange world. This extract, as you have probably realised, is the moment when Frankenstein's monster comes to life. There might appear to be little that can be said about the passage apart from drawing attention to its 'spooky' qualities, but if we are going to get somewhere in our analysis – and bring it to life – we will have to add something to the simple impression that it is frightening.

As always, in order to gain control of a passage, we need to return to basics, to look for a society-versus-the-individual tension. We can start with the behaviour of Frankenstein, in particular the fact that it is not exactly conventional behaviour to spend one's time trying to create life. There is, therefore, an immediate sense in the passage of wayward individualism. We can add that Frankenstein is experimenting with science: a scientist is presumably meant to work for the general good of society, but in the behaviour of Frankenstein we are offered a sense of the dangerous implications of scientific invention that is unrestrained by moral considerations. The larger issue in this text would, therefore, seem to be the nature and danger of unfettered individualism.

This general sense of what is being conveyed in the passage is confirmed by all the details. The speaker is isolated, locked away from society. It is a night-time world he occupies, where even his candle is nearly extinguished: we are a world away from the sanity of daylight. He is far from calm and rational, indeed his anxiety is almost 'agony'. The impression, then, is of someone in an extreme psychological state. When the 'lifeless thing' starts to move it is with a 'convulsive motion': there is again a sense of an irrational, violent force that threatens the rational order of society. What such details confirm, of course, is the sense of a society/individual tension, but we are already beginning to flesh this out in a way that will provide us with a framework for discussing more. We are now, therefore, ideally placed for looking at how the extract continues, and for adding to our sense of the serious issues that are raised within this work of gothic horror. But we are also in a position to make sense of the details of the passage, and how they point to a larger issue.

Example 3:   Charles Dickens's *Our Mutual Friend* (1864–5)

This scene from *Our Mutual Friend* takes place at a dinner-party held by the Veneerings:

> Mr and Mrs Veneering were bran-new people in a bran-new house in a bran-new quarter of London. Everything about the Veneerings was spick and span new. All their furniture was new, all their friends were new, all their servants were new, their plate was new, their carriage was new, their harness was new, their horses were new, their pictures were new, they themselves were new, they were as newly married as was lawfully compatible with their having a bran-new baby, and if they had set up a great-grandfather, he would have come home in matting from the Pantechnicon, without a scratch upon him, French polished to the crown of his head.

This is funny, but what else can we say? Let's start with the fact that this is a married couple who have just arrived in society. The elaborate and enormous list of their possessions provides a wonderful impression of the society of the day, not just because it lists the things they have bought but because it conveys a vivid sense of a consumer society endlessly buying. We would probably be right in assuming that the novel is, at least in part, a critique of a society that is overwhelmed by material goods. The worry is, of course, what happens to important values when people become obsessed with superficial things: the name 'Veneering' obviously suggests a concern with the mere surface of life.

But, if Dickens is criticising the society of his day, it is a complex critique, for there is tremendous energy, even delight and enjoyment, in Dickens's description of how the Veneerings spend their money. He seems both fascinated and repelled by this new kind of consumer society where money can, seemingly, buy anything. But there is more to it than this: the Veneerings aren't just interested in spending money, they are also interested in buying themselves middle-class respectability. They not only have a new child but everything about the creation of that child is legal and moral. Perhaps the cleverest detail of all is the final detail about the great-grandfather who, if they had decided to buy one, would have arrived from the shop 'without a scratch on him'. Even people, it seems, are reduced to the status of commodities in this commodity-based society. What we can establish, therefore, from this one paragraph of *Our Mutual Friend* is Dickens's view of the society of his day, and his view of how individuals are regarded within this society.

Example 4: George Eliot's *The Mill on the Floss* (1860)

All three examples so far have focused on characters, but characters seen in a social context. In such cases it is relatively easy to spot an individual-versus-society tension. Not all passages, however, are going to feature a character. Sometimes you will be confronted by a passage that describes a setting. We want to look at three examples here, one by Thomas Hardy and one by Joseph Conrad, but first an extract from George Eliot's *The Mill on the Floss*:

> Journeying down the Rhône on a summer's day, you have perhaps felt the sunshine made dreary by those ruined villages which stud the banks in certain parts of its course, telling how the swift river once rose, like an angry, destroying god sweeping down the feeble generations whose breath is in their nostrils and making their dwellings a desolation. Strange contrast, you may have thought, between the effect produced on us by these dismal remnants of commonplace houses, which in their best days were but the sign of sordid life, belonging in all its details to our own vulgar era – and the effect produced by those ruins on the

castled Rhine which have crumbled and mellowed into such harmony
with the green and rocky steeps, that they seem to have a natural fitness,
like the mountain pine . . .

We very much doubt whether you would ever be set a passage as
difficult to discuss as this; most readers are likely to find it totally
perplexing. We have deliberately chosen an extreme passage,
however, to show just how easy it is to get hold of what is going on
in any passage of description.

What everyone can probably make out here is that the narrator
describes some ruined villages on the banks of the Rhône, and then
compares them with the far more picturesque ruined castles on the
banks of the Rhine. With a passage of description, the way to gain
access to it is to ask yourself what it is saying about society, about the
constitution and condition of social life. If there are no characters in
the passage, you might also have to ask yourself what the passage is
saying about nature. In the case of this passage, there are ruined
villages that have been destroyed by the River Rhône. Can you see
how that immediately gives us an idea of the frailty of the social
order? People bond together in small communities for mutual
protection, but a destructive nature is simply indifferent to
humanity's need for security. It seems reasonable to suggest,
therefore, that George Eliot is interested in the social orders that
people put together while at the same time being aware of the
fragility of what people achieve.

That gives us a very general idea of her area of concern, but
other details in the passage allow us to achieve a little more precision.
In emphasising these dreary villages, Eliot indicates her interest in the
trials and tribulations of ordinary life. She is attracted by, but less
interested in, the more attractive ruined castles. Yet there is
something a little incongruous in her assumption that the reader is
familiar with what can be seen on the banks of the Rhône (this is,
after all, the Victorian period when, unlike today, the vast majority of
her readers would not have had any experience of travelling abroad).
The strategy seems to be to establish a feeling of connectedness with
the reader, as if the narrator and her reader are both sophisticated
people who have seen the world. Implicit in this is a sense of
independence, including the financial independence to be a traveller,
that is far removed from the lot of those who live a 'sordid life' in
'commonplace houses'. In this we can see the novel defining (or to be
more precise, as this passage appears well into the novel,

reformulating) its area of concern. It is concerned with ordinary social life, it is aware of how such a life is played out against a background of the relentless onslaught of nature, and it is concerned with the possibilities for the self within that society. The narrator and her readers are travellers; the lives of the characters in 'commonplace houses' are far more cramped and constrained.

Example 6:   Thomas Hardy's *The Return of the Native* (1878)

Our approach with a descriptive passage, as you can see, is to look for the ways in which it embodies familiar areas of concern in fiction – but in the very act of identifying these familiar issues we begin to gain a sense of the distinctive way in which the individual novelist is addressing these questions. In order to underline how this works in relation to a descriptive passage, let's look now at the first two sentences of Thomas Hardy's *The Return of the Native*:

> A Saturday afternoon in November was approaching the time of twilight, and the vast tract of unenclosed wild known as Egdon Heath embrowned itself moment by moment. Overhead the hollow stretch of whitish cloud shutting out the sky was as a tent which had the whole heath for its floor.

This might appear just as puzzling as the previous extract from *The Mill on the Floss*, but we should be able to sort out a response very quickly.

The thing to ask yourself, as with any descriptive passage, is what does it say to us about society, about the constitution and condition of social life. If there are no characters in the passage, you might also have to ask yourself what the passage is saying about nature. Looking at this passage from *The Return of the Native*, we cannot, to begin with, see that it is saying anything about society, but we can see that it is saying a great deal about nature. The most obvious point is that the heath is untamed and untameable. The description of it as an 'unenclosed wild' makes it clear that it is not fenced off into fields: here is an area of wildness where society has not imposed its pattern. And when Hardy writes that it 'embrowned itself moment by moment', he seems to suggest that the heath has an active life force of its own. At the same time there is clearly something rather disturbing about this, as if a malignant force is at work here.

It is in order to safeguard themselves against natural forces that people join together in societies: they create a social order that is in some way in competition with nature. This idea is suggested in the words 'Saturday afternoon', 'November' and 'the time of twilight'. Such details suggest the ways in which people order experience. They impose a calendar on the year, they structure the week, and they name the different parts of the day: they order the world through time. The same impulse is apparent when Hardy compares the sky to a tent and the heath to the floor of a tent: an idea from social life is used metaphorically to help make sense of the natural world. It is a form of social discourse that is imposed upon nature. It looks, therefore, as if the passage as it continues will deal with the way people and society attempt to control nature, with how language helps us construct and control an ordered vision of the world, but how nature resists or lies outside such control.

Example 6:   Joseph Conrad's *Heart of Darkness* (1902)

As you can see, the things to consider are how a passage presents a sense of the constitution and condition of society, what it says about nature, and how it sees individuals faring in the society in which they find themselves. If you can establish your bearings at the outset and see the ways in which a passage in its opening lines reflects a common pattern in novels, then that gives you the basis for establishing the distinctive qualities of the extract you are being asked to consider. We want to illustrate this once more in relation to a descriptive passage combined with some suggestions about how you might set about discussing the opening of Joseph Conrad's *Heart of Darkness*:

> The *Nellie*, a cruising yawl, swung to her anchor without a flutter of sails, and was at rest. The flood had made, the wind was nearly calm, and being bound down the river, the only thing for it was to come to and wait for the turn of the tide.

As we have said before – and it is worth saying it again since so many students do find it hard to get into prose analysis – the thing to ask yourself with a descriptive passage is what does it say about society, about the constitution and condition of social life. If there are no characters in the passage, you might also have to ask yourself what the passage is saying about nature. A quick glance at this passage, where the ship is having to wait for the turn of the tide, suggests that nature is what we should look at first. The idea of the ship having to wait for the tide suggests an immense natural force that both dwarfs and controls all the movements of people within society. As with many novels, therefore, we have an idea of the conflict between people and the social order they represent and the force of nature.

But does this short extract enable us to say anything about the society they construct? One thing that is apparent is that, as in the opening of *The Return of the Native*, there is a desire to name and label: Conrad names the ship, and then defines what kind of ship it is. Implicit in naming is an idea that if we can name the world then we can control it. Again, then, we begin to think about the kind of order that people create in life. This becomes more complicated, however, when we consider the actual name of the ship. Given that the novel has such a weighty title as *Heart of Darkness*, there is something more than a touch absurd about it starting with the words 'The *Nellie*'. The larger idea we can extrapolate is that there is something rather absurd about all human pretensions to name, order and control life.

Example 7:   James Joyce's 'Araby', from *Dubliners* (1914)

We have gone into quite a lot of detail in our discussion of each of the passages so far. We want to move through the last four examples a lot more quickly, putting all our emphasis on how easy it is to spot a tension in a passage. This is a paragraph from a short story by James Joyce from his collection of stories, *Dubliners*:

> The former tenant of our house, a priest, had died in the back drawing-room. Air, musty from having been long enclosed, hung in all the rooms, and the waste room behind the kitchen was littered with old useless papers. Among these I found a few paper-covered books, the pages of which were curled and damp: *The Abbot*, by Walter Scott, *The Devout Communicant* and *The Memoirs of Vidocq*. I liked the last best because its leaves were yellow. The wild garden behind the house contained a central apple-tree and a few straggling bushes under one of which I found the late tenant's rusty bicycle-pump.

The tension must be between the individual and society. Let's start by considering what the passage is saying about society.

The impression is thoroughly depressing. There is a sense of being trapped in a musty room. The books in the room might have introduced a note of escape into the priest's life, but the titles of the books suggest stifling religious themes. And it is not only the pages of the books that are 'curled and damp': there is something rather mildewed about the whole atmosphere. Indeed, even the garden seems in decay, for it can only muster 'a few straggling bushes'. Nature seems to gasp for air in this world of a 'rusty bicycle-pump'.

What about the individual? There's not much evidence to go on, but, in the detail about the narrator's liking for the yellow pages of the book, there seems a touch of romance, as if he would like to escape from this gloomy world that is associated with death. A simple individual-versus-society tension has, therefore, enabled us to see the pattern in this extract very quickly. If we looked at the continuation of this extract we would discover more material consistent with the pattern we have detected so far, but we would also start to add complications and nuances to that basic tension.

Example 8:   Doris Lessing's *Martha Quest* (1952)

In the meantime, Martha, in an agony of adolescent misery, was lying among the long grass under a tree, repeating to herself that her mother was hateful, all these old women hateful, every one of these relationships, with their lies, evasions, compromises, wholly disgusting. For she was suffering that misery peculiar to the young, that they are going to be cheated by circumstances out of the full life every nerve and instinct is clamouring for.

We again need to look for an individual-and-society tension. It is easy to see this pattern here. Society is represented by Martha's mother and the other old women. Martha, by contrast, is an adolescent longing for a 'full life'. She doesn't want to compromise with society, she doesn't want to be 'cheated by circumstances'. The following paragraphs would undoubtedly enable us to fill out this initial impression. Our duty as critics is to see the general in the particular, to see how, although the passage is dealing with one girl at odds with her mother, it is dealing with much broader issues of individual aspirations, the idealism of youth and the rigidity of the social order. In other words, we need to see the large issue embodied in the particular characters.

Example 9:   Jean Rhys's *Wide Sargasso Sea* (1966)

So it was all over, the advance and retreat, the doubts and hesitations. Everything finished, for better or for worse. There we were, sheltering

> from the heavy rain under a large mango tree, myself, my wife Antoinette and a little half-caste servant who was called Amélie. Under a neighbouring tree I could see our luggage covered with sacking, the two porters and a boy holding fresh horse, hired to carry us up 2,000 feet to the waiting honeymoon house.

We could again start by looking for an individual-versus-society tension, but if this approach doesn't help, we can fall back on asking ourselves what the passage says about society, about the constitution and condition of social life. There are characters in this passage, but we might want to consider what the passage is saying about nature.

Let's start, in fact, with the point that they are sheltering from the heavy rain under a mango tree. The couple involved have just got married. On the one hand, therefore, we have an image of the relentless force of nature, and on the other we have the social institution of marriage. There does, however, seem something rather remote and inaccessible about their 'honeymoon house'. These details tell us all we need to know: we are clearly being offered an impression of the fragile social order people construct. Even on the basis of this brief passage, however, we could take our ideas further by picking on one or two more details. There is the man and his wife, but also their mixed-race servant. The society the man describes is, therefore, hierarchical, with masters and servants, and also organised along the line of colour. The implication seems to be that this is how a certain kind of white, Western European organises his life, even when he is in the tropics (where mango trees grow), but there is likely to be a problem as this tropical setting is so far away from the comforts and security of middle-class western society. Already we can see nature wrecking the plans to get up to the honeymoon house.

Example 10: Toni Morrison's *Sula* (1974)

> After five years of a sad and disgruntled marriage BoyBoy took off. During the time they were together he was very much preoccupied with other women and not home much. He did whatever he could that he liked, and he liked womanizing best, drinking second, and abusing Eva third. When he left in November, Eva had $1.65, five eggs, three beets and no idea of what or how to feel. The children needed her; she needed money, and needed to get on with her life. But the demands of feeding her three children were so acute she had to postpone her anger for two years until she had both the time and energy for it. She was confused and desperately hungry. There were very few black families in those low hills then.

Looking for an individual-versus-society tension, we could argue that it is BoyBoy who is most at odds with society, for he obviously hates the restrictions that are placed upon his freedom within the institution of marriage.

The real focus of the passage, however, is upon his wife Eva. What is so effective in this extract is the way in which it suggests that she is just so busy and exhausted providing for her children that for two years she doesn't have time to think about herself as an individual. As with every novel, it is your job as a critic to see the general in the particular, to see that this is not just the story of one woman having a hard time. Implicit in this one woman's story is a far broader sense of the particular demands that are placed upon women by society, how they are trapped in a way that men are never trapped, and often simply too busy to have an idea of themselves as individuals. Eva, however, is doubly disadvantaged: as the last sentence makes clear, they are a poor black family, so Eva is likely to feel the full weight of white oppression as well as male oppression. In a situation like this, we are likely to see the novelist presenting an impression of society as ungenerous and uncaring, something we can spot in the language emphasising Eva's hardship – how she is abused, how everything is acute, how she is desperately hungry. In addition, we are likely to see a particularly hard fight on the part of the woman to become recognised, and to value herself, as an independent individual.

STRATEGIES FOR TACKLING A PASSAGE OF PROSE
1. Get hold of the passage as a whole.
2. Look for a tension, particularly in terms of a conflict between the individual and society.
3. Think about how the passage presents a sense of the constitution and condition of society.
4. If there are no characters in the passage, ask yourself what the passage is saying about nature – about how fragile, by implication, the social order is.
5. Use the idea of a tension to interpret the details.
6. Think about the implications of the details, how they point to the wider issues embodied in the particular examples in the text.

12

Building a response

ONE of the main things we have established so far is just how much novels have in common; they return to a handful of themes again and again, in particular showing individuals in conflict with society. The other thing we need to be aware of, however, is just how little different novels have in common. If we consider D. H. Lawrence's *Sons and Lovers* and James Joyce's *A Portrait of the Artist as a Young Man*, there is a sense in which they tell the same story: both deal with young men who are at odds with their fathers and both deal with the first sexual experiences of these young men. But one only needs to glance at the two novels to see that they are a world apart, that the two writers have totally different ways of writing. It is this – an author's distinctive manner – that we need to look at in practical criticism, for it is the author's distinctive manner that enables him or her to give a fresh twist to familiar themes.

This is something that should become very clear in this and the next chapter as we look in detail at a number of passages. We will start by looking for a tension, but then the focus will be on every aspect of how the writer brings his or her ideas to life. Try to see the logic of the method we employ: a limited number of steps, but each step making a decisive contribution to the building of a case. In this chapter we look at passages by Virginia Woolf and Edmund Gosse.

Step 1: Reading and thinking

'No going to the Lighthouse, James,' he said, as he stood by the window, speaking awkwardly, but trying in deference to Mrs Ramsay to soften his voice into some semblance of geniality at least.

Odious little man, thought Mrs Ramsay, why go on saying that?

. . .

'Perhaps you will wake up and find the sun shining and the birds singing,' she said compassionately, smoothing the little boy's hair, for her husband, with his caustic saying that it would not be fine, had dashed his spirits she could see. This going to the Lighthouse was a passion of his, she saw, and then, as if her husband had not said enough, with his caustic saying that it would not be fine tomorrow, this odious little man went and rubbed it in all over again.

'Perhaps it will be fine tomorrow,' she said smoothing his hair.

All she could do now was to admire the refrigerator, and turn the pages of the Stores list in the hope that she might come upon something like a rake, or a mowing-machine, which, with its prongs and its handles, would need the greatest skill and care in cutting out. All these young men parodied her husband, she reflected; he said it would rain; they said it would be a positive tornado.

But here, as she turned the page, suddenly her search for the picture of a rake or a mowing-machine was interrupted. The gruff murmur, irregularly broken by the taking out of pipes and the putting in of pipes which had kept on assuring her, though she could not hear what was said (as she sat in the window), that the men were happily talking; this sound, which had lasted now half an hour and had taken its place soothingly in the scale of sounds pressing on top of her, such as the tap of the balls upon bats, the sharp, sudden bark now and then, 'How's that? How's that?' of the children playing cricket, had ceased; so that the monotonous fall of the waves on the beach, which for the most part beat a measured and soothing tattoo to her thoughts and seemed consolingly to repeat over and over again as she sat with the children the words of some old cradle song, murmured by nature, 'I am guarding you – I am your support', but at other times suddenly and unexpectedly, especially when her mind raised itself slightly from the task actually in hand, had no such kindly meaning, but like a ghostly roll of drums remorselessly beat the measure of life, made one think of the destruction of the island and its engulfment in the sea, and warned her whose day had slipped past in one quick doing after another that it was all ephemeral as a rainbow – this sound which had been obscured and concealed under the other sounds suddenly thundered hollow in her ears and made her look up with an impulse of terror.

They had ceased to talk; that was the explanation. Falling in one second from the tension which had gripped her to the other extreme which, as if to recoup her for her unnecessary expense of emotion, was cool, amused, and even faintly malicious, she concluded that poor Charles Tansley had been shed. That was of little account to her. If her husband required sacrifices (and indeed he did) she cheerfully offered up to him Charles Tansley, who had snubbed her little boy.

It takes some time to work out what is going on here, to realise, for example, that it is Charles Tansley and not the boy's father speaking at the opening of the passage. And some details might puzzle us: what is meant by the reference to the young men who 'parodied her husband'? Most awkwardly of all, the 'Lighthouse', a detail that is obviously of central importance, is likely to baffle us at the moment.

This doesn't matter, however. If we start to consider the passage in our usual logical way, we will eventually be able to fit the Lighthouse and all the other details into our developing response.

Step 2:   Starting an essay. Summarise the passage, establish your sense of the central opposition in the passage, set up the controlling idea for your essay as a whole

The extract starts with Charles Tansley stating that a projected trip to a lighthouse will have to be cancelled because of poor weather. His bluntness annoys Mrs Ramsay, who comforts her son James and tries to distract him with a cutting-out game. She reflects on the fact that Tansley copies her husband, but in a more extreme form. She then reflects on the sound of men's conversation and other sounds that she hears, but this ceases and she listens to the sound of the waves, a sound that is often consoling but sometimes terrifying. The passage ends with her feeling that her husband has 'shed' Charles Tansley, a fact that gratifies her because of the manner in which Tansley has snubbed James. The central difficulty we are going to encounter with this passage will be deciding what to say about Mrs Ramsay's response to the sounds she hears, particularly the sound of the sea. But this is something that we can delay thinking about. What we need to do first is to look for a familiar pattern in the passage.

More often than not, this means looking for an individual-versus-society pattern. The individual at the centre of this passage is Mrs Ramsay. But where is society? It seems reasonable to suggest that Tansley is the voice of society. He has a cold insensitivity to the needs of the child and is lacking in emotional imagination. As against such fact-based thinking, Mrs Ramsay represents individual warmth and compassion. With such a complex passage, this is probably about as far as we can proceed at this stage; we can return later to questions of the broader implications of the extract.

Step 3:   Look more closely at the opening of the passage, trying to see how the author brings the theme to life

Any words or images associated with society at large are likely to be countered by the words and images associated with Mrs Ramsay. Tansley's opening comment, for example, is negative and crushing, whereas everything Mrs Ramsay says is positive and encouraging. Woolf then describes him as 'speaking awkwardly', a detail that is complemented by the reference to Mrs Ramsay speaking 'compassionately'. It could be described as a difference between hardness and softness: Tansley tries to 'soften his voice', but can't manage to do so. As against this, Mrs Ramsay is presented as 'smoothing the little boy's hair'. Such gentleness contrasts with the word 'caustic', which is used twice in the same paragraph, once in relation to Tansley and once in relation to Mrs Ramsay's husband. To underline the contrast, Woolf then repeats the image of the mother 'smoothing' the boy's hair. It is so different from the behaviour of Tansley, who 'rubbed it in all over again'.

The basic opposition, then, as we had already established, is between the world at large and Mrs Ramsay, but a look at just a few details has already given us a fuller understanding of the difference between the world's hardness and Mrs Ramsay's kindness.

Step 4: Look at another section of the passage, trying to build on your analysis of the passage's details

We haven't considered the Lighthouse yet. How does this relate to the pattern we have established? It isn't really all that difficult to work out its significance. Primarily a lighthouse must suggest hope and reassurance, a light that guides in the surrounding darkness. For James, it is a dream that is going to be realised. Or which could be realised, if it wasn't for the fact of bad weather and the readiness of people such as Tansley to crush dreams. There is probably more that could be said about the Lighthouse, but for the moment we have a quite sufficient sense of its place in the pattern we have been establishing.

What we might also want to consider is the significance of the child's cutting-out game. With a detail like this a degree of inventiveness on the part of the reader is required. What strikes us is that there is a rather unusual relationship between the mother and son and the world at large; it is reflected in the way that they cut out everyday objects and rearrange them into the shapes and patterns they want. The child's activity, therefore, creates an impression that is consistent with everything we have established so far about the distance between these two people and the world. James is playing with images from this world that exists outside himself. There is a refrigerator, an image that underlines an idea of coldness, and there are garden tools, Woolf specifically drawing attention to their 'prongs'. At a surreptitious level, such images reinforce the sense of a hostile, sharp world. Yet, with some careful cutting, such hostile images can be tamed and made safe.

We have again managed to add to our initial impression. The reservation you might have, of course, is that this step forward in our reading required a considerable degree of ingenuity. But ingenuity is probably the wrong word, for we have not ventured into far-fetched ideas. All we have done is look at the details in a way that is consistent with, and yet enables us to add to, our initial impression.

Step 5:   Look at another section of the passage, trying to build on your analysis of the passage's details

We want to stress again how simple the steps are in building a case: establish a tension, then, on the basis of looking at a few details, try to fill out your sense of that tension. Repeat this manoeuvre until you feel you have got hold of a passage as a whole. If you dash about all over a passage, you are likely to tie yourself up in knots. It is much better to proceed sequentially through the passage. Look at a detail, and then try to extrapolate a sense of its place in the passage's general scheme. Don't make the mistake of speculating first and then looking for the evidence afterwards.

In this passage from *To the Lighthouse*, we started with an idea of Mrs Ramsay versus the world. Our consideration of a number of details means that we now have a far fuller impression of both Mrs Ramsay and the social world she occupies. Everything about this world seems cold and sharp. If we look at the comment about the young men who 'parodied her husband', we can add yet more to this overall impression. What Woolf literally means by the phrase is that Mr Ramsay has a number of young followers who emulate his tone and manner. It extends, therefore, the idea of his hardness, but it now becomes specifically an idea of *male* hardness. This adds an additional dimension to everything we have said so far: it is the female Mrs Ramsay against the male world at large.

This impression is underlined by the reference to the 'gruff murmur' of men's voices at the start of the next paragraph, the image of the men's 'pipes', and the children's game of cricket. Can you see how the world beyond Mrs Ramsay is a male world of conversation, pipe-smoking and sport? Even the repeated 'How's that?' in the game of cricket reflects this, for it suggests an approach to life of constant questioning and challenging. It is the approach to life that we associate with Mr Ramsay and Tansley. The paragraph has, then, by its careful selection of details added to our sense of the world that Mrs Ramsay contends with.

But we haven't really come to terms with Mrs Ramsay yet. Consider the fact that she finds it comforting to hear the men talking, and that she is always aware of the presence, and needs, of the children. She seems to play a traditional woman's role, taking care of business at the domestic level, and always having to think about the needs of the men and children in her life. The men can absorb themselves in their own concerns, but the woman, by contrast, has to reach out. Indeed, as she hears the waves pounding, we are told that she is constantly aware of her role as a guard and support to others.

Step 6:   Look at how the passage concludes

But there is more to it than this. The paragraph about the waves is long, and so far we are only half-way through it. What do we say about the violent imagery that now appears in this paragraph? Mrs Ramsay is sometimes comforted by the sound of the sea, but she is also aware of its destructiveness. In addition, it makes her think of her own life as insignificant: there is so much all around her, yet she has just slipped from one small task to another all day. What we might also notice is the extraordinary length of the sentence in which these ideas are conveyed. It is so long that it almost runs out of control. As such, it might suggest an idea of incipient chaos that could easily consume the world.

But where does this get us? How do we pull all these strands together? As always, when things get tough the thing to do is to revert to basics. We need to fall back upon the pattern of the individual and society. Or, if this doesn't work, we need to ask ourselves what the passage is saying about society, about the constitution and condition of social life. As an extension of this, we might also need to ask ourselves what the passage is saying about nature.

The simple point that needs to be made in relation to this paragraph is that the references to the sea suggest vividly the dangerous and chaotic nature of experience. Indeed, the images are so extreme, and the sentence so long and involved, that even Mrs Ramsay is unnerved by thoughts of this larger chaos. But any passage that deals with the disorder of experience is also likely to consider how people contrive to organise their daily lives. In this extract there are two different ways: the male approach – cold, rational and impersonal – and the way of Mrs Ramsay – emotional, seemingly trivial, but probably far more effective. The difference between the two approaches is spelt out in the last sentence: her husband requires 'sacrifices', but she only cares about who 'had snubbed her little boy'.

Step 7:   Sum up your sense of the passage as a whole

It probably isn't too fanciful to conclude that Mrs Ramsay is a kind of living lighthouse – a beacon of light in a dangerous world, offering guidance and protection to those travelling through life. That might seem a rather pretentious conclusion, but if it is at all convincing it is because it is consistent with the pattern of ideas that we have been developing. It is this kind of consistency of thinking that you need in examining a passage. Start with a simple tension, and then interpret details in the light of that tension. As you do so, your sense of the significance and implications of the passage will steadily develop. By the end you should be able to see the general in the particular, should be able to see what large issues are being examined in this specific set of circumstances.

Step 1:   Reading and thinking

The main principle of our approach is that it is possible to build a complicated case if one sticks to a simple method. Our analysis of the extract from *To the Lighthouse* went into a lot of detail, but we now want to look at a second passage rather more quickly with a greater stress on the mechanics of 'how to do it'. It is an extract from Edmund Gosse's *Father and Son*:

> My Father and I were now great friends. I do not doubt that he felt his responsibility to fill as far as might be the gap which the death of my Mother had made in my existence. I spent a large portion of my time in his study, while he was writing or drawing, and though very little conversation passed between us, I think that each enjoyed the companionship of the other. There were two, and sometimes three aquaria in the room, tanks of sea-water, with glass sides, inside which all sorts of creatures crawled and swam; these were sources of endless pleasure to me, and at this time began to be laid upon me the occasional task of watching and afterwards reporting the habits of animals.
>
> At other times, I dragged a folio volume of the 'Penny Cyclopædia' up to the study with me, and sat there reading successive articles on such subjects as Parrots, Parthians, Passion-flowers, Passover and Pastry, without any invidious preferences, all information being equally

welcome, and equally fugitive. That something of all this loose stream of knowledge clung to odd cells of the back of my brain seems to be shown by the fact that to this day, I occasionally find myself aware of some stray useless fact about peonies or pemmican or pepper, which I can only trace back to the 'Penny Cyclopædia' of my infancy.

It will be asked what the attitude of my Father's mind was to me, and of mine to his, as regards religion, at this time, when we were thrown together alone so much. It is difficult to reply with exactitude. But so far as the former is concerned, I think that the extreme violence of the spiritual emotions to which my Father had been subjected, had now been followed by a certain reaction. He had not changed his views in any respect, and he was prepared to work out the results of them with greater zeal than ever, but just at present his religious nature, like his physical nature, was tired out with anxiety and sorrow. He accepted the supposition that I was entirely with him in all respects, so far, that is to say, as a being so rudimentary and feeble as a little child could be. My Mother, in her last hours, had dwelt on our unity in God; we were drawn together, she said, elect from the world, in a triplicity of faith and joy. She had constantly repeated the words: 'We shall be one family, one song. One Song! One Family!' My Father, I think, accepted this as a prophecy, he felt no doubt of our triple unity: my Mother had now merely passed before us, through a door, into a world of light, where we should presently join her, where all things would be radiant and blissful, but where we three would, in some unknown way, be particularly drawn together in a tie of inexpressible benediction. He fretted at the delay; he would fain have taken me by the hand, and have joined her in the realms of holiness and light, at once, without this dreary dalliance with earthly cares.

He held this confidence and vision steadily before him, but nothing availed against the melancholy of his natural state. He was conscious of his dull and solitary condition, and he saw, too, that it enveloped me. I think his heart was, at this time, drawn out towards me in an immense tenderness. Sometimes, when the early twilight descended upon us in the study, and he could no longer peer with advantage into the depths of his microscope, he would beckon me to him silently, and fold me closely in his arms. I used to turn my face up to his, patiently and wonderingly, while the large, unwilling tears gathered in the corners of his eyelids. My training had given me a preternatural faculty of stillness and we would stay so, without a word or a movement, until the darkness filled the room. And then, with my little hand in his, we would walk sedately downstairs, to the parlour, where we would find that the lamp was lighted, and that our melancholy vigil was ended. I do not think that at any part of our lives my Father and I were drawn so close to one another as we were in that summer of 1857. Yet we seldom spoke of what lay so warm and fragrant between us, the flower-like thought of our Departed.

We need to read the passage carefully, probably at least twice. Then we need to search for a tension. We should be able to identify this in the opening lines of the passage. We can, for the moment, ignore subsequent complications. Our answer is going to prove most effective if we proceed through the passage sequentially rather than jumping from one end to the other in pursuit of details to consider. A great help with this passage is the fact that it consists of four paragraphs. In addition to an introduction and a conclusion, our essay should consist of four main paragraphs, one devoted to each paragraph in the extract. If a passage isn't in four paragraphs, the sensible approach is to divide it into four roughly equal sections; this produces four manageable chunks on which to get to work.

Step 2:   Starting an essay. Summarise the passage, establish your sense of the central opposition in the passage, set up the controlling idea for your essay as a whole

Summarising the passage involves saying in about ten lines what is going on at an obvious factual level. In this passage, the narrator speaks about his relationship with his father. His mother has died and he feels very close to his father. He recalls some of his interests as a child, and then goes on to speak about his father's religious beliefs and how, in the year following the death of his mother, he and his father grew closer together. We have suggested that you look for a tension between the individual and society; sometimes, though, the tension will be implicit rather than explicit. Here, for example, the child seems very much at one with his father (remember that society is not just the world at large, that the family is a social institution). When we are offered a harmonious picture, however, we might well suspect that there are more stresses and strains present than might be apparent at first sight.

In the particular example, we get the impression that the closeness between the father and son that isn't going to last. One clue to this is that the child has experienced a loss, and now feels a lack in his life. As such, the concept of a perfect family order is flawed. The father finds comfort in religion, but it is quite possible that the child isn't going to share the father's conviction of God's order. What we can establish at the outset, therefore, is that the author is dealing with the stresses and strains of family life. The references to God raise the additional question of how the individual adjusts to a traditional source of authority. Taking this one step further, God the father and the child's actual father have parallels; if the child rejects either or both it is more likely to be in a spirit of sorrow than anger.

Step 3: Look more closely at the opening of the passage, trying to see how the author brings the theme to life

The pattern we have presented could be described as the order of the family and the order of religion, and the child as a potential rebel against both. We now need to focus on a number of details in the opening paragraph to see how this tension is brought to life. Most of the details, however, suggest how close the child is to his father: they are friends, they share a room, they communicate even when they are not speaking directly to each other. And the father provides the child with tasks, specifically monitoring the habits of the creatures in the aquaria. It is as if the father is grooming the child to inherit and take on his work. It all creates a feeling of well-being.

To such an extent, indeed, that we might well feel that there are no negative signals in this paragraph. If we look a little more closely, however, we might have some reservations even in the very first sentence: 'My father and I were now great friends'. The author is describing how they became great friends after the death of the mother, but the sentence none the less manages to suggest that this is a temporary situation, that it might not last. In addition, there is tentativeness of 'I think that each enjoyed the companionship of the other'. It is as if the author looks at himself as another person, a person who is not his true self. These are, of course, minor details, but they manage to create a slight feeling of unease, a sense that the harmony of this household is not as perfect as it seems and that it might not last forever.

Step 4: Look at another section of the passage, trying to build on your analysis of the passage's details

Let's move to the next paragraph, which deals with the child's reading of the *Penny Cyclopaedia*. What on earth can we do with the list of 'Parrots, Parthians, Passion-Flowers, Passover and Pastry'? In order to answer the question, as always we need to resort to basics. Do the details support the sense we have established so far of the reassuring nature of the young child's life or do they disrupt the neat pattern in some way. At one level, of course, the image of a child absorbed in a big encyclopaedia is a familiar and cosy impression of childhood. At the same time, however, the child obviously has a voracious appetite for knowledge, and such openness of mind might eventually clash with the religious conformity of the father. The actual details in the line reinforce this impression. One of the topics is 'Passover', but it is simply tucked away in the list as if it is of no more significance than anything else in life. The overall effect, therefore, of listing 'Parrots, Parthians' and so on is to create a sense of a free-ranging mind that is almost bound to come in conflict with the father's sense of religious authority.

Step 5: Look at another section of the passage, trying to build on your analysis of the passage's details

Obviously we could have looked at other details in the previous paragraph, but we picked just one to illustrate how every detail is significant; every detail, however minor, will in some way be reflecting and extending the central concerns of the passage. It is essential to work on the details, therefore, but it is also essential to pull back at the end of each paragraph to consider what it is now possible to say that couldn't have said before. In relation to this passage, we now feel that we have a better understanding of the teeming variety of the world. The father keeps 'all sorts of creatures' locked up in tanks, as if he wants to contain and control the world, but in paragraph two there is a sense of more knowledge than can be contained within the father's religious framework of beliefs.

Paragraph three looks more closely at the father's religious convictions, in particular the way in which the father's beliefs are put on trial when the mother dies. But what paragraph three also offers us is an increasing number of indications that the child is not entirely at one with his father. For example, the narrator writes, 'He accepted the supposition that I was entirely with him in all respects'. He is, it is becoming clear, now at a distance from his father, but he can also look back and see that sense of distance coming into existence. There are the first stirrings of rebellion here against both his literal father and God the father.

Step 6: Look at how the paragraph concludes

The father, with his tanks, is a scientist, or at least an amateur scientist, but in the last paragraph the child almost holds the father's faith up as a kind of scientific specimen for our dispassionate examination. He can now see how it was the loss of his mother that united the father and son, but now he looks at these events from a distance, almost as if through a microscope.

Step 7:   Sum up your sense of the passage as a whole

The examination of a very small number of details has enabled us to come a long way. We started with nothing more than a picture of the father and child, but within four paragraphs we have gained a considerable understanding of the role and nature of religious faith in Victorian society. And we have also begun to grasp how one person at least found himself moving away from religious faith. It is a rebellion that has more than a little to do with the young man's attraction to science. All of this is now clear, but at the same time we need to be aware that the passage doesn't state any of this directly: at no stage does it openly discuss scientific or religious thinking in Victorian Britain, nor does it state that the child is moving away from his father. But our work on the details has enabled us to see the general in the particular, to see the broader issues in this specific set of circumstances. By the end of any passage one should have arrived at a sense of the nuances and implications of the tension with which one started.

BUILDING A RESPONSE TO A NOVEL

1. Build your response in paragraph steps.
2. Remind yourself how much all novels have in common in terms of an individual-versus-society pattern.
3. But then remind yourself that what we are after is the author's distinctive way of treating familiar themes.
4. Start by summarising the passage, and establishing a central tension, so as to set up the controlling idea for your essay.
5. Look closely at the opening of the passage, trying to see how the words and phrases used bring the theme to life.
6. Move on to the next section, building your analysis by looking at the details but then pulling back to comment on the larger issues.
7. Proceed logically, but don't be afraid to push your ideas on the basis of the evidence examined.
8. At the end of each paragraph you should be able to add to your overall sense of the issues in the passage.
9. By the end of your analysis you should feel you have achieved a sense of what the passage is saying and how it works.

13

Discussing a detail, building a case

IN this chapter we want to reinforce the points made in the previous chapter, but with rather more emphasis on *how* to discuss a detail and on *how* to link impressions together in such a way as to be sure that you are building a strong case. The extracts considered are from F. Scott Fitzgerald's *The Great Gatsby* and Emily Brontë's *Wuthering Heights*.

Step 1: Reading and thinking

About half-way between West Egg and New York the motor road hastily joins the railroad and runs beside it for a quarter of a mile, so as to shrink away from a certain desolate area of land. This is a valley of ashes – a fantastic farm where ashes grow like wheat into ridges and hills and grotesque gardens; where ashes take the forms of houses and chimneys and rising smoke and, finally, with a transcendent effort, of ash-grey men, who move dimly and already crumbling through the powdery air. Occasionally a line of grey cars crawls along an invisible track, gives out a ghastly creak, and comes to rest, and immediately the ash-grey men swarm up with leaden spades and stir up an impenetrable cloud, which screens their obscure operations from your sight.

But above the grey land and the spasms of bleak dust which drift endlessly over it, you perceive, after a moment, the eyes of Doctor T.J. Eckleburg. The eyes of Doctor T.J. Eckleburg are blue and gigantic – their retinas are one yard high. They look out of no face, but, instead, from a pair of enormous yellow spectacles which pass over a non-existent nose. Evidently some wild wag of an oculist set them there to fatten his practice in the borough of Queens, and then sank down himself into eternal blindness, or forgot them and moved away. But his eyes, dimmed a little by many paintless days, under sun and rain, brood on over the solemn dumping ground.

The valley of ashes is bounded on one side by a small foul river, and, when the drawbridge is up to let barges through, the passengers on waiting trains can stare at the dismal scene for as long as half an hour.

There is always a halt there of at least a minute, and it was because of this that I first met Tom Buchanan's mistress.

The fact he had one was insisted upon wherever he was known. His acquaintances resented the fact that he turned up in popular cafés with her and, leaving her at a table, sauntered about, chatting with whomsoever he knew. Though I was curious to see her, I had no desire to meet her – but I did. I went up to New York with Tom on the train one afternoon, and when we stopped by the ashheaps he jumped to his feet and, taking hold of my elbow, literally forced me from the car.

'We are getting off,' he insisted. 'I want you to meet my girl.'

The passages considered in the last chapter both featured characters; although there are characters present here, it is primarily a descriptive passage, concentrating on the rather strange landscape in which some of the events of the novel are taking place.

Step 2:   Starting an essay. Summarise the passage, establish your sense of the central opposition in the passage, set up the controlling idea for your essay as a whole

There are four main paragraphs in this extract. In paragraph one, Fitzgerald describes 'a valley of ashes', a desolate area of land between West Egg and New York. In paragraph two, he describes an advertising hoarding, seemingly for an optician called Doctor T.J. Eckleburg. In paragraph three there is a reference to how the train has to stop at a certain point in the valley of ashes, and in paragraph four the narrator talks about Tom Buchanan's mistress. One afternoon, when the train has stopped at the ashheaps, Tom takes the narrator by the arm and leads him from the train to meet her.

We need to establish a tension, but as the details are rather bizarre this might seem difficult. What we need to do, therefore, is ask ourselves some basic questions:

1. Can I see an individual-versus-society tension in this passage?
2. If you can't see an individual-versus-society tension, ask yourself what the passage is saying about society, about the constitution and condition of social life.
3. If there are no characters in the passage, or only passing references to characters, you might want to ask yourself what the passage is saying about nature.

As there are only passing references to characters in this extract, let's concentrate on the social picture and the picture of nature. There is West Egg and New York, and the motor road and the railway, all of which are places and things that people have built. But the railway and the road run through a very curious 'desolate area of land'. It is a valley of ashes. It's not quite clear what is being described in this valley, although it is a reasonable guess that this is a landscape that has been blighted by industry and pollution. It is so strange, however, that in some way it threatens to undermine, or show the truth behind the gloss of, the social world. It is the way in which Fitzgerald describes it that creates this effect. It is, in fact, almost indescribable: 'a fantastic farm', 'like wheat into ridges and hills', and 'grotesque gardens'. In some odd way the debris of industrialisation echoes shapes and impressions from nature, things such as farms, hills and gardens.

What do we make of all this? It is easy to see that Fitzgerald is looking at the social world we have created, the world of the railway and the motor car. But there is another chaotic world behind the social world, which is in fact a product of the social world. It is a kind of living hell, the kind of image we only encounter when we see pictures of poisoned and polluted industrial cities in Eastern Europe. Such a description obviously makes us look at society in a sceptical way: society has only managed to achieve something at the cost of destroying nature. The effect of a passage such as this, therefore, is that it broadens our sense of the themes being dealt with in the novel. The average reader obviously isn't going to pause to work all this out, but at a surreptitious level such passages in a novel make the reader think about the constitution and condition of the social order.

Step 3:   Look more closely at the opening of the passage, trying to see how the author brings the theme to life

The point we have arrived at is that Fitzgerald is examining sceptically the society of his day. It is important to take stock in simple terms like this. Analysis of a complex passage, as in the previous paragraphs of this chapter, can draw you into a complicated argument. In order to re-establish full control of your developing case, you need to sort out and state clearly what it is that you have demonstrated. If every paragraph in your essay tries to clarify matters as it approaches its end, you will find that you can control even the most complicated set of ideas.

The clear view we have arrived at so far – that Fitzgerald looks sceptically at the society of his day – gives us our lead into a fuller consideration of the opening paragraph of this extract. We might decide to look at how the train 'gives out a ghastly creak' and how 'ash-grey men swarm' over the train. There is something disturbing about these images; it is not just the fact that this is the price that has had to be paid for industrialisation, but also the impression the images offer of a kind of nightmare world. It is the sense of a tension that helps us get this in focus: alongside the confident, prosperous image of twentieth-century America is this night-time world where everything is alarming.

Step 4: Look at another section of the passage, trying to build on your analysis of the passage's details

We have the social world and what lies behind the social world. The first paragraph has focused on what lies behind, but the passage is bound to give consideration as well to the nature of the society that has been created. This comes in paragraph two: it focuses on what we build 'above the grey land and spasms of bleak dust'. The most prominent thing that has been built is the grotesque advertising-hoarding featuring the eyes of Doctor T. J. Eckleburg. The ugliness of the hoarding tells us something about the society of Fitzgerald's time, as does the prominence of the advert: this is a commercial society where advertising is a central feature. But why the emphasis on the glasses? The simple explanation is that this is an advertisement for an optician, but there seems to be more to it than that. In order to understand what, we need to fall back on the ideas we have already established. Our emphasis so far has been on the glossy face of American society and the ugliness that lies just behind the surface. Implicit in this contrast is an idea of seeing the truth about modern America. The image of the glasses can, therefore, be linked with the idea of being able to see clearly, being able to see behind the surface. The image, we might say, almost acts to encourage us to look more searchingly behind the appearance.

Step 5: Look at another section of the passage, trying to build on your analysis of the passage's details

We have, so far, only looked at two paragraphs, but we have already made considerable progress in terms of seeing the large issues implicit in a small scene. We have managed to show that this is far more than just a passage of description, that Fitzgerald is offering an analysis and critique of American society. Of course, it might not always be possible to make such rapid progress, but you should always be endeavouring to see the general in the particular in this kind of way. What you need to tell yourself is that 'the large issue' isn't a mysterious or elusive concept. You are simply endeavouring to see how the tiny details encapsulate important themes about everyday life: how society functions, how society treats individuals, and how the social world we have created compares to the natural world it has displaced.

We can see all of this in paragraph three, which starts with an image of 'a small foul river', a river that, presumably, industry has polluted. The train has stopped to let the barges through, but when Fitzgerald writes about the 'drawbridge' that has been raised the word might make us think more of knights and castles than of a bridge over a polluted river. This is probably intentional: there is an ironic gap between a world of medieval castles and the reality of these commuters on a city-bound train. And when the passengers are seen staring at the dismal scene for as long as half an hour, there is a sense of the vacuous emptiness of modern life.

Step 6: Look at how the passage concludes

We now need to move on to the last section of the extract, but before doing so it is worth thinking about how we discussed the previous paragraph. We looked at just three details: the 'foul river', the 'drawbridge' and the passengers staring at the dismal scene. It is a very small amount of evidence, but, because we had established a framework for making sense of these images, we could move decisively from the details to the view of American society implicit in the details. It is this kind of ability to extrapolate a larger case from a few details that you need to cultivate in practical criticism.

But the only way to do this is to work steadily through a passage. In paragraph four of this extract, Tom Buchanan's mistress is introduced. Why? What has this got to do with anything we have said so far? The fact is that if we had tried to answer this question earlier we would probably have managed to get ourselves tied up in knots, but at this point we should be able to see how this follows on naturally from everything we have established so far. We have been talking about the social order and the ugliness just behind the surface of the social order. Absolutely central in an idea of the social order is the institution of marriage, but there is a sordid reality that lies behind the fiction, and the sordid reality here is Tom's extra-marital relationship. There is something offensive in the way he flaunts his mistress. The shallowness of it all is somehow conveyed in the fact that they are seen together at 'popular cafés': it all seems glamorous and dazzling, but we can't help but be aware of the grubbiness behind the gloss.

Step 7:   Sum up your sense of the passage as a whole

We very much doubt whether you would be given such an oblique passage as this for discussion in an examination, but whatever passage is set the same principles always hold true. You have always got to concentrate on explaining and justifying the small details, but what this also means is trying to see the larger vision of society that is conveyed in the brief span of the passage.

Step 1:   Reading and thinking

This is the opening of Emily Brontë's *Wuthering Heights*:

> 1801. – I have just returned from a visit to my landlord – the solitary neighbour that I shall be troubled with. This is certainly a beautiful country! In all England, I do not believe that I could have fixed on a situation so completely removed from the stir of society. A perfect misanthropist's Heaven – and Mr Heathcliff and I are such a suitable pair to divide the desolation between us. A capital fellow! He little imagined how my heart warmed towards him when I beheld his black eyes withdraw so suspiciously under their brows, as I rode up, and when his fingers sheltered themselves, with a jealous resolution, still further in his waistcoat, as I announced my name.
> 'Mr Heathcliff?' I said.
> A nod was the answer.
> 'Mr Lockwood, your new tenant, sir. I do myself the honour of calling as soon as possible, after my arrival, to express the hope that I have not inconvenienced you by my perseverance in soliciting the occupation of Thrushcross Grange: I heard, yesterday, you had had some thoughts -'
> 'Thrushcross Grange is my own, sir,' he interrupted wincing, 'I should not allow any one to inconvenience me, if I could hinder it – walk in!'

The 'walk in' was uttered with closed teeth, and expressed the sentiment, 'Go to the Deuce'; even the gate over which he leant manifested no sympathizing movement to the words; and I think that circumstances determined me to accept the invitation: I felt interested in a man who seemed more exaggeratedly reserved than myself.

When he saw my horse's breast fairly pushing the barrier, he did pull out his hand to unchain it, and then sullenly preceded me up the causeway, calling, as we entered the court:

'Joseph, take Mr Lockwood's horse; and bring up some wine.'

'Here we have the whole establishment of domestics, I suppose,' was the reflection, suggested by this compound order, 'No wonder the grass grows up between the flags, and cattle are the only hedge-cutters.'

Joseph was an elderly, nay, an old man, very old, perhaps, though hale and sinewy.

'The Lord help us!' he soliloquised in an undertone of peevish displeasure, while relieving me of my horse; looking, meantime, in my face so sourly that I charitably conjectured that he must have need of divine aid to digest his dinner, and his pious ejaculation had no reference to my unexpected advent.

It's an arresting opening to a novel; we are already tantalised by a powerful and puzzling character. But it isn't enough to just say 'the opening presents a striking character'. We have to establish a broader picture.

Step 2:   Starting an essay. Summarise the passage, establish your sense of the central opposition in the passage, set up the controlling idea for your essay as a whole

A man called Lockwood is narrating. He describes an encounter with his landlord, Heathcliff. Lockwood also meets Heathcliff's servant, Joseph. If we think in terms of the individual and society, what we might notice is that Lockwood presents himself as someone at odds with society, as someone who wants to escape from the buzz of the world to a lonely and secluded place. We have, therefore, already arrived at a sense of a 'larger issue': the passage seems to be looking at how people relate to, or choose to distance themselves from, society. Lockwood seems to be, but only *seems* to be, a social rebel. The pattern you might see in the opening could, of course, differ greatly from what we have picked out, but this is as it should be. Different readers will latch on to different details and see different patterns of significance. This is possible because a literary text can support a huge number of readings. The particular drift of an initial response is, therefore, up to you, but what you must ensure is that you do get a strong initial grip on a passage, for this gives you a base on which to build.

Step 3: Look more closely at the opening of the passage, trying to see how the author brings the theme to life

In order to help organise our discussion, we will divide the passage into four sections: the opening paragraph, Lockwood's conversation with Heathcliff, Heathcliff leading Lockwood into Thrushcross Grange, and the encounter with Joseph. The pattern in the opening paragraph, as we have established, is Lockwood turning his back on society. But is it as simple as this? How does his manner of speaking strike you? Is there something affected about his whole style and tone? One thing that catches our eye is the way in which every noun in his speech is matched with an appropriate adjective: 'solitary neighbour', 'beautiful country', 'a capital fellow', 'a jealous resolution'. It is as if he is striving for elegant literary balance in his phrasing. This is complemented by the precious quality of everything he says: 'Mr Heathcliff and I are such a suitable pair to divide the desolation between us'. All in all, Lockwood might claim to be a rebel, but as we can see he speaks in the polite, almost mincing, manner of the most refined society.

Step 4: Look at another section of the passage, trying to build on your analysis of the passage's details

The affected manner of Lockwood makes the arrival of Heathcliff all the more impressive, for Heathcliff is genuinely at odds with society. It is apparent from the outset in his surly and aggressive manner. Why is he so abrupt in his declaration that he owns Thrushcross Grange? It seems to us that this is another way of indicating that this is a man who does not observe the social niceties. A position in society usually involves owning property; Heathcliff, to this extent, is a member of the property-owning class, but he doesn't play the game of pretending to be a gentleman. His manner is blunt and direct. We might stop at this point, of course, simply declaring that Brontë has created a memorable character, but it seems necessary to make the step beyond character-reading. It is important to see that a larger theme is implicit here, the whole question of how people conduct themselves in society, and how people relate to or fail to relate to social conventions.

Step 5:   Look at another section of the passage, trying to build on your analysis of the passage's details

> The 'walk in' was uttered with closed teeth, and expressed the sentiment, 'Go to the Deuce'; even the gate over which he leant manifested no sympathizing movement to the words; and I think that circumstances determined me to accept the invitation: I felt interested in a man who seemed more exaggeratedly reserved than myself.
>
> When he saw my horse's breast fairly pushing the barrier, he did pull out his hand to unchain it, and then sullenly preceded me up the causeway, calling, as we entered the court:
>
> 'Joseph, take Mr Lockwood's horse; and bring up some wine.'
>
> 'Here we have the whole establishment of domestics, I suppose,' was the reflection, suggested by this compound order, 'No wonder the grass grows up between the flags, and cattle are the only hedge-cutters.'

We start with Heathcliff's aggression, but this then yields to the, by now familiar, elegant manner of Lockwood. By this stage, however, Lockwood seems absurd. The explanation for this is that there is just such a gap between Heathcliff's bluntness and Lockwood's ornate sentences. One is a total outsider whereas the other is a man caught up in the rigmarole of society. It is a point that is nicely summed up in the ironic voice Lockwood adopts to comment on the fact that Heathcliff only has one servant: 'Here we have the whole establishment of domestics, I suppose'. Irony is an indirect, rather deceitful, highly mannered way of speaking. Heathcliff, of course, would never employ irony: his manner is always totally direct. Where does this get us, however? The point yet again is to see that something far more complex is being offered than just a contrast between two characters. We have to look beyond character and see that this is the beginning of an exploration of the nature of social life, and how individuals see and conduct themselves in relation to society.

Step 6:   Look at how the passage concludes

Heathcliff is obviously a social outsider. Joseph is an almost equally interesting character. He makes no pretence to politeness. But the additional factor here is that Joseph is immediately associated with religion. It is, however, an austere and demanding religion rather than a religion of Christian kindness – or at least this is what we can assume from the manner in which he greets Lockwood. What can we do with such an impression? As always, we need to return to basics. We have the social world and people who are against or outside the social world. A look at these opening paragraphs has enabled us to say a great deal more about the social world as conceived in this novel, how it is essentially the polite world of the gentleman. Joseph, a character from the fringes of society, is one example of a character who isn't a member of polite society. Relating this to our impressions so far, it would appear that Brontë is exploring various kinds of conformist and non-conformist behaviour in society, including Joseph's form of religious non-conformity. The introduction of this character this early in the novel adds, therefore, to our sense of how the novel is offering a broad exploration of the nature of society.

Step 7: Sum up your sense of the passage as a whole

This is about as far as we can go, for again we have spotted the general in the particular; but at every stage we have tried to ensure that our broader speculations follow directly from our consideration of specific details. If you can manage to combine the particular and the general, the small detail and the large idea, in a prose practical criticism essay then you can be sure that you are producing a good piece of work. The way to do this is constantly to question where your points are leading and how they are connected to the larger issue. Look back at this chapter and you will see how simple it is to ask of a detail 'Why? What has this to do with the case so far?', and how simple it is to make sure at the end of each paragraph-step you pull back and sum up the larger idea you have reached.

14

Writing a prose practical criticism essay

BEFORE turning directly to essay-writing, we want to reiterate some points that we made in Chapter 6, points about mistakes to avoid and tips to adopt in essay writing:

(i)   **Avoid story telling.** There is no point in merely repeating what the passage says in your own words. You are meant to be analysing the passage: showing what it is about, how it brings its subject to life, and what it all amounts to.

(ii)   **Don't stray from the point**. Practical criticism in not an excuse or opportunity for writing about your own life. Stick to the extract, stick to the words on the page.

(iii)   **Don't talk about content and style separately.** Far too often candidates say what the passage is about at great length and then comment separately on its formal qualities. Through the entire course of your essay you should be talking about the artistic choices the writer has made, and how these choices help create the meaning and significance of the passage.

(iv)   **Recreate the reading process.** The ideal answer recreates the reading process. You read the passage, form an initial impression of what it is about, but then, as you look more closely and reflect on what you have read, your sense of what the passage is about becomes more subtle.

(v)   **Remember that you are writing an essay.** Far too many examination candidates present their observations in a piecemeal fashion. You must ensure that you are building a case. Get hold of the passage as a whole in an introductory paragraph, and then write four substantial paragraphs (sometimes three or five might be more appropriate), before pulling everything together in a conclusion.

(vi)   **What assumptions can I bring to practical criticism?** If the passage is from a novel there is a good chance that it will feature a character or characters who are in some way at odds with society. If this doesn't seem to be the case, try to work out what the passage is saying about society, about the constitution and condition of society. You might also want to consider how social order as represented in the passage is in some way opposed to or imposed upon the pattern of nature.

(vii) **What do examiners mean when they ask for comments on the style of a passage?** This is an instruction that can mislead candidates. Many assume that the examiner is asking for an impressionistic comment: for example, 'this seems a highly poetic style'. But what the examiner is really asking you to do is to examine how the language in a passage functions in creating the meaning of a passage. At a simple level, an enormously long sentence, for example, might suggest the complexity of the situation or dilemma being presented at that point. At the opposite extreme, the kind of short sentences favoured by D. H. Lawrence manage to convey the fleeting feelings of the characters. The important point to grasp is that style is functional, that the author's manner of writing creates the meaning of the passage.

(viii) **What is the 'large issue' in a passage of prose?** We have suggested repeatedly that you try to look for the 'large issue' in a passage of prose. We hope what we mean by this is clear by now, but there is no harm in reiterating the point. We don't mean that there is a secret meaning in a passage; when the writer is writing about one thing, he or she isn't secretly writing about something else. What we do mean is that if the author presents, say, a family, it isn't just the one family that concerns us; we have to see the general in the particular, how familiar family tensions are reflected in the specific extract. In the same way, if there is a man and a woman in a passage, the larger issue of gender may well be implicit in the scene. You are not, therefore, looking for something that the author has concealed; you are simply trying to grasp the general application of the particular examples, how the particular examples embody the idea or issue that is indicated by the text. In doing this, you need to bear in mind that there is no single correct answer that can be arrived at. Indeed, what makes criticism interesting to read is the fact that every reader will have his or her own idea of the 'large issue' in a passage.

(ix) **Stick to the details.** A reading needs to be inventive, but it mustn't be pure invention. The secret of practical criticism is to keep very close to the details in a text while at the same time showing that you can do interesting things with these details. It isn't as difficult as it sounds if your essay is coherently organised, as a coherently organised essay will steer you along in the right direction.

(x) **What is the examiner looking for?** Simply the following:

---

1. Evidence that you have grasped the sense and significance of the passage.
2. Evidence that you can discuss the extract in some detail, with an awareness of how it brings its subject-matter to life.
3. Evidence that you can build a response to the passage.
4. Evidence that you can express and develop your analysis of the extract in the form of a coherent and literate essay.

If you can offer evidence of all four of these, then you should receive a very good mark for your prose practical criticism.

How to achieve a good mark is something that we now want to consider in rather more detail as we focus on how to write an essay. This is a much shorter chapter than the equivalent earlier one about poetry. This isn't because writing about poetry is more difficult; it is simply because just about everything we said in that chapter also holds true for this chapter. We could repeat all the points we made earlier, but it seems more sensible to suggest that you might read Chapter 8 in combination with this chapter. What we want to do here is look at one example, an extract from the novel *A Story of an African Farm*, by Olive Schreiner. As always, what we are keen to show is that an effective essay structure will do much of the work of reading the passage for you.

Step 1:   Reading and thinking

The room was dark; door and shutter were closed; not a ray of light entered anywhere. The German overseer, to whom the room belonged, lay sleeping soundly on his bed in the corner, his great arms folded, and his bushy grey and black beard rising and falling on his breast. But one in the room was not asleep. Two large eyes looked about in the darkness, and two small hands were smoothing the patchwork quilt. The boy, who slept on a box under the window, had just awakened from his first sleep. He drew the quilt up to his chin, so that little peered above it but a great head of silky black curls and the two black eyes. He stared about in the darkness. Nothing was visible, not even the outline of one worm-eaten rafter, nor of the deal table, on which lay the Bible from which his father had read before they went to bed. No one could tell where the tool-box was, and where the fireplace. There was something very impressive to the child in the complete darkness.

At the head of his father's bed hung a great silver hunting watch. It ticked loudly. The boy listened to it, and began mechanically to count. Tick – tick – tick! one, two, three, four! He lost count presently, and only listened. Tick – tick – tick – tick!

It never waited; it went on inexorably; and every time it ticked *a man died!* He raised himself a little on his elbow and listened. He wished it would leave off.

How many times had it ticked since he came to lie down? A thousand times, a million times, perhaps.

He tried to count again, and sat up to listen better.

'Dying, dying, dying!' said the watch, 'dying, dying, dying!'

He heard it distinctly. Where were they going to, all those people?

He lay down quickly, and pulled the cover up over his head; but presently the silky curls reappeared.

'Dying, dying, dying!' said the watch, 'dying, dying, dying!'

He thought of the words his father had read that evening – 'For wide is the gate, and broad is the way, that leadeth to destruction, and many there be which go in thereat.'

'Many, many, many!' said the watch.

'Because strait is the gate, and narrow is the way, that leadeth unto life, and few there be that find it.'

'Few, few, few!' said the watch.

The boy lay with his eyes wide open. He saw before him a long stream of people, a great dark multitude, that moved in one direction; then they came to the dark edge of the world, and went over. He saw them passing on before him, and there was nothing that could stop them. He thought of how that stream had rolled on through all the long ages of the past – how the old Greeks and Romans had gone over; the countless millions of China and India, they were going over now. Since he had come to bed, how many had gone!

And the watch said, 'Eternity, eternity, eternity!'

'Stop them, stop them!' cried the child.

And all the while the watch kept ticking on; just like God's will, that never changes or alters, you may do what you please.

Great beads of perspiration stood on the boy's forehead. He climbed out of bed and lay with his face turned to the mud floor.

'Oh, God, God! save them!' he cried in agony. 'Only some; only a few! Only for each moment I am praying here one!' He folded his little hands upon his head. 'God! God! save them!'

He grovelled on the floor.

Oh, the long, long ages of the past, in which they had gone over! Oh, the long, long future, in which they would pass away! Oh, God! the long, long, long eternity, which has no end!

The child wept, and crept closer to the ground.

Read the passage twice, making sure that you are reading it actively, looking for a pattern, looking for a tension. As it is a substantial passage, a number of issues will be raised, but there is no point trying to work out every twist and turn in advance. Instead, concentrate on the opening, trying to find a tension. Here, for example, there is the dark room and the little boy awake in the dark room: this seems to set up a significant pattern, a pattern that we should be able to build on as the passage continues.

As it is a long passage, it is a good idea to divide it into four stages at this point:

(i)   paragraph one, where the child is asleep in the room;
(ii)   the short paragraph in which the child listens to the tick of the watch;
(iii) the longer paragraph beginning 'The boy lay with his eyes wide open';
(iv)   the final section where the child becomes agitated.

At one level it is a trivial scene – as children, we have all experienced nights rather like this – but it is your job as a critic to move, when you can, to a sense of the larger issues that are being dealt with here. Don't worry if you can't see a large issue at the outset. This is the reason why we write essays: an essay is an investigative probe. A coherent, structured essay will lead you towards the right answers.

Step 2:   Starting an essay. Summarise the passage, establish your sense of the central opposition in the passage, set up the controlling idea for your essay as a whole

In summarising the passage, make sure that you limit yourself to what the passage actually says. This passage is set in South Africa;

you might have your own views on the past and present history of South Africa, but the examiner doesn't want to hear your political opinions. Stick to the facts at this stage. When you have written your summary, devote the next sentence to your sense of the tension in the passage. If you can add another sentence, a sentence that offers a broader comment on the overall significance of what you have encountered, then it is a good idea to do so, but if you can't, the sense of a tension is quite enough to be going on with.

Let's try to put these ideas into practice. A boy lies awake in a dark room. He hears the ticking of his father's watch which, after a while, seems to be repeating the word 'dying'. The child thinks of the words from the Bible that his father read earlier that evening. He then begins to think of the millions of people throughout the world and throughout history who have died or are dying. He becomes agitated, asking God to save all these condemned people. There is a sense at the outset of one little individual in a dark and threatening world. Larger issues seem to be implicit in this situation: most obviously, there is the sense of everybody on their own in the world. Though not quite on their own: there is a reference to the child's father. Most people fit into the context of a family. And there are also references to God; God provides a sense of comfort and security in a dangerous world. This is, then, more than just a child's nightmare: the passage raises questions about the self, and how the self relates to the world at large.

Step 3: Look more closely at the opening of the passage, trying to see how the author brings the theme to life

We now have a steady opening paragraph: the first paragraph of our essay has got hold of the passage and, at the same time, set up a framework that will help us organise our subsequent impressions. These subsequent impressions can start to appear in our second paragraph. We need to look at a number of the details to see how they bring to life the ideas we have established so far, but we can also feel confident that examination of these details will enable us to extend and develop our initial ideas. As our case advances, at the end of each paragraph we will need to spell out how it has advanced. One way of putting it as follows: say to yourself, what is it that I can say at the end of this paragraph that I couldn't have said at the end of the previous paragraph of my essay? If you make sure that you actually write down what you know now that you didn't know before, then you will be totally in control of the essay and the argument.

In the first few lines of this extract from *A Story of an African Farm*, the most obvious thing to look at is the darkness. The child occupies a frightening world. His father is there, but the father, who appears burly and intimidating, isn't a reassuring figure. Even the fact that his arms are folded suggests that he is wrapped up in himself, that he is not the kind of father who would reach out and comfort his child. As against the immensity of the night and the immense size of the father, we have the 'small hands' of the child. He is small and vulnerable, and his 'black curls' add to this sense of childish innocence.

Three details are picked out in the room: the worm-eaten rafter, the deal table and the Bible. The reference to wood-worm in the rafter suggests something rotten in the supports of the roof that is meant to cover and protect the child. That might, of course, strike you as a far-fetched interpretation, but it is a legitimate interpretation of the detail because it fits in with the general pattern we have been developing. The detail adds to the sense of the insecurity of the shelters that are provided for us in a frightening world. We can't think of much to say about the deal table apart from the fact that its plainness helps create a sense of the plain lives of these characters. It is also straightforward and dependable, something they can rely upon in the same way that they rely upon the Bible, for the Bible offers them some sense of a larger purpose in their spartan existence.

Can you see the simplicity of the method we have followed here? A handful of details, all interpreted in the light of our initial pattern, but in thinking about these details we have arrived at a much fuller sense of the nature of these people's lives and a more general sense of how people sustain themselves under difficult circumstances. In particular, we have a sense of the important role that religion can play in people's lives.

Step 4:   Look at another section of the passage, trying to build on your analysis of the passage's details

We have started to build a case. Our opening paragraph set the issue up and the second paragraph of our essay has, on the basis of looking at a few details, moved the case forward. What matters is that we are firmly in control of both the passage and our argument, but it is the strict discipline of our essay structure that has enabled us to establish and maintain this degree of control. There is no point in trying to run before we can walk; there is no point in tying the essay up in complicated knots at this early stage. The complications can come along as the essay develops; in the ideal essay, each paragraph is a little more complicated than the paragraph that has preceded it.

We should be able to see the relevance of this point as we consider the section of the passage that deals with the ticking of the watch. A lot of readers might find this detail puzzling. How can it be related to anything we have said so far? As always, when a detail proves difficult, it is best to go back to basics. Does the watch add to our sense of a frightening world or does it tell us something about the child in this world? The answer is probably ambiguous, that the watch tells us about both the world and the child. We can start with the fact that a watch is obviously a useful thing. Look at how the child counts in time with the watch. One of the ways in which we impose a structure upon life is by counting, by dividing the day into hours, minutes and seconds. A watch, therefore, like religion, is one of the tools that people use to help them structure experience.

But the watch doesn't just divide the day into hours. In this passage, it makes the child think of the enormity of time, that the ticking of the watch has gone on relentlessly for ever. There is now no structure, just a repeated tick; and, with this, his thoughts turn to just how many people have died during the course of history. The detail of the watch expands, therefore, on the themes we have already noticed of the frightening vastness of the world and how people structure their lives. Yet, although it gestures in both directions, the detail at this stage probably does more to indicate and expose the frailty of the supporting structures that we rely upon. One of these supporting structures is religion. The child's thoughts turn to religion, but the religion suggested in the words his father has been reading is far from comforting: the stress is not on the saving power of Christ but on the number of sinners in the world. Where this gets us, then, in terms of advancing our case as we conclude a paragraph of our essay, is that religion in this society, like time, adds to the sense of a frightening world.

Step 5: Look at another section of the passage, trying to build on your analysis of the passage's details

Our method of writing an essay is almost like assembling a jig-saw: the best place to start is with setting out the frame. Then, focus on the details, seeing how the details fit together, and where they fit into, and how they contribute to, the whole picture. Steadily the complete picture will take shape. The two points to bear in mind are that it is essential to keep on turning to details from the passage, and it is equally essential to keep on taking stock of how the overall case is advancing.

Let's turn now to this paragraph from the extract:

> The boy lay with his eyes wide open. He saw before him a long stream of people, a great dark multitude, that moved in one direction; then they came to the dark edge of the world, and went over. He saw them passing on before him, and there was nothing that could stop them. He thought of how that stream had rolled on through all the long ages of the past – how the old Greeks and Romans had gone over; the countless millions of China and India, they were going over now. Since he had come to bed, how many had gone!

This is a nightmare vision of human destruction, suffering and death throughout the course of history. The child ponders morbidly on the fact of death. Again, then, we have the sense of a vulnerable child in a huge universe. And it is again the case that religion offers no help, for religion only promotes a sense of individual worthlessness. It seems reasonable to assume that the novel as a whole will deal with this child trying to break free, trying to assert himself as an individual as he grows up. But it is also possible that he is doomed before he even begins, because the religious and social framework in which he has been raised encourages only a sense of sinfulness and the insignificance of the individual. But a practical criticism exercise doesn't require us to anticipate what happens next. Taken in isolation, there is plenty to consider about the complex nature of the relationship between the individual and the society – including the values and beliefs of that society – in which he exists.

Step 6:   Look at how the passage concludes

In the final lines of the passage we see the child sweating, grovelling on the floor, crying, and keeping close to the ground. He is begging God to save some of the people who have died, are dying and will die. What do we make of this? What strikes us is the fact that the child is making a simple plea for kindness. It is a hard world in which he has been brought up, his father we can assume is a hard man, and we have been offered an impression of a hard God. But the child is making a plea for a softer attitude. It is the voice of someone who is at odds with the world in which he finds himself.

Step 7: Sum up your sense of the passage as a whole

We started with the idea of an individual in conflict with society. And we have finished with an idea of an individual in conflict with society. But our steady progress throughout the passage has enabled us to fill out our sense of what it means for this child to find himself alone in a frightening world. We have established a great deal about how this society is constituted, in particular how religion is perceived in this society, and we have learnt a lot about the child's desperation. It is this sense of having got hold of the full picture that should be your goal in practical criticism.

And at that point a practical criticism essay would stop. But as we have said throughout this book, practical criticism is not the end but the beginning of criticism. In a practical criticism exercise you don't need to speculate about a novel as a whole, but a practical criticism exercise that has worked well provides you with a solid start for a full analysis of a novel. *A Story of an African Farm* isn't, in fact, primarily about this young boy, who is a subsidiary character in the novel. It is about a young girl called Lyndall, who feels imprisoned by the iron-bound conventions of Boer life, and her struggles to attain independence of action and belief. Can you see how our discussion of the extract from the novel provides a very good way into discussing the situation in which Lyndall finds herself? The great advantage of looking closely at a passage is that it helps you define the issues in a book in a far more subtle and thorough way than if you approached the issue in general terms. If we say that Lyndall feels trapped by religion, that doesn't really tell us all that much, but our examination of this passage about a young boy conveys a complex sense of just how it must have affected a child to be brought up in that kind or religious and social context. It is always the case that close exploration of small areas of the text is going to provide you with the fullest and most perceptive understanding of the large concerns of a text.

Part Three
Drama

15

Understanding an extract from a play

THE third option on many practical criticism papers, alongside writing about a poem or passage of prose, is writing about an extract from a play. This is what we are going to deal with in the final three chapters of this book. We are devoting less space to drama than to poetry or prose simply because nearly everything we have said so far also applies to drama: it is essential to get hold of the extract as a whole, it is essential to focus on details in order to build your case, and it is essential to present your case in the form of a coherent essay. If, therefore, we don't, in these three chapters, spell out every step of how to construct a response, try to see how principles established earlier are just as important here.

Our starting point with a play is a little different, however. It again depends upon searching for a tension, and spotting this tension in the opening lines of an extract, but in order to make sense of what is going on it helps to know a little about the conventional structure of a play. A play falls into three stages: exposition, complication and resolution. In the early part of a play, the exposition scenes, the situation and issue are established. More often than not, some problem develops that disrupts the routine business of life. In a Shakespeare history play, for example, a group of noblemen may decide to challenge the authority of the king. At the opening of Shakespeare's *King Lear*, a tragedy, there is an alteration in the status quo when the king decides to hand over power to his children. In Shakespeare's comedies, such as *A Midsummer Night's Dream*, the daily order of society is disrupted when characters in love start behaving in a reckless manner. What we see at the beginning of a play, therefore, is a stable situation that is destabilised.

In the complication stage of a play, which is usually the longest section, we begin to see the consequences of the disruption that has taken place. In some plays everything becomes topsy-turvy; the whole social order is thrown into chaos. This is resolved, however, in the resolution stage of a play. In a Shakespeare comedy, the characters in love sort themselves out. The comedies always end with marriage, symbolising the way in which wild romantic impulses have been domesticated within a social institution, the social institution of marriage. In a tragedy, however, things do not end joyfully: the disruption within society has been so extreme that one or more of the central characters is pushed to the 'brink, pushed to the point where there is no possibility of restoring the order that used to exist. A tragedy, consequently, ends with death.

It is the idea of disruption that, more than anything else, provides a way of focusing a sense of what is going on in an extract from a play. The assumption we can always bring to an extract is that the passage will in some way suggest a routine order that exists or has existed in society, and, at the same time, examine the disruption that has taken place or which is about to take place. As we begin to read a passage, therefore, we should be looking for an impression of a stable situation and also for details that suggest change and disruption. Anything that provides a sense of uneasiness or conflict in an extract is exactly the kind of detail we should seize upon. We can see how to apply these ideas as we look at this extract from a seventeenth-century play, *Volpone* by Ben Jonson.

Step 1:   Reading and thinking

Volpone (the word means fox), a wealthy Venetian, pretends to be dying so that his potential heirs will bring him presents. Mosca (fly), his servant, persuades each of the would-be heirs in turn that he is the one who will inherit. In this extract, Voltore (vulture) pays his visit, followed by Corbaccio (raven):

MOSCA.   Sir, Signior Voltore is come this morning
             To visit you.
VOLPONE.   I thank him.
MOSCA.   And hath brought
             A piece of antique plate, bought of St Mark,
             With which he here presents you.

VOLPONE.   He is welcome.
Pray him to come more often.

MOSCA.   Yes.

VOLTORE.   What says he?

MOSCA.   He thanks you and desires you see him often.

VOLPONE.   Mosca.

MOSCA.   My patron?

VOLPONE.   Bring him near, where is he?
I long to feel his hand.

MOSCA.   The plate is here, sir.

VOLTORE.   How fare you, sir?

VOLPONE.   I thank you, Signior Voltore.
Where is the plate? mine eyes are bad.

VOLTORE.   I'm sorry
To see you still thus weak.

MOSCA. [aside]   That he is not weaker.

VOLPONE.   You are too munificent.

VOLTORE.   No, sir, would to heaven
I could as well give health to you as that plate!

VOLPONE.   You give, sir, what you can. I thank you. Your love
Hath taste in this, and shall not be unanswered.
I pray you see me often.

VOLTORE.   Yes, I shall, sir.

VOLPONE.   Be not far from me.

MOSCA.   Do you observe that, sir?

VOLPONE.   Hearken unto me still; it will concern you.

MOSCA.   You are a happy man, sir; know your good.

VOLPONE.   I cannot now last long –
                            You are his heir, sir.

VOLTORE.   Am I?

VOLPONE.   I feel me going – uh! uh! uh! uh!
I am sailing to my port – uh! uh! uh! uh!
And I am glad I am so near my haven.

MOSCA.   Alas, kind gentleman. Well, we must all go –

VOLTORE.   But, Mosca –

MOSCA.   Age will conquer.

VOLTORE.   Pray thee, hear me.
Am I inscribed his heir for certain?

MOSCA.   Are you?
I do beseech you, sir, you will vouchsafe
To write me i' your family. All my hopes
Depend your worship. I am lost
Except the rising sun do shine on me.

VOLTORE.   It shall both shine and warm thee, Mosca.

MOSCA.   Sir,
I am a man that have not done your love
All the worst offices. Here I wear your keys,
See all your coffers and your caskets locked,
Keep the poor inventory of your jewels,

Your plate, and moneys; am your steward, sir,
Husband your goods here.

VOLTORE.   But am I sole heir?

MOSCA.   Without a partner, sir, confirmed this morning;
The wax is warm yet, and the ink scarce dry
Upon the parchment.

VOLTORE.   Happy, happy me!
By what good chance, good Mosca?

MOSCA.   Your desert, sir;
I know no second cause.

VOLTORE.   Thy modesty
Is loath to know it; well, we shall requite it.

MOSCA.   He ever liked your course, sir; that first took him.
I oft have heard him say how he admired
Men of your large profession, that could speak
To every cause, and things mere contraries,
Till they were hoarse again, yet all be law;
That, with most quick agility, could turn,
And re-turn; make knots, and undo them;
Give forkèd counsel; take provoking gold
On either hand, and put it up. These men,
He knew, would thrive with their humility.
And, for his part, he thought he should be blessed
To have his heir of such a suffering spirit,
So wise, so grave, of so perplexed a tongue,
And loud withal, that would not wag, nor scarce
Lie still, without a fee; when every word
Your worship but lets fall, is a chequin!
[*Another knocks.*]
Who's that? One knocks. I would not have you seen, sir.
And yet – pretend you came in and went in haste;
I'll fashion an excuse. And, gentle sir,
When you do come to swim in golden lard,
Up to the arms in honey, that your chin
Is borne up stiff with fatness of the flood,
Think on your vassal; but remember me:
I ha' not been your worst of clients.

VOLTORE.   Mosca –

MOSCA.   When will you have your inventory brought, sir?
Or see a copy of the will? – Anon.–
I'll bring 'em to you, sir. Away, be gone,
Put business i' your face.
[*Exit Voltore.*]

VOLPONE.   Excellent, Mosca!
Come hither, let me kiss thee.

MOSCA.   Keep you still, sir.
Here is Corbaccio.

VOLPONE.   Set the plate away.
The vulture's gone, and the old raven's come.

Start by reading the passage slowly and carefully at least twice. Read it actively, looking for the subject, looking for a tension. It is a good idea to divide an extract into four parts so that, when you begin to write, you have material selected for each paragraph of your essay. But the most important thing you have to do at the outset is to try to get hold of the extract as a whole. Concentrate on the clues that are offered to you. An extract will often be preceded, as here, by a few lines introducing the characters and the situation. These aren't, strictly speaking, stage directions, but they are very useful directions to you as someone trying to make sense of the passage. Sometimes the passage will be preceded by actual stage directions, and these are again useful clues to help you get started. In nine cases out of ten, it should be possible to establish a sense of a tension from these introductory words, the words that appear before the dialogue in the play commences. If you can't find a tension, or if there are no introductory words to the extract you have to consider, then you will obviously have to turn to the actual words of the play, but here again it should be possible to find a tension within the first ten to twelve lines.

In the case of *Volpone*, we are going to start with our preliminary comments about the characters and the situation:

> Volpone (the word means fox), a wealthy Venetian, pretends to be dying so that his potential heirs will bring him presents. Mosca (fly), his servant, persuades each of the would-be heirs in turn that he is the one who will inherit. In this extract, Voltore (vulture) pays his visit, followed by Corbacio (raven).

We have suggested that the two things to look for in an extract are indications of a settled state of affairs within society and indications of disruption and change. If we consider the opening reference to Volpone as a wealthy Venetian, that might suggest the settled life of a prosperous man, but the details that follow throw this idea into disarray, particularly the fact that he pretends he is dying. He pretends to be dying in order to obtain presents from his relatives. He is avaricious, and the names of the relatives, one a vulture and the other a raven, suggest they are equally avaricious, indeed they are like birds of prey waiting to swoop on the corpse. What pattern of ideas can we extrapolate from this? The proper state of affairs in society, we can assume, would be that a wealthy man should act in a dignified and generous way. Similarly, in a well-conducted society the behaviour of relatives would be prompted by love rather than self-interest. The tension in the passage, therefore, would seem to be between how things should be and how they actually are, between moral and immoral behaviour, and between proper conduct and corrupt conduct.

Step 2:   Starting an essay. Summarise the extract, establish your sense of the central opposition in the extract, set up the controlling idea for your essay as a whole

The passage presents Mosca welcoming Voltore to Volpone's home. Voltore soon displays his corrupt personality, his grasping desire to acquire Volpone's fortune, but Volpone himself is both avaricious and wily. Mosca, working on behalf of Volpone, manipulates Voltore with clever speeches. The tension, quite clearly, is between any idea of moral conduct and the grasping immorality of these characters. As with poetry and prose analysis, we need to grasp the 'large issue' that the passage is dealing with. It is relatively easy to spot this here. It must be obvious that Jonson isn't just ridiculing Voltore as one corrupt individual. The play isn't a character study of some corrupt characters. On the contrary, the play is exploring human weakness and folly, in particular the lust for wealth and the malignant effect this has upon the human personality. It is a play that is concerned with a form of moral rottenness in society.

Step 3:   Look more closely at the opening of the extract, trying to see how the author brings the theme to life

If you can get this far you have a solid foundation on which to build your case. You now need to start adding to this initial impression, and the way to do so, as always, is by picking out and commenting upon details in the extract. Remember that your analysis is going to build through a sequence of substantial paragraphs; you don't, therefore, need to run before you can walk. A case can be allowed to accumulate steadily and logically. The second paragraph of your essay, in particular, where you might look at the first quarter of the extract, need make only the most modest advance on what you have established in your first paragraph.

    You might, for example, decide to look more closely at the characters' names. As we can see, the characters are named after animals. Some students spotting this might think they have done all they need to do in merely noting the point, but you can't just spot a detail and leave it at that. You have got to do something with the detail; to be more precise, you have got to come up with a theory about the detail that enables you to connect it with everything you have said about the extract so far. This means that you have to establish the connection between the detail and your overall view of the extract.

Let's put these principles into action here. The first and most obvious consequence of giving the characters animal names is that it indicates the way in which they lack the kind of dimension that distinguishes human beings as human. They lack any sense of a conscience or any idea of moral responsibility. They have no finer instincts, only animal-like instincts. Giving them animal names also serves to highlight the main features of their personalities. Volpone is as wily and vicious as a fox. His relatives, Voltore and Corbacio, are literally birds of prey. Most interesting of all, however, is Mosca the fly, for like a fly he flutters around filth, feeding off filth in a parasitic manner. Such names tell us a great deal about how characters are going to be presented in this play. We aren't going to be confronted by complex psychological characterisation; on the contrary, we are going to be offered caricature-like representations, characters drawn in such a way as to exemplify in bold terms some of the worst human failings.

In piecing these impressions together, can you see how in the case of a play (and this is more true of drama than it is of poetry or prose), we are like detectives searching for the clues that will enable us to make sense of what is going on? This is a legitimate comparison because it acknowledges a central feature of a play, that it has to communicate information very quickly and directly to a audience. When we read a poem, we can reread it until we see it as a whole. In the case of a novel, we might be lost for a while, but the novelist has hundreds of pages in which to establish what matters. But in the theatre, the play begins and in seconds we have to absorb and interpret a great deal. The playwright has, therefore, to provide a mass of clues, and we really are detectives piecing the clues together, sorting out what is going on and what it all means. This is obviously most true at the start of a play, but with any extract from any play clues are being dangled in front of the audience; a large part of the response to an extract is, therefore, going to involve responding to and interpreting clues.

The point about watching a play on the stage leads us on to another aspect that you must always bear in mind when writing about drama. With a poem or passage of prose, we are responding to what we read. In the case of a play, we are also responding to words, but in addition we are responding to what we see. Obviously this isn't literally true when we discuss a drama extract in an examination, but it is important to understand that there is a visual dimension to the extract being examined. Try to imagine how the extract might be staged, how it would look on the stage. But you need to be careful how you handle this visual element. There's no point is saying, if I was the director I would have the actor stand here and read his or her lines in a certain tone. You are not being asked to imagine how you might direct the play. What you should be trying to do in a consideration of the 'look' of the extract is endeavouring to see how the staging of the play might reflect the issues that you have been discussing in your response. For example, if the characters move around the stage in a giddy way then this is an effective way of representing a chaotic state of affairs that has developed in the play. Similarly, separations and divisions within a society, or within a family, can be underlined by grouping the characters on the stage in certain patterns. The objective in looking at staging is, therefore, to see how the staging adds to our grasp of the meaning of an extract.

How does this apply to the first part of this extract from *Volpone*? The obvious point is that Voltore has an antique plate in his hand and Volpone grabs it. In a play that is about greed and the desire for possessions, it helps to have a physical manifestation and symbol of these desirable material goods present on the stage; and it is an even better idea to have Volpone grabbing the plate. If we didn't speak English we would, in seeing this moment acted out on stage, none the less grasp the theme of the play from this one visual impression. We wouldn't, of course, understand every nuance of the theme, but that is why we need to work on the words on the page, as only close examination of the details can enable anyone to form a full impression.

Step 4:   Look at another section of the extract, trying to build on your analysis of the extract's details

So far we have looked at the extract up to the point where Volpone grabs the plate. Let's look now at the exchanges between Volpone, Voltore and Mosca:

> VOLPONE.   You give, sir, what you can. I thank you. Your love
> Hath taste in this, and shall not be unanswered.
> I pray you see me often.

VOLTORE.	Yes, I shall, sir.
VOLPONE.	Be not far from me.
MOSCA.	Do you observe that, sir?
VOLPONE.	Hearken unto me still; it will concern you.
MOSCA.	You are a happy man, sir; know your good.
VOLPONE.	I cannot now last long –
	You are his heir, sir.
VOLTORE.	Am I?
VOLPONE.	I feel me going – uh! uh! uh! uh!
	I am sailing to my port – uh! uh! uh! uh!
	And I am glad I am so near my haven.
MOSCA.	Alas, kind gentleman. Well, we must all go –
VOLTORE.	But, Mosca –
MOSCA.	Age will conquer.
VOLTORE.	Pray thee, hear me.
	Am I inscribed his heir for certain?

Up until this point Volpone's words have not really betrayed his grasping personality; he has played the part of a sick man, and only the act of seizing the plate has betrayed his true self. He continues to speak here in a way that could be regarded as quite straightforward. He thanks his relative, commends the love of his relative, and says that he hopes to see him often. The thing is, however, that we know things Voltore doesn't know; we know this is all a pretence. It is this that allows us to stand back from the extract and think about its significance.

But it isn't enough to just say what a rogue Volpone is; we have to see how the deception is consistent with the ideas we have developed so far. The point is that Volpone's speech again suggests an idea of a moral rottenness in society. Nothing is as it seems; polite and friendly words cannot be trusted. It is as if there is no such thing as honest behaviour, for every villain can make a pretence of playing the part of an honest man. Something as slight as Volpone's false behaviour in this speech suggests, therefore, a general untrustworthiness about all words and all conduct. We might, indeed, feel that Jonson has a very jaundiced and cynical view of human behaviour. His cynicism is most neatly illustrated at the moment when Volpone seems very close to death. His speech about 'sailing to my port' is exaggerated, to alert the audience to his play-acting, but Voltore is not in on the pretence and, even when Volpone seems about to die, shows no compassion, only an interest in his possible inheritance. It is this kind of juxtaposition of (apparent) death and selfishness that marks the extent of human corruption.

Step 5:   Look at another section of the extract, trying to build on your analysis of the extract's details

The passage continues with Mosca ingratiating himself with Voltore, and Voltore, basking in the thought that he is now a rich man, feeling well-disposed towards Mosca. Mosca's speeches are fascinating, however, because he knows what is going on. He appears to grovel before Voltore but is, in fact, totally detached from everything he says. This is funny as we see it on the stage, as it is amusing to see one character manipulating another, but what complicates the whole issue is the fact that we are in on the joke. It places us in a powerful position as moral judges who can see further and more clearly than the characters. But there is also something unnerving about the ease with which Volpone and Mosca can play their parts; the worrying thing is that it undermines language itself. When Mosca speaks of his hopes, and uses words like 'beseech' and 'vouchsafe', these words that seem to have the ring of religious and legal truth are emptied of meaning. In his next speech Mosca speaks of 'keys', 'coffers', 'caskets', 'jewels', 'plate' and 'money'. These words are not in doubt. The conclusion that all this amounts to is that we can trust nothing except the existence of material objects, that all words relating to morals and beliefs are a sham.

Step 6:   Look at how the extract concludes

We started with a sense of how things should be in society and how they actually are. We advanced to a sense of the moral rottenness of society, but the larger issue we seem to have arrived at now is that nothing is trustworthy. Morality exists as a concept constructed through language, but if everything is a sham is there such a thing as moral behaviour? Given these observations on the duplicitous nature of language, it is appropriate that the extract, in its last quarter, features a long speech from Mosca. The essence of this speech is that Voltore is a lawyer, and that, as a lawyer, he has made many noble speeches, but none of these have ever been prompted by a concern for the truth. They were speeches made in order to earn money, and in which he has given 'forkèd counsel', in other words used his powers of speech to promote any cause with a total disdain for the truth. Where does this get us? We have suggested that Jonson calls language into doubt in this extract as a whole; at the end, he criticises the law as a profession where words have very little connection with morality or truth.

Step 7:   Sum up your sense of the extract as a whole

We have come a long way. We have managed to do so because we have pursued the large issue implicit in the scene rather than getting lost in all the details. Jonson contrasts a moral society and an immoral society. One of the foundation stones of a well-run society is the rule of law: it ensures fairness for all and justice for all. But Jonson has exposed the law as just part of the general sham. Now it might be that you feel you could not spot this much in a passage, but is this really the case? There are two points to bear in mind. First, we managed to prove a lot by moving carefully and steadily through the extract. Up until the stage where we looked closely at Mosca's final speech we hadn't really realised it was about lawyers, and we certainly had no idea how this speech related to the case we had made up to that point. What we are saying, therefore, is that an argument might be fairly complicated by the end of your essay, but it is a case of building the argument in steps, adding one impression to another, so that a complicated argument can emerge. It doesn't have to be complicated from the word go; indeed, it is much more likely that you will be in control of the argument if it begins in the simple fashion we have illustrated.

The second point to bear in mind is that the examiner is not looking for a devastatingly complete and complex analysis of the extract. What the examiner is looking for is evidence that you can work from the evidence and can piece a case together. In the case of this extract, if you managed to establish in your first paragraph that it is about good and bad behaviour, and then wrote four solid paragraphs showing how the passage illustrates good and bad behaviour, then you would be doing enough to achieve a good mark. What we have been trying to demonstrate is how things can be pushed a little further. But we do want to make the point as emphatically as possible that a coherent essay that builds a case, even if it can't push things that little bit more, is bound to get a good mark. The pattern to follow is the pattern we have stressed throughout this book: establish a tension, look at the details, and build a case from these details, a case that enables you to develop and complicate your initial sense of the tension in the passage.

TACKLING AN EXTRACT FROM A PLAY

1. Remember all plays employ a basic three-part structure of exposition, complication and resolution.
2. Look for a tension in the extract, a pattern of the established order of society and the disruption of that settled order.
3. Divide the extract into four sections and use the paragraph steps to frame your analysis.
4. Focus on a handful of details, connecting them to your overall view of the extract.
5. Think about how the staging reflects the larger issue you see in the piece.
6. Towards the end of your analysis push your ideas on further: think about the implications of the issues raised.

16

Building a response

THERE are three stages in putting together a practical criticism answer: getting hold of the extract, building a response, and writing an essay that will help structure and direct your response. In this chapter we focus on how to build your response to an extract from a play.

Step 1: Reading and thinking

This is the opening of Henrik Ibsen's play *Ghosts*:

> [*A spacious garden-room, with one door to the left, and two doors to the right. In the middle of the room a round table with chairs about it. On the table lie books, periodicals, and newspapers. In the foreground to the left a window, and by it a small sofa, with a work-table in front of it. In the background, the room is continued into a somewhat narrower conservatory, which is shut in by glass walls with large panes. In the right-hand wall of the conservatory is a door leading down into the garden. Through the glass wall one catches a glimpse of a gloomy fjord-landscape, veiled by steady rain.*
>
> ENGSTRAND, *the carpenter, stands by the garden door. His left leg is somewhat bent; he has a clump of wood under the sole of his boot.* REGINA, *with an empty garden syringe in her hand, hinders him from advancing.*]

REGINA. [*in a low voice*] What do you want? Stop where you are. You're positively dripping.
ENGSTRAND. It's the Lord's own rain, my girl.
REGINA. It's the Devil's rain, *I* say.
ENGSTRAND. Lord! how you talk, Regina. [*Limps a few steps forward into the room.*] What I wanted to say was this –
REGINA. Don't clatter so with that foot of yours, I tell you! The young master's asleep upstairs.
ENGSTRAND. Asleep? In the middle of the day?
REGINA. It's no business of yours.
ENGSTRAND. I was out on the loose last night –
REGINA. I can quite believe that.

ENGSTRAND. Yes, we're weak vessels, we poor mortals, my girl –

REGINA. So it seems.

ENGSTRAND. – and temptations are manifold in this world, you see; but all the same, I was hard at work, God knows, at half-past five this morning.

REGINA. Very well; only be off now. I won't stop here and have *rendezvous* with you.

ENGSTRAND. What is it you won't have?

REGINA. I won't have any one find you here; so just you go about your business.

ENGSTRAND. [*advances a step or two*] Blest if I go before I've had a talk with you. This afternoon I shall have finished my work at the school-house, and then I shall take to-night's boat and be off home to the town.

REGINA. [*mutters*] A pleasant journey to you.

ENGSTRAND. Thank you, my child. To-morrow the Asylum's to be opened, and there will be fine doings, no doubt, and plenty of intoxicating drink going, you know. And nobody shall say of Jacob Engstrand that he can't keep out of temptation's way.

REGINA. Oh!

ENGSTRAND. You see, there are to be any number of swells here to-morrow. Pastor Manders is expected from town, too.

REGINA. He's coming to-day.

ENGSTRAND. There, you see! And I should be cursedly sorry if he found out anything to my disadvantage, don't you understand?

REGINA. Oh! Is that your game?

ENGSTRAND. Is what my game?

REGINA. [*looking hard at him*] What trick are you going to play on Pastor Manders?

ENGSTRAND. Hush! Hush! Are you crazy? Do *I* want to play any trick on Pastor Manders? Oh no! Pastor Manders has been far too kind to me for that. But I just wanted to say, you know – that I mean to set off home again to-night.

REGINA. The sooner the better, say I.

ENGSTRAND. Yes but I want to take you with me, Regina.

REGINA. [*open-mouthed*] You want me – ? What are you talking about?

ENGSTRAND. I want to take you home, I say.

REGINA. [*scornfully*] Never in this world shall you get me home with you.

ENGSTRAND.
We'll see about that.

REGINA. Yes, you may be sure we'll see about it! I, who have been brought up by a lady like Mrs Alving! I, who am treated almost as a daughter here! Is it me you want to go home with you? – to a house like yours? For shame!

ENGSTRAND. What the devil do you mean? Do you set yourself up against your father, girl?

REGINA. [*mutters without looking at him*] You've said often enough I was no child of yours.

ENGSTRAND. Stuff! Why should you trouble about that?

REGINA. Haven't you many time sworn at me and called me a – ? *Fi donc*!

ENGSTRAND. Curse me now, if I ever used such an ugly word.

REGINA. Oh! I know quite well what word you used.

ENGSTRAND. Well, but that was only when I was a bit on, don't you know? Hm! Temptations are manifold in this world, Regina.

REGINA. Ugh!

ENGSTRAND. And besides, it was when your mother rode her high horse. I had to find something to twit her with, my child. She was always setting up for a fine lady. [*Mimics*] 'Let me go, Engstrand, let me be. Remember I've been three years in Chamberlain Alving's family at Rosenvold.' [*Laughs*] Mercy on us! She could never forget that the Captain was made a Chamberlain while she was in service here.

REGINA. Poor mother! You very soon worried her into her grave.

ENGSTRAND. [*turns on his heel*] Oh, of course! I'm to be blamed for everything.

As we pointed out in the previous chapter, in the case of a play (far more so than with poetry or prose), we are responding to clues, clues that are present in what we see in front of us and clues that are present in what the characters say. We're not going to mention in this chapter what *Ghosts* is about, what the revelation is that comes in the course of the play; its subject-matter was controversial at the time of the play's appearance and is still fairly controversial today. But if we revealed 'the secret' of the play, that would provide a key that unlocked many of the details in the text. It's much better if we side-step this revelation and put ourselves in the position of an audience, an audience who don't know the play and who are having to work hard at the clues in order to form an impression.

It's little things that are important to an audience, like the opening words in Ibsen's stage directions, 'A spacious garden-room'. We know immediately that we are dealing with relatively wealthy people. But why a garden-room, which is presumably a conservatory, rather than, say, a drawing-room? The point to grasp is that this kind of detail, even if we are unaware of it doing so, is surreptitiously establishing ideas in our minds. The interesting point about a garden-room as the setting is that it hints at a tension between the structure of life within the house – in other words, life within the social order – and life outside the house – that is to say, life that has more to do with nature. Instantly, therefore, before the characters have even appeared, and without giving it a moment's thought, the audience has already established some important points about this play. The audience has already realised what social class the play is going to focus on, and has also, in very broad terms, got an inkling of the play's likely theme, how in some way it is likely to look at the life we construct within society.

Step 2:   Starting an essay. Summarise the extract, establish your sense of the central opposition in the extract, set up the controlling idea for your essay as a whole

The setting is the garden-room of a fairly prosperous family (they employ a carpenter and a maid). Beyond the windows there is a 'gloomy fjord-landscape' and steady rain. Engstrand, the carpenter, dripping with rain, enters the room and encounters Regina, the maid. He jokes about how he was out the night before but back at work first thing in the morning. He refers to an Asylum that is being built (the word 'asylum' was used more broadly in the past than it is today; it simply meant a refuge and needn't imply mental illness). Engstrand also says that he intends to go home before Pastor Manders arrives. The real surprise in the passage comes, however, when it is revealed that Engstrand is Regina's father.

In looking for a tension, focus on the opening directions. We have already established that the garden-room is a significant setting, and this becomes even more apparent if we consider the view from the window. It is a fjord-landscape, but this is described as gloomy rather than beautiful, and, in addition, there is 'steady rain'. The tension would seem to be between the well-ordered life of the house – the books, periodicals and newspapers on the table indicate the cultured life of the owners – and something more gloomy the other side of the windows. The windows, we might conjecture, lock nature out and keep it at a safe distance, but the room then becomes a kind of prison where people are locked in.

Step 3:   Look more closely at the opening of the extract, trying to see how the author brings the theme to life

In the previous chapter we suggested that in any play you should be able to detect a pattern of the established order of society and disruption of that settled order. The established order is life within this room; the danger that will disrupt is hinted at in the view outside. What we need to look at in our overall analysis is both the established order of this society and the nature and force of the disruption that Ibsen presents. The best way of doing this, as we have stated all along, is to look at a handful of details. On this occasion, however, to underline just how few details it is possible to work from, we want to concentrate as clearly as possible on a series of small points.

Why is Engstrand's left leg somewhat bent? Why does Ibsen make the character lame? If you can't think of an answer, think about the pattern we have established so far: a secure life within the house but something rather disturbing beyond the windows. The characters, we might say, protect themselves by surrounding themselves with glass and sheltering inside, but glass can easily be broken. Uncomfortable reality is never all that far away. Engstrand's damaged leg is just one example of how everything within society isn't as well-ordered as it might initially seem. There is always evidence of, and reminders of, a less than perfect world.

Why does Regina confront Engstrand with a garden syringe? It would be easy to overlook such a minor detail as this, but it is in fact very effective, for it is a military image of Regina challenging an invader. There is again, therefore, a sense of a confrontation between the social world and alien forces, and the social world, even if only with a garden syringe, immediately leaps to defend itself.

Why is Engstrand dripping with rain? The simple answer is because it is raining, but Ibsen didn't have to make it rain. As always, the detail must be related to our sense of the passage as a whole, and what we can say is that it is a further illustration of raw and messy nature forcing its way into this family's house.

Why do they talk about the Lord's rain and the Devil's rain? We don't know. We don't, of course, really know why any of the details are in the text, but in each case we are trying to work out a plausible theory that makes the details fit in with, and advance, our overall sense of the passage. We might, just for a moment here, think that Engstrand is a religious man, but the reference to God looks more like a cliché that is met by another cliché about the devil. What we might also notice, however, is that Engstrand uses the word 'Lord' in the kind of way that people use phrases like 'Oh God' in conversation. What that might suggest is that religion features in these people's lives, but hardly in a significant way. Religion has, in fact, become merely incidental in conversation. Can we relate this to our overall view? The point seems to be that, while religion has traditionally acted as a support to people, it is no longer central in the lives of these people. It seems that wealth and social position matter far more.

Why is the young master asleep in the middle of the day? Alarm bells should ring here. There is obviously something wrong about the young master being asleep at midday. Various hints in the extract have suggested that the prosperity of these people is the product of hard work, so there seems something amiss in the young man sleeping at this hour. We don't, however, yet know the reason: he could be ill or he could be lazy. But we don't need to know at this stage: the detail as it stands suggests the vulnerability of the ordered life within this room. Everywhere we turn there are hints of flaws and weaknesses in the safe order that has been established.

Step 4:   Look at another section of the extract, trying to build on your analysis of the extract's details

The straightforward nature of our method of analysis should be apparent by now: look for a tension, look at details, see how these details extend and complicate the initial sense of a tension. In our analysis of the opening of *Ghosts* we are considering no more than twenty details altogether. But this consideration of details needs to be accompanied by repeated stock-taking: at the end of each paragraph it is essential to ask how consideration of further details has advanced one's overall understanding of an extract. In other words we are not looking at the details just for themselves. In the case of *Ghosts*, we started with an idea of life inside the house and life beyond the window. What we have now achieved is a fuller understanding of the vulnerability of the order that has been established within this house.

Why does Regina use a French word? Regina, rather awkwardly, says, 'I won't stop here and have *rendezvous* with you'. Her use of the French word is an attempt to distance herself from the rough reality of Engstrand, and to associate herself with a more sophisticated life style. But there is something so contrived and amateurish about her use of the word that it manages to suggest again the frailty of the social order.

Why the stage direction that Engstrand 'advances a step or two'? We have mentioned how important it is with a play to report on how it would appear on a stage. Physically in this play we have had Engstrand coming from outside the room and being challenged by Regina with the garden spray. He is an intruder, an alien force. The sense of him as a threat is now visually reinforced by having him advance on Regina.

Why the references to the school-house, the Asylum, and intoxicating drink? This is a well-ordered society. It builds schools to educate people. It also builds asylums in order to look after and shelter the more vulnerable people in society. But the need for an asylum also indicates potential problems within society. If, for example, the asylum houses illegitimate children then this raises the spectre of illicit sexuality within society. It is interesting that the text at this point mentions 'intoxicating drink'. This is another dangerous force, another threat to the social order. We are no more than twenty to thirty lines into the play, yet already the idea of dangerous forces that threaten the social fabric is being signalled to us in a variety of ways.

Why is there a reference to Pastor Manders? Pastor Manders seems to be a social figure as much as he is a religious figure. He is part of the orderly framework of society.

Why does Engstrand go on about returning home? It is as if Engstrand wants to return to a world where he feels more safe and secure. He has found life away from home too full of temptation (in particular, he has been a drinker). Regina speaks to him as if he is a rogue, but in fact he appears to be a rather more complex figure.

Step 5:   Look at another section of the extract, trying to build on your analysis of the extract's details

Why is Engstrand revealed to be Regina's father? This comes as a total shock. We are forced to reconsider the relationship between the two. She has been treating him like a servant, but he is now revealed to be her father. As always, when a detail proves difficult to interpret, return to basics. We have been dealing with bourgeois life and threats to this bourgeois life. Something has gone terribly wrong in the social order here, for the father and child have become separated and estranged. She feels more at home in her employer's household and prefers not to acknowledge her father. Again, then, the whole social structure of this community seems very unstable. Social life is built around the family, but in this community families have become divided and are in conflict. What we can add is that, as this revelation of a divided family is so central at the start of the play, the play as a whole might well focus to a quite considerable extent on questioning and undermining the myth of the family in middle-class life.

Why has Engstrand denied he is her father? A secure social order is, traditionally and invariably, a patriarchal social order: men govern and lead in a responsible fashion. But something seems to have gone wrong in this society. It is Mrs Alving who owns and runs the house.

The young master is in bed. Engstrand has failed in his duties as a father. Male authority is, clearly, not functioning at all well.

How does Regina respond? Everybody needs to be part of a secure order. In the absence of a father, Regina has accepted a place in the Alving family.

Why does Engstrand refer to Regina's illegitimacy? There is sex inside marriage and there is sex outside marriage. Engstrand's remark forces us to consider again the existence of a dangerous force, the force of illicit sexuality, that can be seen to threaten the values of the family, indeed the whole fabric of middle-class life in this community.

Step 6:   Look at how the extract concludes

We have made a great deal of progress very quickly. We started with life inside the room and life outside the room. We then moved on to a sense of the vulnerability of middle-class life, but what we have now established is a sense of the nature of the threats to middle-class life. Primarily it seems to be sex that threatens the social order. We have, therefore, come a long way in a very few steps, but the point to grasp is that it is the simple step-by-step nature of our progress that has enabled us to prove so much.

How does Engstrand regard his past behaviour? He seems genuinely remorseful, but at the same time there is something just a little too pat about his sentence beginning 'Temptations are manifold in this world.'

Why does Regina respond with 'Ugh'? She is repelled by the tone of this repentant sinner. She does not want to return home with him, and we can see her point: there is no way in which he can suddenly reconstruct an imagined idyll of family life. Regina has found a secure niche with the Alving family, but is, given her background, conscious of the fragility of the security she has found.

What is Engstrand's attitude towards Regina's mother? His attitude is cruel and spiteful; he mocks her social affectations. But we can sympathise with her need for status as it has provided her with a greater degree of security than any man ever could.

Why was she 'worried' into 'a grave'? There is again a sense of male aggression, male cruelty and male sexual desire as dangerous and destructive forces within life. People try to create safe havens to protect themselves from dangerous forces, but sometimes there is an additional victim, a child, who has to live with the consequences.

Step 7: Sum up your sense of the extract as a whole

We have established a good sense of the larger issues in this extract.
We started with life inside and outside the room, but we now have a
full sense of the constitution and condition of the social order and an
equally full understanding of the threats to this established order. If
you now went on to read the rest of this play, you would probably be
surprised at just how much of it has been anticipated and prepared
for in this opening episode. This is, of course, evidence of Ibsen's skill
as a dramatist. But when there is so much in an extract it becomes all
the more important to have a critical method that enables you to get
hold of and control what is going on in the text. When it comes down
to it, the great attraction of the method we have been illustrating is
that it enables you to do justice to the complexity of an extract.

BUILDING A RESPONSE TO A PLAY: STRATEGIES TO
EMPLOY
1. Build your response in paragraph steps.
2. Start by getting hold of a pattern of the established order of
society and the disruption of that order.
3. Interpret the details of the text in the light of that pattern.
4. Remember you are not interested in the details for their own
sake but in how they point to the larger issue.
5. Examine the stage directions for clues.
6. Take stock at the end of every paragraph, asking how the
details have advanced your understanding of the extract as
a whole.
7. Try to do justice to the complexity of the extract by
controlling and developing your argument: begin simply
and then build on that base step by step.

17

Writing a drama practical criticism essay

THIS very short chapter repeats the advice we have already given in the earlier chapters about writing an essay. Throughout this book we have explained a method and then provided illustrations of possible readings. In this chapter, however, we want to stress the bare steps of the method of essay writing. We look at a specific passage, but do not attempt to offer a comprehensive reading; all we offer is some pointers about how you might set about tackling this extract.

Step 1: Reading and thinking

The extract is from George Bernard Shaw's *Arms and the Man*. The scene is set in a lady's bedchamber in Bulgaria in 1885. Raina, the young woman who lives here, has been admiring a portrait of her young man. She is startled when she hears gun shots outside her window. She blows out her candle. A few seconds later she becomes aware that there is somebody in her room.

> [*Then she lights a candle; and the mystery is at an end. He is a man of about 35, in a deplorable plight, bespattered with mud and blood and snow, his belt and the strap of his revolver-case keeping together the torn ruins of the blue tunic of a Serbian artillery officer. All that the candlelight and his unwashed unkempt condition make it possible to discern is that he is of middling stature and undistinguished appearance, with strong neck and shoulders, roundish obstinate looking head with short crisp bronze curls, clear quick eyes and good brows and mouth, hopelessly prosaic nose like that of a strong minded baby, trim soldierlike carriage and energetic manner, and with all his wits about him in spite of his predicament: even with a sense of the humour of it, without, however, the least intention of trifling with it or throwing away a chance. Reckoning up what he can guess about Raina: her age, her social position, her character, and the extent to which she is frightened, he continues, more politely but still determinedly*] Excuse my disturbing you; but you

recognise my uniform? Serb! If I am caught, I shall be killed. [*Menacingly*] Do you understand that?

RAINA. Yes.

THE MAN. Well, I don't intend to get killed if I can help it. [*Still more formidably*] Do you understand that? [*He locks the door quickly but quietly.*]

RAINA. [*disdainfully*] I suppose not. [*She draws herself up superbly, and looks him straight in the face, adding, with cutting emphasis*] Some soldiers, I know, are afraid to die.

THE MAN. [*with grim goodhumour*] All of them, dear lady, all of them, believe me. It is our duty to live as long as we can. Now, if you raise an alarm –

RAINA. [*cutting him short*] You will shoot me. How do you know that *I* am afraid to die?

THE MAN. [*cunningly*] Ah; but suppose I don't shoot you, what will happen then? A lot of your cavalry will burst into this pretty room of yours and slaughter me here like a pig; for I'll fight like a demon: they shan't get me into the street to amuse themselves with: I know what they are. Are you prepared to receive that sort of company in your present undress? [*Raina, suddenly conscious of her nightgown, instinctively shrinks and gathers it more closely about her neck. He watches her and adds pitilessly*] Hardly presentable, eh? [*She turns to the ottoman. He raises his pistol instantly, and cries*] Stop! [*She stops.*] Where are you going?

RAINA. [*with dignified patience*] Only to get my cloak.

THE MAN. [*passing swiftly to the ottoman and snatching the cloak*] A good idea! I'll keep the cloak; and you'll take care that nobody comes in and sees you without it. This is a better weapon than the revolver: eh? [*He throws the pistol down on the ottoman.*]

RAINA. [*revolted*] It is not the weapon of a gentleman!

THE MAN. It's good enough for a man with only you to stand between him and death. [*As they look at one another for a moment, Raina hardly able to believe that even a Serbian officer can be so cynically and selfishly unchivalrous, they are startled by a sharp fusillade in the street. The chill of imminent death hushes the man's voice as he adds*] Do you hear? If you are going to bring those blackguards in on me, you shall receive them as you are.

[*Clamour and disturbance. The pursuers in the street batter at the house door, shouting*] Open the door! Open the door! Wake up, will you! [*A man servant's voice calls to them angrily from within*] This is Major Petkoff's house: you can't come in here; [*but a renewal of the clamour, and a torrent of blows on the door, end with his letting a chain down with a clank, followed by a rush of heavy footsteps and a din of triumphant yells, dominated at last by the voice of Catherine, indignantly addressing an officer with*] What does this mean, sir? Do you know where you are? [*The noise subsides suddenly.*]

LOUKA. [*outside, knocking at the bedroom door*] My lady! my lady! get up quick and open the door. If you don't they will break it down.

[*The fugitive throws up his head with the gesture of a man who knows that it is all over with him, and drops the manner he has been assuming to intimidate Raina.*]

THE MAN. [*sincerely and kindly*] No use, dear: I'm done for. [*Flinging the cloak to her*] Quick! wrap yourself up: they're coming.

RAINA. Oh, thank you. [*She wraps herself up with intense relief.*]

THE MAN. [*between his teeth*] Don't mention it.

RAINA. [*anxiously*] What will you do?

THE MAN. [*grimly*] The first man in will find out. Keep out of the way; and don't look. It won't last long, but it will not be nice. [*He draws his sabre and faces the door, waiting.*]

RAINA. [*impulsively*] I'll help you. I'll save you.

THE MAN. You can't.

RAINA. I can. I'll hide you. [*She drags him towards the window.*] Here! behind the curtains.

THE MAN. [*yielding to her*] There's just half a chance, if you keep your head.

RAINA. [*drawing the curtain before him*] S-sh! [*She makes for the ottoman.*]

THE MAN. [*putting out his head*] Remember –

RAINA. [*running back to him*] Yes?

THE MAN. – nine soldiers out of ten are born fools.

RAINA. Oh! [*She draws the curtain angrily before him.*]

THE MAN. [*looking out at the other side*] If they find me, I promise you a fight; a devil of a fight.

　[*She stamps at him. He disappears hastily. She takes off her cloak, and throws it across the foot of the bed. Then, with a sleepy, disturbed air, she opens the door. Louka enters excitedly.*]

One interesting point about this passage is that the intruder is Serbian. When we considered this passage some years ago with a group of students, there was a fairly general assumption that the play was set in a romantic fairy-tale world. The comments about war in the passage seemed worth considering, but, because of the setting, they seemed rather distant from real life. Since then, however, we have all become familiar with the tragic events in the former Yugoslavia. Consequently, when we last looked at this passage with a group of students, the fact that the soldier is a Serb made the play seem urgent and relevant to modern life. This might seem an irrelevant point to make, but one thing that it underlines is how the meaning of a text can change in the light of the assumptions and expectations a reader brings to it. This should remind us that, in constructing a reading of any text, we are not putting together an objective analysis of the poem, passage of prose or play. Every reader is offering his or her own sense of what is going on in an extract, and there will often be disagreements between different readers about what is important and of central significance.

This does not mean, however, that the reader has absolute freedom. You can't just make up ideas about what you are reading in a reckless way. Everything you say must be based upon the evidence of the words on the page. But this still leaves you considerable freedom to read the passage as you wish. In a sense, you are like a barrister: the facts are there in the passage, but different barristers could construct different, indeed totally opposed, readings of the evidence. Practical criticism is, therefore, an activity where there is plenty of room for inventiveness and creative reading. Indeed, it is the examination candidate who manages simultaneously to read a passage in both a solid, sensible way and an inventive, creative way who is likely to receive the best mark.

Solidity can be achieved primarily through being in control of an essay-writing method that works well. There is everything to be said for a practical criticism answer that is constructed in six paragraphs: one paragraph of introduction, four substantial paragraphs of analysis ,and one paragraph of conclusion. You must be aware of the fact that you need to build a case, but an effective essay method will help you do this, as it will encourage you to take stock at the end of each paragraph. Keep the structure of an essay simple, therefore. And let this simple structure do a lot of the work of organising your case. At all costs, avoid the kind of disorganised essay where you tie yourself up in knots. An organised essay structure will enable you to concentrate your energy on the important task, which is doing justice to the text.

Step 2:   Starting an essay. Summarise the extract, establish your sense of the central opposition in the extract, set up the controlling idea for your essay as a whole

The first paragraph is where you can deal with, and dispose of, the 'story' of the extract. When you have told the story once, probably in about ten lines at the most, you will have got it out of the way; this should help you avoid the temptation of retelling the story throughout your answer. When you have told the story, look for a tension. What we have suggested is that plays set an idea of a settled life against disruption of that settled life. In the case of *Arms and the Man*, war and the arrival of the young man in the woman's bedroom are clear indications of disruption. If you can, try to see a larger issue that underlies the tension you have spotted. In a lot of plays, a cold dose of reality shatters middle-class complacency; there seems more than a trace of this in this opening scene from *Arms and the Man*.

Step 3: Look more closely at the opening of the extract, trying to see how the author brings the theme to life

You have set up your broad pattern: Raina's settled existence is disrupted by this man in her bedroom. In order to build upon this idea you need to look at details, that is either details that tell us more about the life that Raina normally leads or details that tell us more about the soldier. You might, for example, want to consider his appearance when he enters the room. And what do you make of his one menacing comment to Raina? Why does Shaw state that the young man can see the humour of his position? How does Raina initially respond to the intruder? Why is she so disdainful? And why does she raise the point about soldiers not being afraid of dying? If you considered these or similar points, the conclusion you might well arrive at is that the soldier is a realist whereas Raina is a romantic, or at least that she has a lot of romantic illusions about soldiers and war.

Step 4: Look at another section of the extract, trying to build on your analysis of the extract's details

Look at some more details. At the end of the last paragraph we arrived at the idea of the realistic character and the romantic character. The logical thing to do now is to build on this insight. What further evidence can you find of his realism and her romanticism?

Step 5: Look at another section of the extract, trying to build on your analysis of the extract's details

As you look at more details, you should be able to find nuances and complications in the realist/romantic pattern. Possibly the soldier might be exposed as a bit of a romantic himself. We are not saying this is the case, simply making the point that examination of the evidence may well push the case along in unexpected directions. What you would obviously need to pick up and consider are all the references to war. You would need to explain the difference between his attitude to fighting and her attitude. One is a romantic, the other a realist, but perhaps the man isn't as much of a hard-headed realist as he claims.

Step 6:   Look at how the extract concludes

The whole time you should be doing more than assessing the two characters. A play is not a character study. The characters are merely devices that the writer employs to make possible an exploration of larger themes. Towards the end of this extract, therefore, when she decides to protect him, try to see the larger issues involved, the extent to which she might still be playing a romantic game but also a certain satisfaction she derives as a woman in, for once, having this kind of power over a man.

Step 7:   Sum up your sense of the extract as a whole

Most of our argument about *Arms and the Man* has been constructed around the twin poles of romanticism and realism. All the differences between the two people, and all the contention between the two, makes sense in these terms, but at the end of the last paragraph we stumbled on another difference between these two figures. It is the obvious difference that he is a man and she is a woman, and there is a gender battle going on here; at the end of this extract it is interesting that she usurps from the male his usual prerogative of power. That would, in fact, be a good point on which to finish. We started with a tension, a look at the details enabled us to fill out our sense of the tension, and at the end of our essay we have, in the comments about gender, found a new twist to our theme. It is a point that connects with everything we have said so far, for up until this point in her life Raina has thought of men as warriors and been content to play the traditional role of the patient woman at home. But the arrival of a real soldier begins to turn her ideas inside out, and begins to move her away from her usual timid female role.

That, as we say, would amount to more than enough material for a very substantial essay. But, as we have also said throughout this book, practical criticism is an exercise where there is plenty of scope for inventive and creative reading. If you wanted to, you could get more out of this extract by seeing what more can be done with this gender theme. It might be felt, for example, that there is something disturbing, rather than amusing, about the way in which the man violates the woman's space. It could be said that Shaw is insensitive to the potential meanings of the scene he has chosen to present. The reservation about Shaw's stance is also evident in his assumption that a woman is inevitably a romantic whereas the man is a realist. There is something complicated in all this: the extract seems designed to challenge outdated myths about war and masculinity, but there is a way in which Shaw, in his presentation of the heroine as bimbo and in his inability to recognise that the man's intrusion has unpleasant sexual implications, seems to display some old prejudices. Our point is that Shaw seems to challenge old ways of thinking, but we suspect that Shaw bases his own world view on traditional concepts of masculinity and femininity. In other words, an avowedly radical and debunking text is not as radical and debunking as it might at first appear.

We have touched on these points simply to illustrate that, whatever clear path you steer through an extract, it is usually possible to take those ideas one stage further. But it is always a logical progression, a position that emerges from the case that you have taken care to build slowly and steadily. You don't, however, have to take things as far as we have taken them here. Indeed, it might be several years before you can tease out a huge variety of implications from a passage. What matters far more than the ability to push the case as far as it can go is the basic ability to build a solid case. Indeed, all that the examiner wants to see in a practical criticism exercise, regardless of whether you are dealing with poetry, prose or drama, is that you can construct your own coherent, well-organised case from the evidence, from the details of the text.

Further reading

THE main point of the preceding chapters has been to offer you a method for tackling practical criticism – how to get hold of the text and then how to build a response by using paragraph steps. The ideal answer, we have suggested, recreates the reading process, moving from an initial impression to a more subtle sense of the text. It is a method that allows you to reflect on the details of the poem or passage or extract and discuss their relationship to the larger issue in the text, to the big idea that the author is dealing with.

A moment's thought will tell you that the method we have outlined is not only a way of writing about literary texts, it is also a way of shaping and organising your reading. Very often students want to develop their critical skills by reading more widely, but then are disappointed because they get so little out of tackling, say, a Dickens novel or a Shakespeare sonnet or a Caryl Churchill play. Little seems to be gained by going through the book, and so students give up doing what they are supposed to do, which is enjoy reading. But you cannot really enjoy reading texts if each time you open a book you feel at a loss as to what to make of it. The method we have described for tackling practical criticism should help you overcome this problem and give you good reason to read more widely and more adventurously.

How? The answer is really quite straightforward. In almost every chapter of this book we have stressed a number of simple points that should carry you through the most difficult text. Because we do believe they will actually help you read with a purpose, that is read actively and also think about the text, we'll list them here:

DO remember how much all poems have in common, how they deal with familiar oppositions such as love and death, order and disorder, harmony and lack of harmony.

DO remember how much all novels have in common, how they often present a pattern of individuals in conflict with the social order, or how they deal with how fragile the social order is as it confronts the world of nature.

DO remember how much all plays have in common with their common theme of the disruption of the social order and their pattern of exposition, complication, resolution.

And then

DO remember how little texts have in common, and that we are after is the author's distinctive manner, the different way of writing that gives familiar themes a fresh twist.

DO look for the broad pattern in the text, the big idea or issue it is treating.

But

DO look at how the text develops from some simple basis towards more complex ideas.

DO look at the details of the text, and how they serve to bring the theme to life.

DO think about what new angle the text gives to a familiar issue or problem, and the questions it raises.

If you are starting on a new text, you may even find it worthwhile to reread one of the earlier chapters so as to set yourself up. There is little point in reading a book aimlessly: you will be far better off reading it critically in the way we have suggested, really getting your ideas to work for you, really seeing what is going on in the text. In turn you will find this developing your critical sense and critical confidence, so that you will start to handle texts – and language – with ease. We mention language here because, quite obviously, it is central to both criticism and texts. As you become more conscious of how texts work, and of how writers give their familiar themes a distinctive manner, so you will see how to use the method we have outlined to suit your own purposes, to develop your own ideas. If you want evidence of this, look back to Chapter 8 and see how the three student essays all use a similar essay format but use it to develop their own critical view of the poem.

We have implied above that you might find it helpful to draw up a reading list, or you might be given suggestions for further reading by one of your teachers or lecturers. Obviously you do not want to draw up a massive list that you will never get through. You might start with something like the following:

a Jane Austen novel – say, *Mansfield Park*;
a Shakespeare play – say, *Othello*;
a twentieth-century poet – say, Wilfred Owen.

That would give you much to read, and much to think about. But there are other ways you might want to expand your reading experience. Most students, when they get to university, claim to have read very little poetry. In turn that makes them lose confidence at the start of their degree work just when they need the opposite, just when they need to be able to draw upon some broader purposeful reading. You might, then, draw up a list of poets and read one poem from each of them:

John Donne – either the love poems or the religious poems;
George Herbert;
Shakespeare's sonnets;
Alexander Pope – try the opening part of *The Rape of the Lock*, dealing with the fashionable world and how a woman's lock of hair is stolen at a card game;
John Keats – one of the odes;
S. T. Coleridge – try 'Kubla Khan';
William Wordsworth – you might read the opening page of *The Prelude*, a long autobiographical poem dealing with the relationship between the author and nature;
Christina Rossetti – look at one or two sonnets;
T. S. Eliot – have a go at *The Waste Land* and its picture of modern life;
Philip Larkin – same topic as Eliot but much more approachable;
Adrienne Rich – a more recent poet;
Seamus Heaney – a more recent poet;
Carol Ann Duffy – a more recent poet.

You will find most of these in *The Norton Anthology of Poetry*. It is a large volume, but don't be put off by this. As you refine your critical reading method you will find your way through such volumes with relative ease. What, though, will also help is if you have a picture of the various periods of English Literature such as the following (all dates are approximate):

Old English or Anglo-Saxon Literature
The period before the Norman Conquest in 1066;
the language is more like German than English;
most famous poem is the epic poem *Beowulf*, about the killing of a monster by the hero Beowulf.

Middle English or Medieval Literature
From roughly 1066 to 1500;
Chaucer is the central figure;
also important are the miracle plays – plays about biblical history and the great poems *Sir Gawain and the Green Knight* and *Piers Plowman*.

Renaissance Literature
from 1500 – 1660;
the term 'renaissance means' 'rebirth' – what is referred to is the renewed interest in the classics but also a new sense of the importance of human potential;
central figures are Shakespeare, Spenser, Milton, Donne, Sidney;
central event which ends the period is the Civil War of 1642–51, a time of great change as we shift into a more secular society.

Sub-divisions are:
the Elizabethan Age (1558–1603: Elizabeth I was on the throne);
the Jacobean Age (1603–25: James I was on the throne; Jacobean is the adjective for James's reign);
the Caroline Age (1625–49), relating to the reign of Charles I;
the Commonwealth Period or the Puritan Interregnum (1649–60) when Oliver Cromwell led the country.

Neo-classical Period
The years 1660–1785, but usually sub-divided into the following three areas:

Restoration Literature
From 1660 to 1700;
refers to the restoration of Charles II;
major poet is Dryden;
also important are Bunyan and Restoration Comedy by Wycherley
and Congreve;
women prose writers include Margaret Cavendish and Mary Wroth.

Augustan Literature
From 1700 to 1745;
takes its name from the original Augustan Age under the Roman
emperor Augustus when Virgil, Horace and Ovid wrote;
during 1700–45 writers such as Pope, the major figure, imitated their
classical forerunners.

Age of Sensibility
From 1745 to 1785;
central figures are Dr Johnson, Fielding, Richardson;
the name stresses the idea that literature is moving away from the sort
of correctness we get in Pope towards an emphasis on instinct and
feeling.

Romantic Period
From 1785 to 1830;
central poets are Wordsworth, Coleridge, Keats, Shelley, Byron;
central novelists and prose writers are Jane Austen, Mary Shelley and
Mary Wollstonecraft;
important events were the French Revolution of 1789 and the
Reform Bill of 1832.

Victorian Period
From 1830 (or 1837, the accession of Queen Victoria) to 1901, the
death of Queen Victoria;
central novelists include Dickens, Charlotte and Emily Brontë,
George Eliot, and, at the end of the period, Thomas Hardy;
major poets include Tennyson, Robert Browning, Elizabeth Barrett
Browning and Gerard Manley Hopkins;
important influences include Charles Darwin's theory of evolution
and many works dealing with economic, class and religious changes;
also notable for the early feminist movement.

Edwardian Literature
From 1901 to 1914, from the death of Victoria, who was followed by Edward VII, to the start of the First World War;
poets writing in this period include W. B. Yeats and Thomas Hardy; central dramatist is George Bernard Shaw;
novelists include Thomas Hardy, Joseph Conrad and Henry James.

Georgian Period
From 1910 to 1936 (the reign of George V, following Edward VII); the 'Georgian' poets included Rupert Brooke, Walter de la Mare, John Masefield.

Modern Period
From 1914 onwards;
a term usually applied to literature written since the beginning of the First World War, so it covers the Georgian period but nobody would call them modern writers – modern implies experimental in terms of form and subject matter, where the Georgians are largely traditional; major modern poets include W. B. Yeats, Wilfred Owen, T. S. Eliot, W. H. Auden, Wallace Stevens, Sylvia Plath, Adrienne Rich, William Carlos Williams;
major modern novelists include Joseph Conrad, James Joyce, D. H. Lawrence, Virginia Woolf, Doris Lessing, E. M. Forster;
dramatists include George Bernard Shaw, Sean O'Casey, Samuel Beckett, Caryl Churchill, Harold Pinter and Tom Stoppard.

Postmodern Period
sometimes applied to the period after the Second World War (1939–45);
writers include Thomas Pychon, Salman Rushdie, Ian McEwan, Toni Morrison, Angela Carter.

We do not, of course, claim that the above list is a very full or representative picture: it is just meant to outline the traditional areas into which critics have divided English Literature. The picture itself is changing as the new critical theories we mentioned in Chapter 9 redefine our understanding of the way literature and society work. However, the list may help you see what the big blocks of literature are and also provide you with some suggestions for further reading.

At this point we have reached the very edge of practical criticism and how it fits into the larger discipline of English Literature. The next move you may want to take in your reading is, indeed, to get an overview of English Literature and, more broadly, the criticism that is now being produced. If this is the case, we recommend that you have a look at our book *Literary Terms and Criticism: Second Edition* (also published by Macmillan, 1993). This, you will discover, is the companion volume to the present book; the two are intended to complement one another and to offer you the two parts of literary study that you need to know about: one is the broader picture of *Literary Terms and Criticism* of how everything fits together; the other is the picture we offer in this book of how to analyse a text closely and arrive at a critical reading of it.

Index